SEEK: SCIENCE EXPLORATION, EXCITEMENT, AND KNOWLEDGE

A Curriculum in
Health and Biomedical Science
for Diverse 4th and 5th Grade Students

Edited by
Lucille Lang Day, PhD

Staff of Health and Biomedical Science for a Diverse Community

Co-Directors
Lucille Lang Day, PhD
Bertram H. Lubin, MD

Curriculum Developer and Program Coordinator
Laura McVittie Gray

Program Coordinators
Ava Holliday
Patricia Mielbeck
Sarah Reede

Curriculum Consultants
Leticia Marquez-Magaña, PhD
Marlene Wilson

Evaluators
Rita Gaber,
Kensington Research Group

Joseph Malloy, PhD,
Kensington Research Group

Presenters
High School Interns,
FACES for the Future,
Children's Hospital &
Research Center Oakland

College Interns,
Biology Scholars Program,
University of California at
Berkeley

Advisory Committee

Katharine Barrett
Charles Carlson
Mary Dean
Mary Frazier, RN
Marion Fredman
Charles Howarth
Caroline Kane, PhD

Do Kim
Janet King, PhD
Leslie Louie, PhD
Alexander Lucas, PhD
Tomás Magaña, MD
Leticia Marquez-Magaña, PhD
Gina Moreland

Laurie Schumacher, PhD
Barbara Stebbins, PhD
Kimberly Turner
Gordon Watson, PhD
Marlene Wilson

We are grateful to Tomás Magaña, MD, and Barbara Staggers, MD, co-directors of FACES for the Future, and to Caroline Kane, PhD, director of the Biology Scholars Program, for partnering with us to provide the many high school and college interns who have presented the SEEK curriculum in classrooms and after-school science clubs.

Published by
Children's Hospital Oakland Research Institute
5700 Martin Luther King Jr. Way, Oakland, CA 94609

Book editor: Lucille Lang Day, PhD
Book designer: Debbie Dare

Copyright © 2010 by Children's Hospital Oakland Research Institute

ISBN: 978-0-9828252-0-4

This publication was made possible by a Science Education Partnership Award (SEPA), Grant Number R25RR020449, from the National Center for Research Resources (NCRR), a component of the National Institutes of Health (NIH). Its contents are solely the responsibility of the authors and do not necessarily represent the official views of NCRR or NIH. Additional support for this SEPA-funded project was provided by Grant Number UL1RR024131-01 from NCRR.

SEEK: SCIENCE EXPLORATION, EXCITEMENT, AND KNOWLEDGE

A Curriculum in Health and Biomedical Science for Diverse 4th and 5th Grade Students

CONTENTS

2 Introduction

FOURTH GRADE INSTRUCTIONAL UNITS

Nutrition: Balance and Imbalance
- 4   Lesson 1: Energy Balance
- 16   Lesson 2: Energy Out = Living + Moving
- 20   Lesson 3: Energy In: Everyday Healthy Foods
- 26   Lesson 4: Energy In: High Calorie Foods
- 32   Lesson 5: Energy Balance and Your Health

Traumatic Brain Injuries
- 36   Lesson 1: Protecting Your Brain
- 41   Lesson 2: Making Neurons
- 48   Lesson 3: Building a Brain
- 54   Lesson 4: Testing Reaction Time
- 59   Lesson 5: Treating Brain Injuries

Infectious Diseases
- 64   Lesson 1: Epidemic Outbreak
- 73   Lesson 2: Classifying Microorganisms
- 77   Lesson 3: Killing Microbes, Part I
- 82   Lesson 4: Killing Microbes, Part II
- 87   Lesson 5: The Body Fights Back

Environmental Toxics
- 91   Lesson 1: Lead Poisoning
- 95   Lesson 2: Test the Alternatives
- 99   Lesson 3: Mercury Poisoning
- 112   Lesson 4: Air Pollution, Part I
- 116   Lesson 5: Air Pollution, Part II

FIFTH GRADE INSTRUCTIONAL UNITS

Nutrition and Diabetes
- 119   Lesson 1: You're the Doctor!
- 126   Lesson 2: Testing for Starch
- 130   Lesson 3: Your Digestive System
- 136   Lesson 4: The Role of Insulin
- 140   Lesson 5: Diabetes and a Diverse Community

Asthma and Lung Disease
- 144   Lesson 1: Your Respiratory System
- 148   Lesson 2: Do You Have Asthma?
- 154   Lesson 3: LeapFrog Asthma Books
- 158   Lesson 4: Lung Disease and Cigarette Ads
- 164   Lesson 5: Preventing Lung Disease

Heart Disease
- 169   Lesson 1: The Heart As a Pump
- 175   Lesson 2: The Circulatory System
- 180   Lesson 3: Exploring Blood Pressure
- 186   Lesson 4: Heart Rate and Exercise
- 191   Lesson 5: Conducting a Heart Experiment

Genetics and Sickle Cell Anemia
- 195   Lesson 1: DNA and Your Cells
- 201   Lesson 2: See Your DNA
- 206   Lesson 3: Plant Parenthood
- 211   Lesson 4: Trait Inheritance
- 216   Lesson 5: Sickle Cell Anemia

INTRODUCTION

Lucille Lang Day, PhD
Staff Scientist
Children's Hospital Oakland Research Institute
Former Director, Hall of Health

Bertram H. Lubin, MD
President and CEO
Children's Hospital & Research Center Oakland

The **SEEK** (**S**cience **E**xploration, **E**xcitement, and **K**nowledge) Curriculum is a joint project of Children's Hospital Oakland Research Institute and Children's Hospital's Hall of Health Museum. Development of the curriculum was funded by a Science Education Partnership Award (SEPA), entitled Health and Biomedical Science for a Diverse Community, from the National Center for Research Resources at the National Institutes of Health.

The focus of this 4th and 5th grade curriculum is diseases and health conditions that disproportionately affect minorities. This differs from the more typical foci of an elementary school curriculum in health and human biology, which are "healthy lifestyles" and "basic human physiology." Focusing on diseases and other medical conditions, such as brain injuries and poisoning from environmental toxics, is part of what makes this curriculum innovative. Information on healthy lifestyles and basic physiology is covered, of course, in the context of teaching about the diseases and conditions.

Although the curriculum focuses on diseases and health conditions affecting minority communities, the lessons are appropriate for all children, regardless of their ethnicity. This is because the health conditions that afflict minorities—such as heart disease, diabetes, asthma, and obesity—are, in fact, found widely in the general population as well.

The curriculum includes eight instructional units, four for fourth grade and four for fifth grade:

Fourth Grade Instructional Units:
1. Nutrition: Balance and Imbalance
2. Traumatic Brain Injuries
3. Infectious Diseases
4. Environmental Toxics

Fifth Grade Instructional Units:
1. Nutrition and Diabetes
2. Asthma and Lung Disease
3. Heart Disease
4. Genetics and Sickle Cell Anemia

Each unit consists of five, one-hour lessons, for a total of 40 lessons, 20 each for fourth grade and fifth grade.

The goals for student learning are:

1. Students will be able to carry out a simple scientific investigation. The curriculum engages students in the scientific process and group problem solving, enabling them to use critical thinking skills. They practice observing, questioning, making predictions, hypothesizing, planning experiments, identifying and controlling variables, collecting data, measuring, estimating, making graphs, and drawing conclusions.

2. Students will be able to describe a variety of healthcare and biomedical science careers. The curriculum uses role-playing and guest speakers to introduce careers. The lessons can be presented without guest speakers, but are enhanced by guests who can tell the students what they do in a typical day, what kind of training they needed, and what research is currently underway in their fields.

3. Students will be able to give examples of current topics of biomedical research. Guest speakers provide information about current research. In addition, many of the experiments afford the opportunity to relate what the students are doing to cutting-edge research.

4. Students will report engaging in healthy behaviors such as eating more vegetables and exercising more often. The lessons provide information on how to avoid the health conditions studied and give students the opportunity to role-play healthy behaviors. Some of the practical skills covered are hand washing, eating a balanced diet, getting plenty of exercise, not smoking, and avoiding secondhand smoke.

5. Students will be able to define basic terms related to the human body such as "cell" and "artery" and will be able to explain the function of organs and organ systems such as "heart" and "immune system." The curriculum takes a "learn by doing" approach to teach scientific concepts and terminology. Students learn through experiments, games, group problem solving, and other activities. Worksheets reinforce the lessons.

All of the lessons address California Science and/or Mathematics Standards, as well as the Health Framework for California Public Schools. Over a four-year period (2005 to 2009), the curriculum was tested in classrooms and after-school science clubs in Oakland, Berkeley, and Concord, California. For all eight instructional units, on pre- and post-tests developed by the project, the experimental group made statistically significant gains that exceeded those of the control group.

Many teachers and other educators have contributed ideas to the SEEK Curriculum, and many scientists and healthcare professionals have checked it for accuracy. To all of these people, we are grateful. A special thanks goes to the staffs at Fruitvale and Hoover Elementary Schools in Oakland, where the curriculum was first piloted, and to Marsha Treadwell, PhD, and Eileen Murray of the Talking Drums Project at Children's Hospital for collaborating with us on the genetics unit. The curriculum draws on many sources, including previously existing curricula and the work of other SEPA projects. These sources are acknowledged in the "References" at the beginning of each lesson plan. Finally, we are grateful to the staff of the Hall of Health, which closed in 2009, for their support of and contributions to this project.

Grade: 4
Nutrition: Balance and Imbalance
Lesson 1: Energy Balance

Lesson Time: 1 hour

Reference: Program Energy, 4th grade lesson: ENERGY IN = ENERGY OUT: http://www.programenergy.org/

Lesson objectives
- Define and explore energy balance.
- Define and explore calories as a unit of energy.
- Explore how energy balances and imbalances affect weight and health.
- Act like a physician prescribing lifestyle changes for children with energy imbalances.

Overview
The presenter explains how food choices and exercise choices can lead to a healthy energy balance. The class reviews calories as a unit for measuring energy. Then the students use calories to estimate energy going into the body through food, and energy going out of the body through exercise. They try to guess the amount of energy in four foods and the amount of energy used in four forms of physical exercise, and they discover that the more energy going out of the body through physical activity, the more energy must go into the body as food. A healthcare worker who treats childhood obesity visits the class. Finally, the students put their energy balance knowledge to work as they solve case studies about children with energy imbalances. Analyzing the energy in and the energy out, groups of students make dietary and physical activity recommendations for their patients.

Occupation of the Day
Pediatrician: Pediatricians are medical doctors who treat children. Becoming a doctor takes four years of high school, four years of college, and four years of medical school. Doctors can specialize in a particular area such as children's medicine, which is also known as pediatrics. A pediatrician who has a patient with an energy imbalance can often refer the patient to specialized programs. Depending on the nature of the imbalance, the doctor may recommend physical exercise or a change of diet.

Key Terms

Energy: The ability to do work. In our bodies, this means the ability of cells to do the work that they need to do to sustain, heal, develop, and move the body.

Cell: The basic unit of structure and function in all living things.

Balance: A state where two things are equal in some way.

Energy balance: A state where the "energy in" matches the "energy out" of the body, i.e., the energy going into the body through food is equal to the energy used to maintain the body and to do physical activity.

Energy imbalance: A state where the energy going into the body as foods does not equal the energy going out of the body through daily living and physical exercise. When the "energy in" is greater than the "energy out," the excess energy from food is stored as body fat. Excess body fat can eventually lead to obesity. When the "energy out" is greater than the "energy in," body fat is used for energy, and the person loses weight.

Energy in: The energy consumed as food.

Energy out: Energy spent maintaining the body and doing exercise.

Calorie: A unit for measuring energy. A scientific calorie is the amount of energy required to raise one gram of water by one degree Celsius. A food calorie is 1,000 times larger than a scientific calorie. It's the amount of energy required to raise 1 liter of water by one degree Celsius.

Physical activity: An activity where someone is moving around and spending energy.

Obesity: A physical condition where a person has dangerous levels of excess body fat. Obesity can lead to serious health issues, including heart disease, diabetes, sleep problems, respiratory problems, and cancer.

Basal Metabolic Rate: The rate at which a resting person uses energy to maintain basic body functions.

Materials

Per class:

"Energy in" estimation visuals:
- 1 empty box of macaroni and cheese
- 1 apple
- 2 cookies
- 1 frozen burrito

"Energy out" estimation visuals:
- 1 jump rope
- 1 picture of a bowling ball
- 1 running shoe
- 1 chair, representing sitting down and doing nothing

Per student:
- 1 "Estimating ENERGY IN" form
- 1 "Estimating ENERGY OUT" form

Per group of 4:
- 100 mini poker chips (or pennies)
- 1 bowl marked "Energy In"
- 1 bowl marked "Energy Out"
- 1 plastic balance scale with two pans
- 4 copies of one case study (Anya, Charlie, Crystal, or Pablo)

Procedure

> **Questions:**
> **What is energy balance?**
> **Why is it important?**

Activity 1: Energy Estimation

1. Introduce the unit, the concept of energy balance, and the concept of a calorie.
2. Pass out the "Estimating ENERGY IN" and "Estimating ENERGY OUT" forms.
3. Show the four food samples and four physical activities.
4. Instruct the students to work in groups of four to estimate the total energy going into the body from the four food items and the energy going out from the four physical activities.
5. Once the estimates are complete, ask each group to share its estimates. Announce the correct amount of energy or calories in each food and physical activity, and ask the students to record it. Actual ENERGY IN for the foods: Mac & Cheese (1 cup prepared) = 410 Cal, 1 apple (medium) = 70 Cal, 2 cookies (chocolate chip) = 200 Cal, and 1 frozen burrito = 370 Cal. Actual ENERGY OUT for the activities (1 hour): jumping rope = 600 Cal, bowling = 175 Cal, jogging = 350 Cal, and sitting = 40 Cal.

Activity 2: Guest Speaker

1. Introduce the guest speaker, a pediatrician or other healthcare worker who treats children with energy imbalances. Ask the guest to speak briefly about his or her education and daily work, to share at least one case where a child had a severe energy imbalance, and to explain how the child was helped to regain energy balance.
2. Encourage the students to ask questions, and ask the guest to stay for additional questions at the end of class.

Activity 3: Energy Balance Case Studies

1. Show the plastic scales and the poker chips. Explain that each poker chip is 50 calories. Using the four foods on the estimation forms, place the total number of calories in the "energy in" side of the scale. Using the four physical exercises, place the appropriate calories in the "energy out" side. Explain that the balanced scale represents a healthy energy balance. The energy going into the body equals the energy going out of the body.
2. Give each group of four students one of four energy balance case studies: Anya, Charlie, Crystal, or Pablo. Each person in the group should have the same case study.
3. Each case study starts with an energy-in and an energy-out total. The students must evaluate whether or not the person is in balance. See case study data sheets.
4. Ask the students to take a closer look at where the patient's energy in and energy out come from. During this section, students must use addition and subtraction skills.
5. Once students have totaled the energy in and the energy out, they should add the correct number of poker chips to each of the energy bowls.
6. The students must help the patient in the case study to achieve energy balance by recommending physical activities or snacks to add to his or her day.
7. Students will then have to add poker chips to the correct energy bowl to reflect the new snacks or physical activities.
8. Once the adjustment to the poker chips has been made, students should weigh their energy bowls. The two bowls should weight the same. If there is a discrepancy in the weights, encourage the group to double check if the number of poker chips in each bowl is correct.

Activity 4: Energy Imbalances and Health

1. Read over the last section of the case study data sheets as a class. Each case study concludes with an unexpected event, such as breaking a leg or catching a cold, that affects energy balance. Students will have to reevaluate energy in and out to determine if the patient is still in balance. Ask the students to offer the patients some advice to help them get back into balance.
2. Discuss health conditions, such as heart disease and diabetes, that can be caused by an energy imbalance resulting from eating more calories than are spent in exercise.
3. Review that when people take in more energy than they spend, they have an energy imbalance. Over time, the body stores the excess food in the form of fat. It takes 3,500 extra calories to make 1lb of body fat. We need some fat to pad, protect, and insulate our bodies, but excess body fat leads to serious health problems, including obesity.
4. Allow time for the students to ask the guest speaker about the health effects of energy imbalances.

Nutrition: Balance and Imbalance
Lesson 1

ENERGY BALANCE

Name: _____

Teacher: _____

Date: _____

ESTIMATING ENERGY OUT

Estimated ENERGY OUT: 1 hour

1) Jumping Rope = _____ Calories

2) Bowling = _____ Calories

3) Jogging = _____ Calories

4) Sitting = _____ Calories

Actual ENERGY OUT: 1 hour

1) Jumping Rope = _____ Calories

2) Bowling = _____ Calories

3) Jogging = _____ Calories

4) Sitting = _____ Calories

ESTIMATING ENERGY IN

Estimated ENERGY IN

1) Mac & Cheese = _____ Calories (1 cup prepared)

2) 1 apple = _____ Calories (medium)

3) 2 cookies = _____ Calories (chocolate chip)

4) frozen burrito = _____ Calories

Actual ENERGY IN1

1) Mac & Cheese = _____ Calories

2) 1 apple = _____ Calories

3) 2 cookies = _____ Calories

4) frozen burrito = _____ Calories

Children's Hospital Oakland Research Institute

Nutrition: Balance and Imbalance
Lesson 1

Name: _____

Teacher: _____

Date: _____

We monitored Anya's ENERGY IN and ENERGY OUT from the last two weeks. Here is the information we got for daily ENERGY IN and OUT:

| ENERGY IN = 1,800 Calories | ENERGY OUT = 2,300 Calories |

1) Is Anya in ENERGY BALANCE right now? _____

2) Put the correct symbol (**>, <** or **=**) between the two ENERGY boxes.

3) If Anya keeps her ENERGY IN and ENERGY OUT exactly where they are right now, will she gain weight, lose weight or stay the same weight? _____

Let's take a closer look...

Where did Anya's ENERGY IN and OUT come from? As you go over her ENERGY, add the ENERGY chips to the correct bowl—either the ENERGY IN bowl or the ENERGY OUT bowl. **1 chip = 50 calories**

ENERGY IN		ENERGY OUT	
Breakfast	500 Calories	Basal Metabolic Rate	1,200 Calories
Lunch	600 Calories		
Dinner	700 Calories	Physical Activity	1,100 Calories
Snack	No snack!		
TOTAL Calories	_____	**TOTAL Calories**	_____

How much more ENERGY IN does Anya need to balance with her ENERGY OUT?

2,300 Calories
- 1,800 Calories

[_____]

Getting in Balance
Anya is out of ENERGY BALANCE by _____ calories.
She needs more ENERGY IN to get into BALANCE. Help Anya make some snack choices so she can get into ENERGY BALANCE.

SNACK	# of SERVINGS	CALORIES
_____	_____	_____
_____	_____	_____
_____	_____	_____
_____	_____	_____
_____	_____	_____

Now adjust your ENERGY IN bowl for the changes to Anya's ENERGY IN.

How many ENERGY chips did you add? _____

Take your ENERGY IN bowl and ENERGY OUT bowl to the balance to see if Anya is really in ENERGY BALANCE now!

What if ...
What if Anya took your advice and added some snacks to her diet to be in ENERGY BALANCE, but she broke her leg trying out a new skateboard trick. Now her ENERGY OUT has decreased. Here are her new daily ENERGY totals.

ENERGY IN = 2,200 Calories	ENERGY OUT = 1,900 Calories

1) Is Anya in ENERGY BALANCE right now? _____

2) Put the correct symbol (**>**, **<** or **=**) between the two ENERGY boxes above.

3) If Anya keeps her ENERGY IN and ENERGY OUT exactly where they are right now, will she gain weight, lose weight or stay the same weight? _____

What advice would you give Anya so she can be in ENERGY BALANCE now?
Circle your answer(s):

Eat More   Eat Less   More Physical Activity   Less Physical Activity

Nutrition: Balance and Imbalance
Lesson 1

Name: _____

Teacher: _____

Date: _____

Pablo "Speed" Martinez
Gender: Male
Age: 10 years old
Activity Level: Lightly Active

We monitored Pablo's ENERGY IN and ENERGY OUT from the last two weeks. Here is the information we got for daily ENERGY IN and OUT:

| ENERGY IN = 2,000 Calories | ENERGY OUT = 1,700 Calories |

1) Is Pablo in ENERGY BALANCE right now? _____

2) Put the correct symbol (>, < or =) between the two ENERGY boxes.

3) If Pablo keeps his ENERGY IN and ENERGY OUT exactly where they are right now, will he gain weight, lose weight or stay the same weight? _____

Let's take a closer look...

Where did Pablo's ENERGY IN and OUT come from? As you go over his ENERGY, add the ENERGY chips to the correct bowl—either the ENERGY IN bowl or the ENERGY OUT bowl. **1 chip = 50 calories**

ENERGY IN		ENERGY OUT	
Breakfast	400 Calories	Basal Metabolic Rate	1,200 Calories
Lunch	500 Calories		
Dinner	600 Calories	Physical Activity	500 Calories
Snack	500 Calories		
TOTAL Calories	_____	**TOTAL Calories**	_____

How much more ENERGY OUT does Pablo need to balance with his ENERGY IN?

$$\begin{array}{r} 2{,}000 \text{ Calories} \\ -\ 1{,}700 \text{ Calories} \\ \hline \end{array}$$

Getting in Balance

Pablo is out of ENERGY BALANCE by _____ Calories.
He needs more ENERGY OUT to get into BALANCE. Help Pablo make some snack choices so he can get into ENERGY BALANCE.

SNACK	# of SERVINGS	CALORIES
_____	_____	_____
_____	_____	_____
_____	_____	_____
_____	_____	_____
_____	_____	_____

Now adjust your ENERGY OUT bowl for the changes to Pablo's ENERGY OUT.

How many ENERGY chips did you add? _____

Take your ENERGY IN bowl and ENERGY OUT bowl to the balance to see if Pablo is really in ENERGY BALANCE now!

What if ...

What if Pablo caught the same cold his sister had and cannot do some of his favorite physical activities. Now his ENERGY OUT has decreased again. Here are his new daily ENERGY totals.

ENERGY IN = 2,000 Calories	ENERGY OUT = 1,600 Calories

1) Is Pablo in ENERGY BALANCE right now? _____

2) Put the correct symbol (**>**, **<** or **=**) between the two ENERGY boxes above.

3) If Pablo keeps his ENERGY IN and ENERGY OUT exactly where they are right now, will he gain weight, lose weight or stay the same weight? _____

What advice would you give Pablo so he can be in ENERGY BALANCE now?
Circle your answer(s):

Eat More   Eat Less   More Physical Activity   Less Physical Activity

Nutrition: Balance and Imbalance
Lesson 1

Name: _____

Teacher: _____

Date: _____

Crystal "Half Pipe" Martinez
Gender: Female
Age: 10 years old
Activity Level: Lightly Active

We monitored Crystal's ENERGY IN and ENERGY OUT from the last two weeks. Here is the information we got for daily ENERGY IN and OUT:

| ENERGY IN = 2,000 Calories | ENERGY OUT = 1,700 Calories |

1) Is Crystal in ENERGY BALANCE right now? _____

2) Put the correct symbol (**>**, **<** or **=**) between the two ENERGY boxes.

3) If Crystal keeps her ENERGY IN and ENERGY OUT exactly where they are right now, will she gain weight, lose weight or stay the same weight? _____

Let's take a closer look...

Where did Crystal's ENERGY IN and OUT come from? As you go over her ENERGY, add the ENERGY chips to the correct bowl—either the ENERGY IN bowl or the ENERGY OUT bowl. **1 chip = 50 calories**

ENERGY IN		ENERGY OUT	
Breakfast	400 Calories	Basal Metabolic Rate	1,200 Calories
Lunch	500 Calories		
Dinner	600 Calories	Physical Activity	500 Calories
Snack	500 Calories		
TOTAL Calories	_____	**TOTAL Calories**	_____

How much more ENERGY OUT does Crystal need to balance with her ENERGY IN?

      2,000 Calories
- 1,700 Calories

[_____]

Children's Hospital Oakland Research Institute

Getting in Balance

Crystal is out of ENERGY BALANCE by _____ Calories.
She needs more ENERGY OUT to get into BALANCE. Help Crystal make some exercise choices so she can get into ENERGY BALANCE.

SNACK	# of SERVINGS	CALORIES
_____	_____	_____
_____	_____	_____
_____	_____	_____
_____	_____	_____
_____	_____	_____

Now adjust your ENERGY OUT bowl for the changes to Crystal's ENERGY OUT.

How many ENERGY chips did you add? _____

Take your ENERGY IN bowl and ENERGY OUT bowl to the balance to see if Crystal is really in ENERGY BALANCE now!

What if ...

What if Crystal had a bad cold for a week and could not do many of her physical activities. Now her ENERGY OUT has decreased. Here are her new daily ENERGY totals.

ENERGY IN = 2,000 Calories	ENERGY OUT = 1,600 Calories

1) Is Crystal in ENERGY BALANCE right now? _____

2) Put the correct symbol (>, < or =) between the two ENERGY boxes above.

3) If Crystal keeps her ENERGY IN and ENERGY OUT exactly where they are right now, will she gain weight, lose weight or stay the same weight? _____

What advice would you give Crystal so she can be in ENERGY BALANCE now?
Circle your answer(s):

Eat More   Eat Less   More Physical Activity   Less Physical Activity

Nutrition: Balance and Imbalance
Lesson 1

ENERGY BALANCE

Charlie "The Board" Jones
Gender: Male
Age: 10 years old
Activity Level: Very Active

We monitored Charlie's ENERGY IN and ENERGY OUT from the last two weeks. Here is the information we got for daily ENERGY IN and OUT:

| ENERGY IN = 1,800 Calories | ENERGY OUT = 2,300 Calories |

1) Is Charlie in ENERGY BALANCE right now? _____

2) Put the correct symbol (**>**, **<** or **=**) between the two ENERGY boxes.

3) If Charlie keeps his ENERGY IN and ENERGY OUT exactly where they are right now, will he gain weight, lose weight or stay the same weight? _____

Let's take a closer look...

Where did Crystal's ENERGY IN and OUT come from? As you go over his ENERGY, add the ENERGY chips to the correct bowl—either the ENERGY IN bowl or the ENERGY OUT bowl. **1 chip = 50 calories**

ENERGY IN		ENERGY OUT	
Breakfast	500 Calories	Basal Metabolic Rate	1,200 Calories
Lunch	600 Calories		
Dinner	700 Calories	Physical Activity	1,100 Calories
Snack	No snack!		
TOTAL Calories	_____	**TOTAL Calories**	_____

How much more ENERGY IN does Charlie need to balance with his ENERGY OUT?

2,300 Calories
- 1,800 Calories
_____

Getting in Balance

Charlie is out of ENERGY BALANCE by _____ Calories.
He needs more ENERGY IN to get into BALANCE. Help Charlie make some snack choices so he can get into ENERGY BALANCE.

SNACK	# of SERVINGS	CALORIES
_____	_____	_____
_____	_____	_____
_____	_____	_____
_____	_____	_____
_____	_____	_____

Now adjust your ENERGY IN bowl for the changes to Charlie's ENERGY IN.

How many ENERGY chips did you add? _____

Take your ENERGY IN bowl and ENERGY OUT bowl to the balance to see if Charlie is really in ENERGY BALANCE now!

What if ...

What if Charlie took your advice and added snacks to his diet to be in ENERGY BALANCE, but he hurt his knee and cannot do some of his favorite physical activities? His ENERGY OUT has decreased. Here are his new daily ENERGY totals.

ENERGY IN = 2,200 Calories	ENERGY OUT = 1,900 Calories

1) Is Charlie in ENERGY BALANCE right now? _____

2) Put the correct symbol (**>**, **<** or **=**) between the two ENERGY boxes above.

3) If Charlie keeps his ENERGY IN and ENERGY OUT exactly where they are right now, will he gain weight, lose weight or stay the same weight? _____

**What advice would you give Charlie so he can be in ENERGY BALANCE now?
Circle your answer(s):**

Eat More   Eat Less   More Physical Activity   Less Physical Activity

Grade: 4
Nutrition: Balance and Imbalance
Lesson 2: Energy Out = Living + Moving

Lesson Time: 1 hour

Reference: Program Energy, University of Colorado, Boulder, Colorado: http://www.programenergy.org

Lesson objectives
- Explore how the body uses energy.
- Observe the effects of physical activity on the body.
- Design and implement an experiment.

Overview
The students reflect on the energy they use in daily life, and they estimate the calories used in a variety of activities. They use pedometers to measure the amount of energy they expend in 15 minutes of outdoor play. When the students return to class, the presenter gives them a healthy snack that matches the amount of energy they used.

Key Terms

Exercise: The activity of exerting your muscles in various ways to keep fit.

Oxygen: A gas in the air that we breathe. Our cells combine it with chemicals from food to release energy.

Pedometer: An instrument that measures how many steps a person takes.

Energy Out: The energy that you use as you live, move, and grow.

Basal Metabolic Rate: The rate at which a resting person uses energy to maintain basic body functions.

Materials

Per class:
- 1 worksheet overhead, optional

Per student:
- 1 worksheet
- 1 pedometer
- 50 calories worth of snack (calorie count is approximate). Only one type of snack is required. Any of the following healthy snacks can be used:
  - 4 saltine crackers
  - 1 small apple
  - 25 raisins
  - 5 pretzel sticks
  - 1 graham cracker square
  - 14 grapes

Procedure

Questions: How do you burn energy?

Activity 1: Experiencing the Two Components of Energy Out

1. Review energy balance, energy in, energy out, and calories. Pass out the worksheets.

2. Look around the room and ask the students what they are physically doing. Ask if they are using energy at that moment. They might say that they are sitting, watching, or doing nothing, and they might suggest that they are not using any energy. Ask them to close their eyes to reflect about everything going on inside of their bodies and minds. Are they digesting food from their last meal? Are they breathing? Are their hearts beating? Are they thinking? Do any of those functions require energy, and if so, how much? How do you know that you are using calories?

3. Explain that moving is fun. For 1 minute lead a fun and active game, Simon Says, that involves jumping and running in place.

4. Afterward ask the students if they spent energy during the game. Ask how they know that they spent energy. What physical sensations did they feel? How did their heart rates change as compared to sitting? What happened to their lungs, skin, and body temperature?

5. Review that the body uses energy in two ways: to live and to move around. Talk about the role of oxygen in energy utilization.

6. With student input, list basic life functions on the board (breathing, sleeping, digesting, thinking, maintaining heartbeat, maintaining body temperature, etc.). Ask the students to guess how much energy they need to live every day. These basic functions add up to about 1,200 calories per day, or 50 calories per hour. This is Basal Metabolic Rate: the calories burned just to stay alive.

7. Write several physical activities on the board. Ask the students to guess how many calories are used in one hour of each activity, and then write the actual number. How close were their predictions? Examples: studying (85 Cal per hour), walking (200 Cal per hr), running (350 Cal per hr), biking (400 Cal per hr), playing soccer (350 Cal per hr), dancing (275 Cal per hr), and watching TV (70 Cal per hr).

Activity 2: Calculating and Experiencing Energy Out

1. Review that someone's level of daily activity determines how much energy should be consumed to have a healthy energy balance. Ask the students how much energy they use during one hour of playtime. Ask them how they could measure the amount of energy that they spend. From the exercise above, they should suggest measuring heart rate, breathing rate, or temperature. Discuss their suggestions.

2. Show a pedometer and how it can be used to approximate the amount of energy that someone uses, depending on information that they enter. Ask the class how they could use pedometers to approximate how much energy they use during 15 minutes of playtime.

3. Divide the class into three groups: a high activity group, a medium activity group, and a low activity group.

4. Give the students pedometers and ask them to walk around the schoolyard according to their group type. The high activity group should walk quickly, the medium activity group should walk moderately, and the low activity group should walk slowly or stand still.

5. After 5 minutes, call the class back together, ask one person from each group for the number of steps on their pedometers, and show how much food is equivalent to that amount of energy. Any food from the list in the materials section can be chosen, for example:
   - Low group: 4 raisins
   - Medium group: 8 raisins
   - High group: 12 raisins

6. Discuss the results.

7. Let the groups do the activity again, so that everyone can do an equivalent amount of exercise and earn the same amount of snack. The low activity group must now exercise vigorously. The medium activity group will continue to exercise moderately, and the high activity group need not exercise at all.

8. Call the class back together and return to the classroom.

9. Work with the students to calculate the number of calories they spent. Everyone should have spent between 40 and 60 calories.
10. Give a 50-Cal snack to each student and discuss the experience. What did they learn?

Extensions:
- Have the students keep a daily log to track their physical activity. Challenge them to exercise at least a half hour a day for a week, and reward those who rise to the challenge.
- Create an exercise activity booklet that the students can share with their families. The booklet should contain suggested activities, games, and outings.

Nutrition: Balance and Imbalance
Lesson 2

ENERGY OUT = living + moving

Name: _____

Teacher: _____

Date: _____

Are you using energy right now? _____

How? _____

Signs of energy use: _____

Benefits of exercise: _____

_____

ENERGY IN		ENERGY OUT
Breakfast	400 Calories	Basal Metabolic Rate for all day burns 1,200 Cal
Lunch	500 Calories	Activity 1 _____ for ____ hr burns ____ Cal
Dinner	600 Calories	Activity 2 _____ for ____ hr burns ____ Cal
Snack	500 Calories	Activity 3 _____ for ____ hr burns ____ Cal
FOOD TOTAL _____ **Cal**		**For a total of** _____ **Cal**

Exercise plan for pedometer activity: _____

_____

_____

Total steps taken: _____   Calories used: _____

Snack: _____

Children's Hospital Oakland Research Institute

Grade: 4
Nutrition: Balance and Imbalance
Lesson 3: Energy In: Everyday Healthy Foods

Lesson Time: 1 hour

Reference: Program Energy, 2nd grade lesson: Reading Food Labels: http://www.programenergy.org

Lesson objectives
- Observe how the energy in food can be measured in calories.
- Observe that different foods contain different numbers of calories.
- Classify foods into food groups in the food pyramid.
- Compare and contrast foods based on caloric density.
- Identify nutrient-rich and nutrient-poor foods.
- Conclude that a healthy and balanced diet includes nutritious foods from all of the food groups.

Overview

The presenter burns a corn chip and a piece of cabbage to show that they contain different amounts of energy that can be measured in calories. As each food burns, it heats a test tube of water. The greater the change in the temperature of the water, the more calories the food contains. Then the students work in groups to categorize and interpret labels from a variety of food types. They organize the labels into food groups from the food pyramid and identify nutrients. Finally, they solve math problems related to calories and make dietary recommendations based on the comparison of frozen dinner packages.

Key Terms

Sugar: A sweet ingredient in food.

Carbohydrates: A component of food that provides energy. Carbohydrates include starch and sugars.

Fat: A component of food that is rich in calories and provides a lot of energy.

Protein: A component of food that builds muscles and provides energy.

Gram: A unit used to measure small increments of weight. About the weight of one paper clip.

Mineral: Nutrients needed for normal growth. One important mineral is calcium.

Fiber: Tough substance that is found in fresh fruits and vegetables and helps with digestion. It cleans out the large intestine.

Nutrients: The substances in your food that your body can use.

Malnutrition: A condition in which the body has trouble functioning because it does not have all the nutrients it needs.

Vitamins: Nutrients that are necessary for the normal functioning of our bodies and for growth and development. Vitamins our found naturally in our food.

Vitamin A: A vitamin found in yellow and orange fruits and vegetables, such as cantaloupes, carrots, and sweet potatoes; vitamin A is essential for growth, vision, and healthy skin.

Vitamin C: A vitamin found in fresh fruits and vegetables, including citrus fruits and red bell peppers, that is necessary for healthy gums, blood vessels, joints, and bones.

Thermometer: A tool used to measure temperature.

Test tube: A small vial used in science labs.

Calorie: A unit for measuring the energy in food. A scientific calorie is the amount of energy required to raise one gram of water by one degree Celsius. A food calorie is 1,000 times larger than a scientific calorie. It's the amount of energy required to raise 1 liter of water by one degree Celsius.

Food group: Foods that are grouped together because they provide similar nutrients.

Materials

Per class:
- 1 test tube stand, 2 ft. tall
- 1 test tube clamp
- 1 thermometer clamp used to hold the food samples
- 20 ml of water in a plastic container
- 2 test tubes, 20-ml capacity
- 1 10-ml graduated cylinder
- 1 thermometer
- 1 scale that measures 1 gram increments
- 1 small corn chip such as a Frito Lay chip
- 1 leaf of green cabbage
- 1 stove lighter
- 1 large tip pan to catch the ashes from the burning food
- 1 large, color FDA Food Pyramid

Per student:
- 1 worksheet on measuring calories in foods
- 1 food-label worksheet

Per group of 4:
- 1 bag containing assorted food labels and food containers. Each bag should contain one label from each of the food groups.

Procedure

> **Questions:**
> How do we know that foods differ in calorie content?
> What makes some foods more nutritious than others?

Activity 1: Different Foods and Different Amounts of Energy

1. Before class, set up the stand, test tube, water, thermometer, and food samples.
2. Start with a brief review of energy, energy balance, energy in, energy out, physical activity, and calories. To balance physical activity and the energy needed to live, we take in calories in food.
3. Ask the students to reflect on their own experience. Does it matter what type of food you eat? Why? Does every food provide the same amount of energy? Why or why not? What foods would you eat if you were about to play a hard game of soccer? What foods would you avoid?
4. Explain that today the class will be food scientists, testing the amount of energy in food and analyzing the contents of food products to determine healthy choices for "energy in." Pass out the worksheet on measuring calories in foods, and narrate the following steps as you perform them.
5. With a gram scale, weigh one Frito Lay chip and an equivalent amount (same weight) of cabbage leaf. Attach the Frito Lay chip to the clamp below and a little to one side of the test tube (instead of directly under it). Ask the students if they think the Frito Lay contains more or less energy than the piece of cabbage. Discuss the students' reasoning.
6. Measure 10 ml of water with a graduated cylinder. Pour the water into the test tube.
7. Measure the temperature of the water in Celsius with a thermometer. Write the temperature of the water on the board.
8. Light the chip and immediately position the clamp so that the chip will burn directly below the test tube.
9. Measure the temperature of the water after the chip burns out. Write the temperature on the board. Ask the students what the difference is between the two temperature readings.
10. Explain that the energy in the chip can be measured in calories. A scientific calorie is the amount of energy required to raise the temperature of one gram of water by one degree Celsius. A food calorie is 1,000 times larger than a scientific calorie. The Frito should heat up the water enough to show about 5 food calories of energy. Ask if a piece of cabbage will have more or fewer calories than the Frito.
11. Repeat steps 5 to 9, replacing the hot water with a new test tube and replacing the chip with a piece of cabbage. Show that the burning cabbage fails to increase the temperature of the water. Therefore, cabbage contains almost no calories.
12. Discuss other foods that you could try and what results you might get.
13. Explain that food scientists have tested thousands of different foods to find out how many calories they contain. Stress that you compared two samples of the same weight.

Activity 2: Are All Energy Balances Equal?

1. Show the students the amount of Frito Lays and the amount of cabbage they would have to eat to take in the energy spent in one busy day. Frito Lays alone or cabbage could meet their energy needs, but would those foods be the best choice? Why, or why not?
2. What other factors besides calories must be considered when planning a meal? Why is it important to eat more than one type of food? Write a list of nutrients on the board: carbohydrates, fats, proteins, vitamins, and minerals.
3. Define a healthy energy balance as an energy balance that includes an active lifestyle and a diverse diet covering all of the food groups and adequate nutrients. Explain that malnutrition is the result of not getting all of the nutrients that one needs.

Activity 3: Food Labels and the Food Guide Pyramid

1. Pass out a food-label worksheet to each student and a bag of assorted food labels to each group. Show the students how to find the calories, serving size, and major nutrients on the food labels. Specifically, the students should pay attention to protein, carbohydrates, fat, calcium, and vitamin C.

2. Point out the grain group on the large Food Pyramid. Then ask each team to locate and choose a food from this group. The students should show their food as they read its name and calorie content to the others in the group.

3. Ask each student to write down the name of the food and the number of calories per serving on the worksheet.

4. Repeat steps 2 and 3 until all six major food groups have been covered: grain, protein, dairy, fruits, vegetables, and oil.

5. Ask the students to compare and contrast the nutrition information for the various food groups. They can compare minerals, vitamins, protein, carbohydrates, fat, and fiber. Encourage them to use math (addition and subtraction) and key words. From this exercise, they should notice that some food types are rich in calories, while other foods have only a few calories. They should also notice that foods have different serving sizes.

6. Pass out two meal containers to each group. Ask the groups to identify the food groups in each meal. Then ask them to compare the two meals based on the number of calories and nutrients they contain.

7. Finally, ask each group to make a dietary recommendation. Which meal would be a wiser and healthier choice?

Nutrition: Balance and Imbalance
Lesson 3

ENERGY IN = Everyday Healthy Foods

Name: _____

Teacher: _____

Date: _____

Step 1: Observations

Do all foods contain the same amount of energy? _____

How do you know? _____

Step 2: Hypothesis

_____ have/has more energy than _____.

(Choose cabbage or Fritos)

Step 3: Plan your test

Step 4: Conduct your test

Trial 1: Frito Burn

Starting temperature: _____

Ending temperature: _____

Temperature difference: _____

Calories: _____

Trial 2: Cabbage Burn

Starting temperature: _____

Ending temperature: _____

Temperature difference: _____

Calories: _____

_____ have/has more energy than _____.

(Choose cabbage or Fritos)

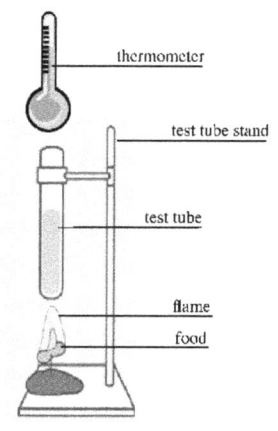

Food Group	Name	Calories
Grains		
Protein		
Fruits		
Vegetables		
Dairy		
Oils		

Nutrients	Meal 1	Meal 2
Macronutrients (protein)		
Minerals (calcium)		
Vitamins (A, D, B, C, K)		
Calories		

Children's Hospital Oakland Research Institute

Grade: 4
Nutrition: Balance and Imbalance
Lesson 4: Energy In: High-Calorie Foods

Lesson Time: 1 hour

References: Program Energy: www.programenergy.org; Sugar Sleuths: Family Health, Lawrence Hall of Science http://lawrencehallofscience.org/familyhealth/activities/sugarsleuths/sugarsleuths.html; Fat experiment: FOSS Food and Nutrition Module http://www.lawrencehallofscience.org/foss/scope/folio/html/FoodandNutrition/2.html

Lesson objectives

- Observe that high-calorie foods tend to contain high levels of fat.
- Observe that the dairy group, the meat and nuts group, and the oil group contain the most calories and the most fat per a given weight of food.
- Discuss how a balanced diet includes foods from all of the food groups.
- Make predictions about the fat content of foods of the same weight but unknown caloric content.
- Draw conclusions based on evidence.
- Conclude that high-calorie foods are high in fat but don't give you the diversity you need to have a balanced diet.
- Measure food samples.

Overview

The presenter shows the class the results of an experiment testing how low-calorie and high-calorie foods interact with brown paper. The students see that high-calorie foods—especially from the meat/nuts, dairy, and oils food groups—tend to leave grease stains. The students receive food samples from a variety of food groups, and they predict which foods contain the most fat, and therefore the most calories. Then they set up experiments to test their predictions. The class discusses sources of excess calories: fat and sugar. The presenter uses Benedict's solution to test food samples for sugar, and students guess the relative sugar content of various beverages. Finally, the class discusses the importance of a balanced diet in helping ensure an overall energy balance.

Occupation of the Day

Nutritionist: A nutritionist is a person who advises people on dietary matters relating to health, well-being, and optimal nutrition. Nutritionists who are registered dieticians plan meals for individuals and groups, such as hospital patients and schoolchildren.

Key Terms

Sugar: A sweet substance that contains 4 calories in every gram.

Nutrients: Important substances that your body needs in order to grow and develop properly.

Starch: A food substance found in grains, potatoes, and root vegetables. It contains 4 calories per gram.

Protein: A food substance found in meat, beans, nuts, eggs, and dairy products. It contains 4 calories per gram.

Oil: A fatty food substance that contains 9 calories per gram. Oil is found in nuts, beans, other plant products, and fish. Oil is the healthiest type of fat.

Fat: A greasy food substance that contains 9 calories per gram. Fats are found in both plants and animals. Everyone needs to eat some fat.

Materials

Per class:

- 1 test tube rack for 50 ml test tubes
- 6 50-ml test tubes with screw-on caps
- 1 pan deep enough to hold the test tube rack in a water bath
- Benedict's Solution
- 1 small graduated cylinder (at least 10 ml)
- 1 eyedropper or small disposable pipette
- Six food samples for the sugar test (about 2 mg or 2 ml each):
    - Table sugar (sucrose)
    - Honey
    - Milk
    - Raisins
    - Cracker
    - Small piece of fruit such as apple
- Empty beverage cans and bottles of various sizes, and for each one a container of sugar to show how much sugar each can and bottle contains
- 8 food samples for the brown squares that will be prepared before class and used in the demonstration. These should be different from the food samples used in class.
- 8 6"x 6" squares of brown paper for the demonstration. Label each square with the food name and the calories per gram. Measure out 2 grams of each food and spread it in a 2-in. circle on the appropriate brown paper square. Leave the squares over night and brush the excess food into the trash before class. The squares can be stacked with wax paper between them.
- At least 8 food samples for the in-class fat tests. About 20 grams of each food type is required. Suggested foods include:
    - Ritz crackers
    - Cereal
    - Oil
    - Fruit
    - Bread
    - Cheese
    - Candy bar
    - White sugar
    - Butter
    - Peanut butter
    - Chips
    - Lettuce

Other foods could include:
    - Low-fat chips
    - Low-fat cheese
    - Nuts
    - Carrots
    - Cookies
    - Salami
    - Cooked chicken
    - Tuna
    - Pretzels
    - Goldfish crackers
    - Granola bar
    - Raisins

Per group of 4:

- 8 6"x6" squares of brown paper
- 16 6"x6" squares of wax paper
- 1 digital food scale
- 2 plastic knives
- 1 permanent marker
- 1 ziplock bag to hold squares of brown paper after the experiment

Procedure

> **Questions:**
> **What foods contain the most fat?**
> **What foods contain the most sugar?**

Activity 1: Fat Test

1. Tape the prepared squares across the top of the board. Below each square write the name of the food, the food group, and calories in large letters on the board, so that everyone can see from across the room.
2. Ask how you could test foods for fat. Discuss as a class.
3. Ask the students to observe the paper squares. What do they notice? What is different about the various squares? What could account for the different sizes of the grease stains? Do the students see any trends? Ask them to write down their observations and conclusions. They should observe that some of the papers have grease stains while others have none. High-calorie foods have more fat and leave larger stains. Foods made of only fat, such as butter, soaked an entire square. High-calorie foods tend to belong to the meat/nuts, dairy, and oils food groups.
4. Discuss how eating only fat could lead to an energy imbalance, and how it could be harmful to your health. Offer the class a challenge. Show food samples from various groups without food labels. Ask them how they would design an experiment to see which foods contain the most fat.
5. Discuss variables that could affect the outcome of the test. Discuss ways to set aside a control as a comparison.
6. Guide the students as they work in groups of four to generate hypotheses, such as the following:
   - Peanut butter contains more fat per gram than a carrot or a pear.
   - Cheese contains more fat per gram than rye bread.
   - Salami contains more fat per gram than lettuce.
7. Each group will test 4 hypotheses involving 8 different types of food. Guide them as they generate their own procedures. For example:
   - Take eight types of food and eight brown paper squares.
   - Label each square of paper with a food name, its food group, and your name.
   - Measure 2 gm of each food using a scale.
   - Place each 2-gm sample on the appropriately labeled square of brown paper.
   - Cut the food up and/or crush it if necessary by putting a clean sheet of wax paper over it and pressing hard.
   - Spread the food around so that it covers the area of a 2-in. circle.
   - Wait one hour. Then brush the excess food into the trash.
   - Observe the differences in the sizes of the grease stains.
   - The foods that leave the larger stains have more fat and more calories.
8. When all of the groups have a procedure, pass out the food samples, brown paper squares, and gram scales. Each group should test 8 foods (2 per student). Assist as they complete the labeling and measuring. At the end of class, after the sugar demonstration, ask students to brush the excess food into the trash. They should then place clean wax paper squares between the brown paper ones to keep them from contaminating each other and put all of the squares into a ziplock bag for storage until the next class.
9. Review that fat gives the body energy, but it lacks the vitamins and minerals that you need from whole grains, fresh fruits, vegetables, lean meat, and low-fat dairy products. A balanced diet includes food from all the food groups, and only moderate amounts of fat and sugar.

Activity 2: Sugar Demonstration

1. Review that a healthy energy balance means that the "energy out" from an active lifestyle equals the "energy in" from nutritious foods from the six food groups. Review the six food groups and point out that calories are found in carbohydrates, proteins, and fats. Remind the class that most people can use

more nutrients in their diets, especially vitamins and minerals. Ask them which foods everyone should eat less of. They should mention fat and sugar.

2. Set up the 6 test tubes on the test tube rack. In the bottoms of the test tubes, put about 2 gm or 2ml of the following foods: table sugar (sucrose), honey, milk, raisins, cracker, fruit. Each sample should be placed in its own test tube. Tell the students that Benedict's solution reacts with milk sugar (lactose), fruit sugar (fructose), and glucose (a sugar found in the bodies of animals and in some plants), but not with table sugar (sucrose) or starch. Ask them to predict which of the six foods will react. To each test tube add 10 ml of water and 15 drops of Benedict's solution. Then cap and shake the test tubes. After the students get a good look at the starting color, place the test tube rack in a pan of hot water (deep enough to submerge the solution in the test tubes) for 5 to 10 minutes. Watch the solution as it changes to green, yellow, orange, red, or brown in the test tubes containing lactose, fructose, or glucose.

3. Discuss the harmful effects of eating excess sugar.

4. Show the beverage bottles/cans. Ask two volunteers to try to line them up according to how much sugar they contain. Then show the correct order and the container of sugar corresponding to each beverage.

5. Discuss how nutritionists advise individuals and groups on dietary matters.

Extension

Tell students to make a list of drinks that they drink at home. Ask them to write down nutrition information that is listed on the drink labels.

Nutrition: Balance and Imbalance
Lesson 4

ENERGY IN = **High Calorie Foods**

Name: _____

Teacher: _____

Date: _____

Fat Experiment

Step 1: Observations

_____

_____

Step 2: Make a hypothesis

_____ have/has more energy than _____.

Step 3: Plan your test

1. Measure 2 gm of each food using a scale
2. Place each 2-gm sample on a separate piece of brown paper.
3. Spread the sample around so that it covers the area of a 2-in circle.
4. Label the paper with the food type and name.
5. Wait one hour. Then brush the excess food into the trash.

Step 4: Conduct your test

Step 5: Draw conclusions (next week!)

Sugar Demonstration

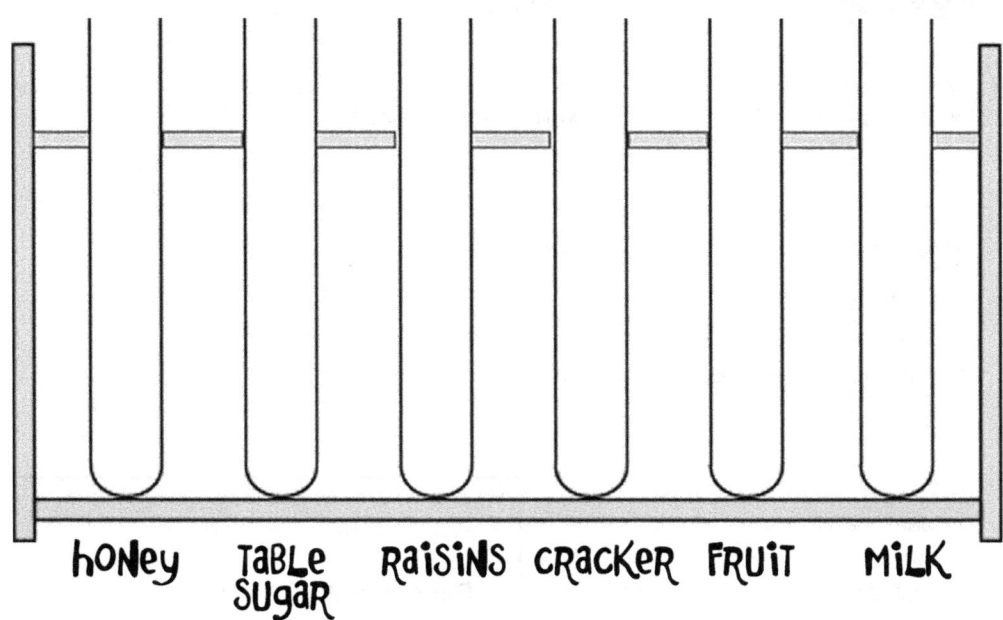

honey   table sugar   raisins   cracker   fruit   milk

Predictions:

Which foods contain **lactose**? _____

Which foods contain **fructose** or **glucose**? _____

Which foods will not react? _____

12 oz of Dr. Pepper
160 empty calories

What are empty calories?

_____

_____

_____

Grade: 4
Nutrition: Balance and Imbalance
Lesson 5: Energy Balance and Your Health

Lesson Time: 1 hour

References: 5-a-day: http://www.5aday.org; American Dietetic Association: http://www.eatright.org/cps/rde/xchg/ada/hs.xsl/nutrition_fgp_ENU_HTML.htm; Kid's Health for Parents: http://kidshealth.org/parent/nutrition_fit/nutrition/lunch.html

Lesson objectives
- Examine the results of an experiment.
- Analyze and graph data.
- Draw conclusions and make recommendations based on reasoning.
- Learn about the career of an exercise physiologist.

Overview
The class measures, compares, and graphs the size of the grease stains from the experiments conducted in the previous lesson. The students meet an exercise physiologist who helps them design their own menus and activity programs.

Occupation of the Day
Exercise Physiologist: Exercise physiologists use physical activity to treat people with illnesses such as obesity, diabetes, and asthma. For their patients, exercise is often the best medicine. Exercise physiologists conduct fitness tests to assess a patient's physical condition. They track heart rate and rhythm, record the oxygen in the blood, and measure blood pressure. They use weights and other instruments to gauge the patient's strength and flexibility. Based on the results of these tests, they prescribe appropriate exercises. Education requirements vary depending on the employment setting. The minimum requirement is a master's degree, but some exercise physiologists have a PhD.

Materials

Per student:
- 1 worksheet
- 1 graph-paper transparency

Per group of 4:
- 8 brown paper squares from the previous lesson
- 1 large piece of graph paper
- 1 box of colored markers
- Pre-cut samples of fresh fruits and vegetables for tasting

Procedure

Question:
How can we keep our meals and physical activities in balance?

Activity 1: Observing Results

1. Ask the students to observe the paper squares from the previous week. What do they notice? What is different about the squares? What could account for the different sizes of the grease stains? Do the students see any trends? Ask the students to write down their observations and conclusions.

2. Pass out overhead transparencies printed with graph paper, so that the students can estimate and compare the sizes of the grease stains. Ask them to place the clear sheet over the brown paper and to count the number of squares that contain grease stains.

3. The students should notice that rich foods from the dairy, meat, nuts, and oils groups leave the largest stains.

4. Help the class to create bar graphs comparing the grease stains.

5. Discuss how the results relate to energy balance.

Activity 2: Exercise Physiologist

IIntroduce the guest speaker, an exercise physiologist who treats childhood obesity. The guest should discuss his or her job, describe what a typical day is like, explain how children's energy imbalances are assessed, and tell how exercise regimens were designed and prescribed for specific patients. The visit should be as interactive as possible. The guest should teach the students stretches, strength building exercises, and simple aerobic exercises, and lead them as they design fun exercise programs for themselves.

Activity 3: Designing a Healthy Energy Balance

1. Hand back all of the worksheets from the first four lessons. Using the information that the students have learned about energy balances, ask them to create their own meal plans and physical education programs. Invite them to try the fruit and vegetable samples to get ideas for foods to include in their menus.

2. Starting with the energy balance examples from lesson 1 and the calorie-expenditure information from lesson 2, the students should devise a list of exercises and meals that balance.

3. Students can work in teams as necessary.

Nutrition: Balance and Imbalance
Lesson 5

ENERGY BALANCE
& Your Health

Name: _____

Teacher: _____

Date: _____

eNeRgy BaLaNce

Energy In _____ Energy Out _____

Food Plan	Exercise Plan
Breakfast _____ _____ _____	**Before School** _____ _____ _____
Lunch _____ _____ _____	**Recess** _____ _____ _____
Dinner _____ _____ _____	**After School** _____ _____ _____

Basal Metabolic Rate (the energy you need outside of exercise): 1,200 Cal

Children's Hospital Oakland Research Institute

Physical Activity Choices

Activity	Time	Energy OUT
Ping Pong	30 minutes	75 Calories
Walking (4 mph)	30 minutes	100 Calories
Skateboarding	30 minutes	75 Calories
Dancing	30 minutes	125 Calories
Riding a bike	30 minutes	200 Calories
Basketball	30 minutes	175 Calories
Jogging	30 minutes	175 Calories
Jumping rope	30 minutes	300 Calories

Snack Choices

Activity	Time	Energy IN
Carrots	1 (1 cup raw carrots)	50 Calories
Banana	1 (1 medium banana)	100 Calories
String cheese	1 (1 oz)	100 Calories
Yogurt	1 (1 cup)	150 Calories
Soda	1 (12 fl oz)	150 Calories
Granola bar	1 (1 medium bar)	100 Calories
Candy bar	1 (1 medium bar)	250 Calories
Ice cream sundae	1 (3 scoops & toppings)	550 Calories

Grade: 4
Traumatic Brain Injuries
Lesson 1: Protecting Your Brain

Lesson Time: 1 hour

Reference: Neuroscience for Kids by Eric Chudler: http://faculty.washington.edu/chudler/injury.html

Lesson objectives
- Make observations and predictions.
- Work as a team on an experiment.
- Explore the fragile nature of the human brain.
- Construct protection for an egg that represents a human head.
- Understand the importance of safety measures such as helmets and seatbelts.

Overview

The presenter discusses helmets and seatbelts with the class to see if the students know how to protect their brains. The presenter compares a brain to the yolk of an egg, then shakes or drops a raw egg to show how different types of accidents can damage your brain. The students do an experiment to see how much padding is needed to protect an egg from cracking in a free fall. Each group gets a different material to tape around an egg. The students predict which eggs will remain intact, and the presenter drops each egg from a height of six feet. The students compare their predictions to the results. Finally, the presenter demonstrates the proper way to wear a helmet.

Key Terms

Skull: The hard bone that covers the brain.

Brain: An organ that controls your body functions, your thoughts, and your movements.

Cerebral fluid: Fluid that surrounds the brain.

Open head injury: A brain injury where the skull cracks open.

Closed head injury: A brain injury where the skull remains intact. The brain may be damaged by bruising and swelling.

Materials

Per class:
- 1 worksheet overhead, optional
- 1 overhead or poster showing various skull injuries, optional
- 1 dozen eggs
- 1 black marker
- 1 Tupperware container with lid
- 1 adult size helmet
- 1 piece of cloth
- 2 1-quart ziplock bags for demonstrations
- 4 MRIs showing traumatic brain injuries (TBIs), optional

Per student:
- 1 worksheet

Per group of 4:
- 1-gallon ziplock bag
- 1 egg (from carton of dozen)
- 1-quart ziplock bag filled with materials that could protect the egg. Each group receives a different material. Materials could include:
  - packaging peanuts
  - cardboard cut into 2-in. squares
  - sponges cut into chunks
  - paper napkins
  - bubble wrap
  - hard plastic plates cut into 2-in. pieces
  - egg cartons cut into 2-in. square pieces
  - plastic garbage bags cut into 4-in. squares
- 1 roll of Scotch tape

Procedure

> **Question:**
>
> How can you protect your brain?

Demonstration: Egg Without a Helmet

1. Put on a helmet. Ask how many students wear a helmet every single time that they bike, skateboard, or roller blade. Write the number of students on the board. Discuss reasons why the other kids don't always wear helmets.

2. Draw a face on an egg. Explain that the egg is like your head. The eggshell is like your skull: it's your built-in protection for your brain. But, like the eggshell, your skull is thin. It cannot withstand hard crashes. Explain that the yolk of the egg is like your brain. Your brain floats in a liquid bath which protects it. The brain is fragile, and it doesn't heal the same way as the rest of the body.

3. Take one egg and shake it vigorously (to ensure that the yolk will break, make a pinprick in this egg before class to break the protective membrane inside). Explain that one type of brain injury is a closed head injury. The skull doesn't crack but the brain smashes against the skull and gets bruised, causing damage. Gently crack the egg into the Tupperware container and show that the yolk is broken.

4. Place an egg in a ziplock bag and press the air out of the bag. Put the ziplock bag into a tupperware container. Explain that the container is a car, and the egg has no seatbelt. Stand on a chair and drop the egg and container on a desk. Show the mess to the class. Explain that another type of brain injury is an open head injury where the skull cracks open. This can happen in a car accident, a fall, a bike accident, or a diving accident. Broken skulls are more dangerous than the other types of bone breaks that occur in accidents, because of the potential for damage to the brain. Also, with any type of brain injury (open head or closed head), the brain can swell, causing serious damage to itself.

5. Ask the students if wearing a hat or a baseball cap can protect someone's head in a bike accident. Take another egg and have a volunteer wrap the egg in cloth simulating a baseball cap. Drop the egg inside a ziplock from the same height and show the class the result.

Activity 1: Designing Protective Gear for Eggs

1. Tell students that they are going to try to build a helmet to protect an egg from damage.

2. Write a list of the different materials on the board and number each one. Ask students to use their previous experiences to predict which materials would make good helmets. They can choose more than one. Each student should state one hypothesis on the worksheet.

3. Split the class into groups of four students. Give each group one egg, some Scotch tape, and a bag of material. Ask the students to design and build a helmet, taping the material to the egg.

4. Allow 15-20 minutes for the helmet construction. Emphasize teamwork. When the groups are ready, show the protected eggs in front of the class and ask the students to predict which eggs will survive.

5. Place each protected egg inside a ziplock bag and drop it onto a desk from six feet above the desk. This will allow students to observe the impact without leaving their seats. Ask the class to make observations about which types of protection worked best.

6. Discuss the egg drop. What properties make a good helmet? Compare these materials to the hard shell and the Styrofoam lining of a helmet. Explain that heads are different from eggs, so the materials used to protect the egg (e.g., a sponge) would not necessarily protect a head.

Activity 2: How to Wear a Helmet

1. Relate the egg drop demonstration to bicycle helmets by saying that helmets work because the hard Styrofoam liner inside breaks instead of your head. The plastic on the outside keeps the helmet sliding with you and not twisting your neck or coming off your head.

2. Demonstrate sliding the helmet on the pavement. Explain that 9 out of 10 bicycle-related deaths are from head injuries. Of those deaths, 8 out of 10 could have been prevented by wearing a helmet.

3. Show the poster, overhead and/or MRIs of various skull injuries (if available).

4. Put on a helmet a number of wrong ways and have the students guess what is wrong. Then show the students the right way:
   - The helmet must be level on your head, covering the forehead.
   - The helmet should be snug and not wobble excessively from side to side.
   - Sliders should be positioned in a V under earlobes.
   - No more than two fingers should fit under the chinstrap.
   - The helmet should not push more than two inches straight back.

   Explain that if you are wearing a helmet and are in an accident, you have to get a new helmet before the next time you ride your bike or skate. Even if you cannot see a crack, you should replace your helmet, because they are not effective for more than one accident.

5. Ask how many students will wear their helmets after doing the experiment and seeing the demonstration.

6. Discuss reasons why you need a brain. Explain that the students will learn about the brain and brain injuries for the next four weeks.

Extensions

Ask the students to make a sign at home that reminds them about the importance of wearing a helmet. The sign can be hung near their bikes or skates.

**Traumatic Brain Injuries
Lesson 1**

PROTECTING Your Brain

Name: _____

Teacher: _____

Date: _____

Do you wear a helmet?   YES   NO   (Circle one)

Why or why not?_____

Egg Drop Experiment

Step 1: Observations

_____

_____

Closed head injury

Open head injury

Questions

_____

_____

Step 2: Hypothesis

_____will make the best protection for the egg because

_____

Step 3: Plan Your Test

1. Material _____

2. Attach material to egg _____

3. Give egg to presenter to drop

4. Observe results

Step 4: Conduct Your Test

Group	Material	Results
1	Packaging peanuts	_____
2	Cardboard	_____
3	Sponges	_____
4	Paper napkins	_____
5	Bubble wrap	_____
6	Hard plastic plates	_____
7	Egg cartons	_____
8	Plastic garbage bags	_____

Step 5: Draw Conclusions

What worked? Why? _____

_____

What didn't work? Why? _____

_____

How do the results relate to preventing brain injuries? _____

_____

Shared Results

With whom can you share this information?

_____   _____   _____

Grade: 4
Traumatic Brain Injuries
Lesson 2: Making Neurons

Lesson Time: 1 hour

References: Neuroscience for Kids: http://faculty.washington.edu/chudler/chmodel.html; Overview of the Nervous System by NASA Quest: http://quest.nasa.gov/neuron/background/nervsys.html; Background information: http://kidshealth.org/parent/general/body_basics/brain_nervous_system.html

Lesson objectives
- Explore the role and function of motor and sensory nerves.
- Create a model of a neuron.
- Explore how neurons interact with one another in nerves to send electrical signals around the body.

Overview
Students learn how neurons send messages through the nervous system to all parts of the body. They make pipe cleaner neurons that they can take home. Then they participate in a role-playing game where they act as neurons sending signals as fast as they can.

Occupation of the Day
Neuroscientist: A scientist who studies the nervous system. Many neuroscientists "wear several hats." For example, a neurosurgeon may also have a Ph.D. in physiology and therefore also be a neuroscientist. He or she may work in the operating room but also have time to perform experiments. There are many career paths that neuroscientists can take, which include: neuroanatomist, neurobiologist, neurochemist, etc.

Key Terms
Neuron: A specialized cell that can receive signals and transmit them to other neurons or muscle cells.

Peripheral nervous system: The part of the nervous system that includes sensory and motor nerves that branch from the central nervous system to the rest of the body.

Central nervous system: The brain and spinal cord.

Cell body: This is the control center of the neuron. Many branches extend from the cell body to receive signals.

Reflexes: The automatic responses of muscles to stimuli.

Sensory nerve: Nerves that react to external stimuli and send signals to the brain.

Motor nerve: Nerves that send signals from the brain to the muscles to make them move.

Materials

Per class:
- 1 worksheet overhead, optional
- Signs that can hang around a student's neck:
  - 1 sign saying "Pain" on one side and "Move" on the other side
  - 1 sign saying "Message"
  - 1 sign saying "Foot"
  - 1 sign saying "Brain"
  - 1 sign saying "Mouth"
  - 4 signs saying "Neuron"

Per student:
- 1 worksheet
- 1 set of pipe cleaners per student and per presenter:
  - 1 full-length black pipe cleaner for the cell body, axon, and synaptic terminal
  - 1 half-length white pipe cleaner for the sheath
  - 3 third-length red pipe cleaners for the branches or dendrites
  - NOTE: Colors of pipe cleaners may vary, but each student should have 1 long one of one color, 1 half-length one of another color, and 3 third-length ones of a different color.

Per pair:
- 1 box of crayons

Procedure

> **Questions:**
> What does the brain do?
> How does the brain receive signals from and send signals to the body?

Introduction

1. Review the function of the brain and nervous system.
2. Explain that the brain performs all of its functions by receiving and sending signals through a network of fibers called nerves. Nerves are bundles of special cells called neurons. There are about 100 billion neurons in our bodies. They transmit signals just like electricity is transmitted through a wire. For example, if you stubbed your toe, your toe would send a pain signal to your brain to tell your brain that your toe was hurt. Neurons also send signals within the brain.
3. People who study how neurons work are called neuroscientists. Establish that "neuro" means "relating to the nervous system."
4. Pass out the worksheets and the crayons. Draw a typical neuron on the board.
5. Explain that first the neuron receives a signal from the brain or another neuron through the branches, or dendrites. Explain that the signal then travels to the cell body, and that the cell body is like the control center of the neuron. Point to the cell body and ask students to label it.
6. Explain that the signal travels through the long part of a neuron, which is like a trunk. Point to the axon.
7. Explain that finally the message is ready to go to the next neuron or a muscle fiber. There are tiny gaps after every neuron. Signals are carried across these gaps to another neuron or muscle. Draw a second neuron on the board and point to the gap.

Activity 1: Pipe Cleaner Neurons

1. Explain that the students will now make neurons out of pipe cleaners. Say that most neurons have this general structure, but sensory neurons are a little different. Demonstrate how to make a neuron out of a pipe cleaner as you test what the students learned about neurons. As you show each part of the neuron, ask what it does.
2. Hold up a finished model in front of the class. Walk through the steps as the students follow along.

3. Hand out the long black pipe cleaners and show the students how to create a cell body by rolling half of the pipe cleaner into a ball.

4. Pass out the red, third-length pipe cleaners and show the students how to add them to the cell body as branches.

5. Hand out the white, half-length pipe cleaners and show the students how to wrap them around the trunk as the sheath. Explain that the sheath acts as insulation like the plastic tubing found around electric wires.

6. In groups, ask the students to discuss what might happen to your neurons if you smash your skull. Assign one person in each group to report to the class. Establish that neurons may be damaged, so that the brain cannot send messages to certain parts of the body.

Activity 2: Sending a Signal

1. Explain that messages can travel in neurons at speeds up to 268 miles per hour. These signals are transmitted from neuron to neuron across gaps called "synapses."

2. Ask for one volunteer to be a neuron with you. Give the student a sign that says "Neuron."

3. Demonstrate that your left hand is the branches and your right arm is the trunk. Show a sign that says "message" and pass the sign from your left hand to your right hand and to the student.

4. Ask for three more students to be neurons, give them signs, and have them practice passing the message down the line. Ask for more students and time how long it takes them to pass the message down the line. Remind them that bundles of neurons form nerves that extend all over your body from your central nervous system, forming your peripheral nervous system, which extends through your entire body including your muscles, internal organs, skin, eyes, nose, mouth, and ears.

5. Ask half of the class to act as one chain of neurons. Explain that the brain receives signals from different parts of the body and sends signals back. Explain that the student on one end the line will be the foot. Give that student a sign that says "foot". Explain that the student at the other end of the line will be the brain. Give that student a sign that says "Brain."

6. Explain that the body has just stubbed the toe. Give the foot a message that says "pain" and ask the students to pass the signal up to the brain.

7. With the rest of the class form another line of volunteers extending from the brain back to the foot. Explain that the brain receives the signal and tells the foot to move. Turn over the pain sign so it says "Move". Give the brain the sign that says "Move" and ask the brain to pass the signal back through the new line of volunteers to the foot. Explain that the neurons that send the message from the foot to the brain are sensory neurons. Explain that the neurons that send the message from the brain to the foot are motor neurons.

8. Time how long it takes the students to send the messages from the foot to the brain and back to the foot. Explain that this is called reaction time. When our nerves are working right, messages are traveling very fast and we react almost instantly.

9. If time permits, try another version of the role-play, where the final student is the mouth rather than the foot. When the brain gets the pain signal it should send a message to "Say ouch."

Extensions

Have the students describe other scenarios that involve their sensory organs sending information to their brains.

Ask the students to write out the path of signals to and from the brain, using scenarios of their choice.

Traumatic Brain Injuries
Lesson 2

MAKING NEURONS

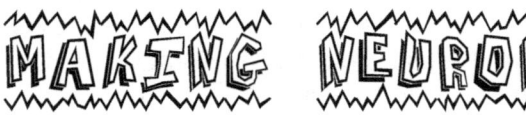

Name: ______________________________

Teacher: ______________________________

Date: ______________________________

The nervous system is made up of nerves.

Nerves are made of specialized cells called ________________________.

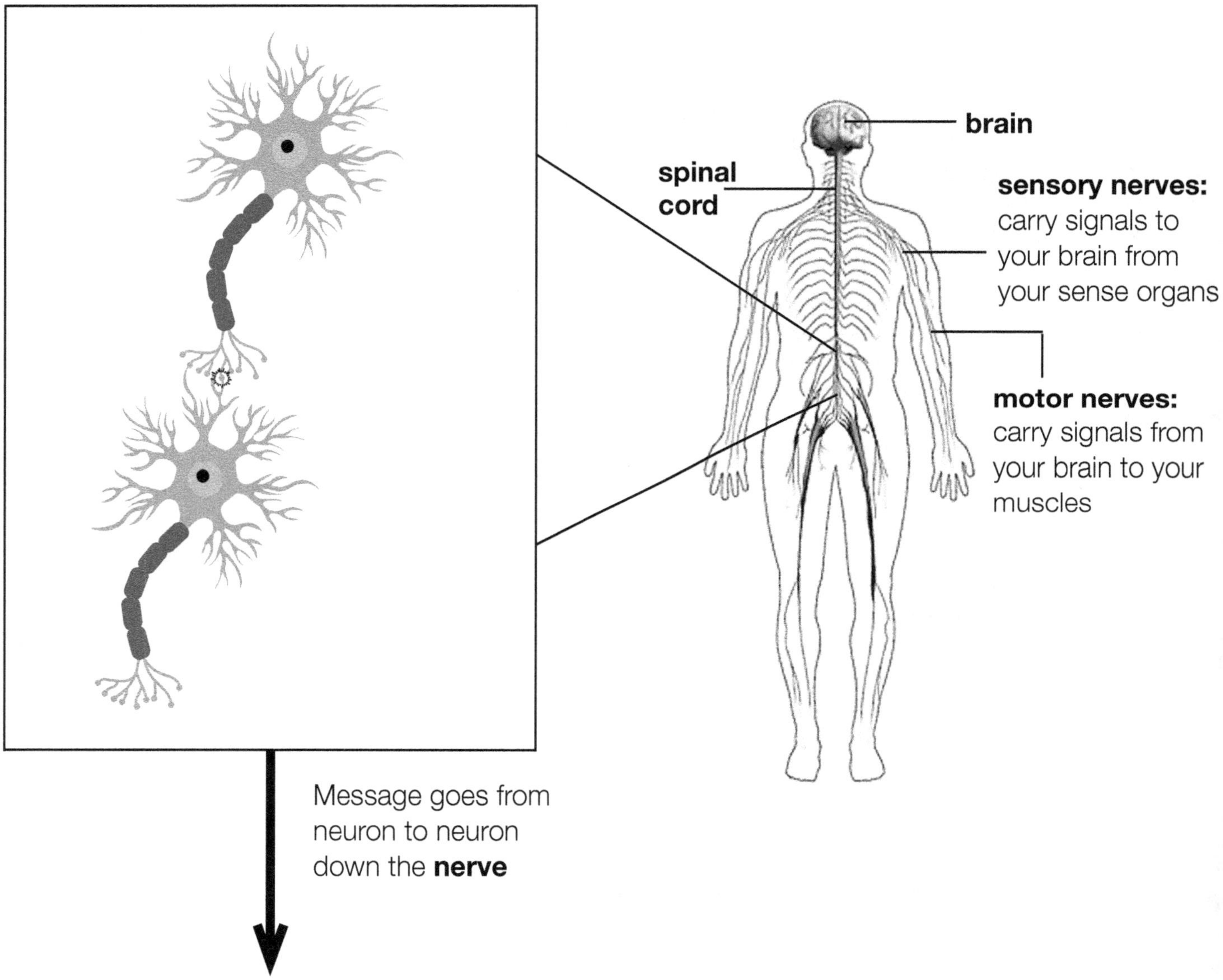
brain
spinal cord
sensory nerves: carry signals to your brain from your sense organs
motor nerves: carry signals from your brain to your muscles
Message goes from neuron to neuron down the **nerve**

Key

Name	Scientific Name
Cell Body	Cell Body
Trunk	Axon
Branches	Dendrites
Sheath	Myelinated Sheath

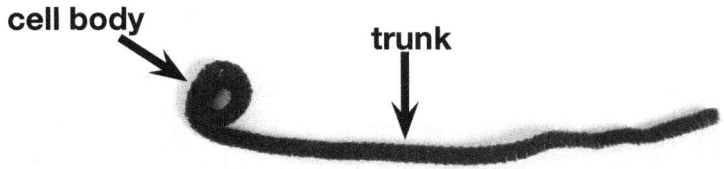

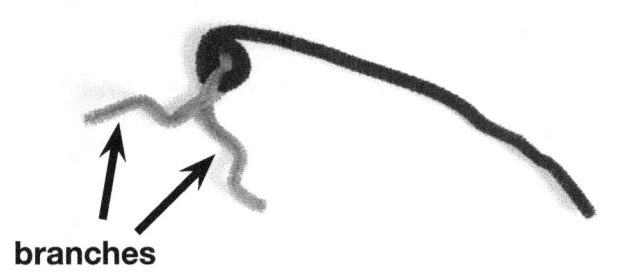

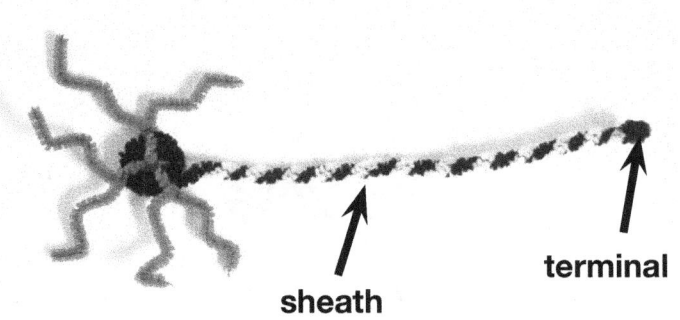

**Traumatic Brain Injuries
Brain Quiz**

1. Take the test and answer the questions.
2. Count up the number of times you answered YES.
3. If you have more "YES" than "NO" answers, you are right-brained.
4. If you have more "NO" than "YES" answers, you are left-brained.
5. If you have an even number of "YES" and "NO" answers, then you use both sides of your brain equally.

Name: _____

Teacher: _____

Date: _____

The PoiNT?

Left-brained people:
- Enjoy math
- Like to be organized and make lists
- Remember people by their names, not their faces
- Can easily memorize facts
- Understand literal meaning

- Are creative, enjoy writing or art
- Are often disorganized
- Remember people by their faces
- Are spatially aware, talk with their hands
- Are "big picture" oriented

Are you Left- or Right-Brained?

1. Do you enjoy creative writing more than math?   YES   NO

2. Do you keep your desk cluttered?   YES   NO

3. Do you remember people better by their faces instead of their names?   YES   NO

4. Do you use a lot of hand motions when you talk?   YES   NO

5. Can you tell about how much time has passed without a watch?   YES   NO

6. Do you like drawing better than writing?   YES   NO

7. Do you put your things in different places after you use them   YES   NO
   instead of always putting them away in the same place?

8. Do you like tests where you must write your own answer better   YES   NO
   than multiple-choice tests?

Grade: 4
Traumatic Brain Injuries
Lesson 3: Building a Brain

Lesson Time: 1 hour

References: Neuroscience for Kids: http://faculty.washington.edu/chudler/chmodel.html; Anatomy of Human Nervous System by Dorothy Starnes: http://idid.essortment.com/anatomynervous_rmej.htm; Neurology Channel: http://www.neurologychannel.com

Lesson objectives
- Be able to identify major parts of the brain.
- Meet a healthcare worker who assesses patients with traumatic brain injuries.
- Understand that the parts of the brain control everything from breathing to complex thought.
- Use diagrams to explore neuroanatomy.
- Create brain models with the four major lobes.
- Know that any injury to a specific part of the brain results in a specific loss of function.

Overview

The presenter shares pictures and models of the central nervous system, and the students brainstorm the functions of the parts. Then the presenter explains a diagram of the brain as the students color a similar one. Next the students use modeling clay to create models of the brain. These models show the four lobes of the brain, the cerebellum, and the brainstem. Finally, the students take a test to see if they are right-brained or left-brained.

Occupations of the Day

Neurologist: A neurologist is a medical doctor who is trained in the diagnosis and treatment of nervous system disorders, including diseases of the brain, spinal cord, nerves, and muscles. Neurologists perform neurological examinations of the nerves of the head and body; muscle strength and movement; balance, walking, and reflexes; and sensation, memory, speech, language, and other cognitive abilities.

Paramedic: A person trained to assist medical professionals and to give emergency medical treatment.

Radiologist: A physician specializing in diagnostic techniques for viewing internal organs and tissues without surgery. Radiological methods include X-ray, MRI, computed tomography (CT) scan, ultrasound, angiography, and nuclear isotopes.

Key Terms

Back lobe: The part of the brain that controls many aspects of vision (a.k.a., occipital lobe).

Brainstem: The part of the brain that controls basic life functions, such as heartbeat, breathing, and blood pressure.

Central nervous system: The part of the nervous system consisting of the brain and spinal cord. It controls and coordinates most functions of the body and mind.

Cerebrum: The largest part of the brain, it includes four lobes that specialize in different functions. The outside of the cerebrum has folds and ridges that increase the total surface area.

Cerebellum: The part of the brain responsible for coordination of movement, posture, and balance.

Front lobe: The part of the brain that controls reasoning, planning, speech, movement (motor cortex), emotions, and problem solving (a.k.a., frontal lobe).

Neuron: A specialized cell that can receive signals and transmit them to other neurons.

Peripheral nervous system: The part of the nervous system that includes sensory and motor nerves that branch from the central nervous system to the rest of the body.

Receptors: Nerve cells that detect conditions in the body's environment.

Side lobe: The part of the brain that deals with hearing and memory (a.k.a., temporal lobe).

Spinal cord: The thick, whitish cord of nerve tissue that extends from the brain down through the spinal column and from which the spinal nerves branch off to various parts of the body.

Top lobe: The part of the brain that controls perception of touch, pressure, temperature, and pain (a.k.a., parietal lobe).

Materials

Per class:
- 1 worksheet overhead, optional
- 1 human brain model
- 1 sheep brain
- 1 poster of brain parts and functions
- Brain Quiz Directions

Per student:
- 1 worksheet
- 1 left-right brain quiz

Per group of 4:
- 2 MRI images of brain injuries affecting specific regions of the brain, optional
- 1 right brain Jell-O mold
- 1 left brain Jell-O mold
- 2 boxes of crayons
- 2 cups of reusable modeling clay
- 12 colored toothpicks including 2 of each of the following colors: plain, red, blue, yellow, green, and purple

Procedure

> **Question:**
> **What happens if you injure one part of the brain?**

Guest Speaker

1. Pass out the student worksheets.
2. Introduce the guest speaker who treats brain injuries. Describe the speaker's educational history and current occupation. Ask the guest to tell about real cases where patients injured specific regions of the brain and lost corresponding body functions. If possible, ask the guest to share MRI images from the cases.
3. Make sure that the guest mentions at least three of the following brain regions: the front lobe (frontal lobe), back lobe (occipital lobe), side lobe (temporal lobe), the brainstem, top lobe (parietal lobe), cerebellum, and spinal cord. Ask the guest in advance to use the terms "front lobe," "back lobe," "side lobe," and "top lobe" in addition to the scientific terms. Ask the students to find the parts of the brain mentioned by the guest on their worksheets.
4. Encourage student questions. Explain that scientists know the different parts of the brain and their functions because they have studied people who have damage to different parts of the brain.
5. If MRIs are available, pass one out to each pair of students. Ask the students what they see.

Activity 1: Brain Labeling

1. Show the sheep brain and various brain models, including a completed clay brain. Briefly review the main parts of the nervous system, including the spinal cord, nerves, and brain. Explain that the brain is divided into two halves and both sides have regions that control specific body functions.
2. Show a poster of the major brain parts. For each part, ask the students to:
   - Perform an action associated with that part.
   - Place their hands on the corresponding part of their heads.
   - Write down the name of the part on the worksheet.
   - Imagine what it would be like to injure that part of the brain.
3. **Brainstem:** Ask the students to find their pulse, placing two fingers on their wrist or just below their jaw line. Explain that basic functions such as breathing, heart rate, and blood pressure are controlled by the brainstem, located at the base of the skull.
4. **Cerebellum:** Ask the students to balance on one foot. The cerebellum, found just above the brainstem, controls coordination and balance.
5. **Back Lobe:** Ask the students to look, roll, or cross their eyes. Explain that vision is controlled by the back lobe at the back of the brain, just above the cerebellum. Note: in steps 5 through 8, the scientific names of the lobes can also be used, but the students should not be expected to memorize these terms or be required to use them.
6. **Top Lobe:** Ask the students to feel the texture of their clothes, hair, or desktop. Explain that touch, pressure, temperature, and pain are all controlled by the top lobe.
7. **Side Lobe:** List a series of random words and ask the students to remember as many as they can. Explain that the side lobe controls memory and hearing.
8. **Front Lobe:** Give the students a simple math problem. Explain that the front of the brain, or front lobe, controls complex thoughts. The right side of the front lobe controls creativity, intuition, and emotions, and the left side controls language and logic.

Activity 2: Brain Molds

1. When the class is ready, distribute 1 left mold, 1 right mold, and 2 cups of modeling clay to each group of four students. Ask the class to work at the same time, filling in each section of the mold with clay. The sections are marked on the mold with a black permanent marker.
2. Show the students how to remove the brain from the molds. Squeeze each mold gently and pull the sides of the clay away from the edge of the mold. Then shake the mold over a desk until the clay falls out.

3. Guide the students as they insert a color-coded toothpick in the correct sections.
4. Carefully show how to unite the left and right clay brains. Explain that the left side of the brain controls the right side of the body, and the right side of the brain controls the left side of the body. These sides are connected by tissue.
5. Have the students complete a short quiz to see if they are right-brained or left-brained.
6. Review the major points of the lesson as a class.

Extensions

Have the students describe other scenarios that involve their sensory organs sending information to their brains.

Ask the students to write out the path of signals to and from the brain, using scenarios of their choice.

**Traumatic Brain Injuries
Lesson 3**

Name: _____

Teacher: _____

Date: _____

What is your Central Nervous System good for?

Guest Speaker

Name:_____ Occupation:_____

What does the speaker do on the job?_____

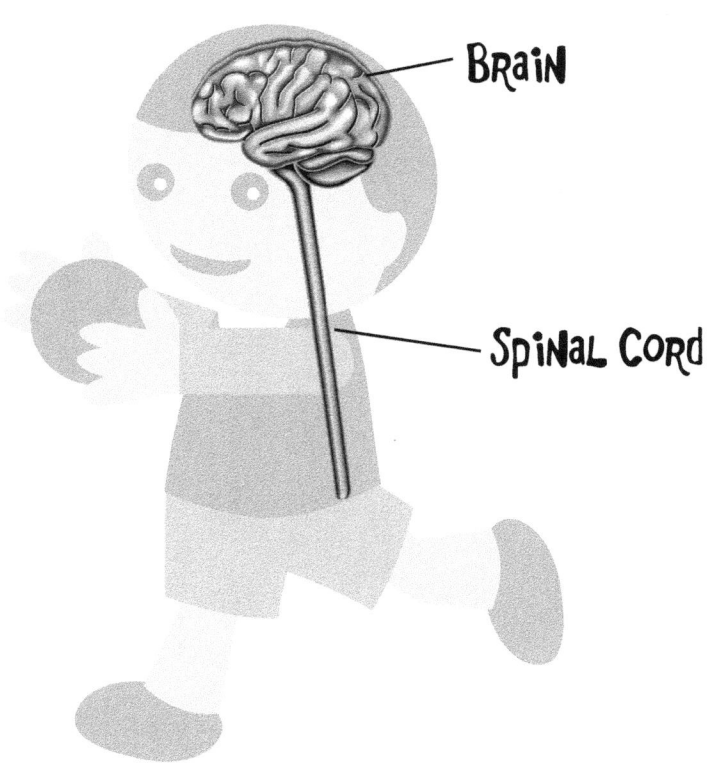

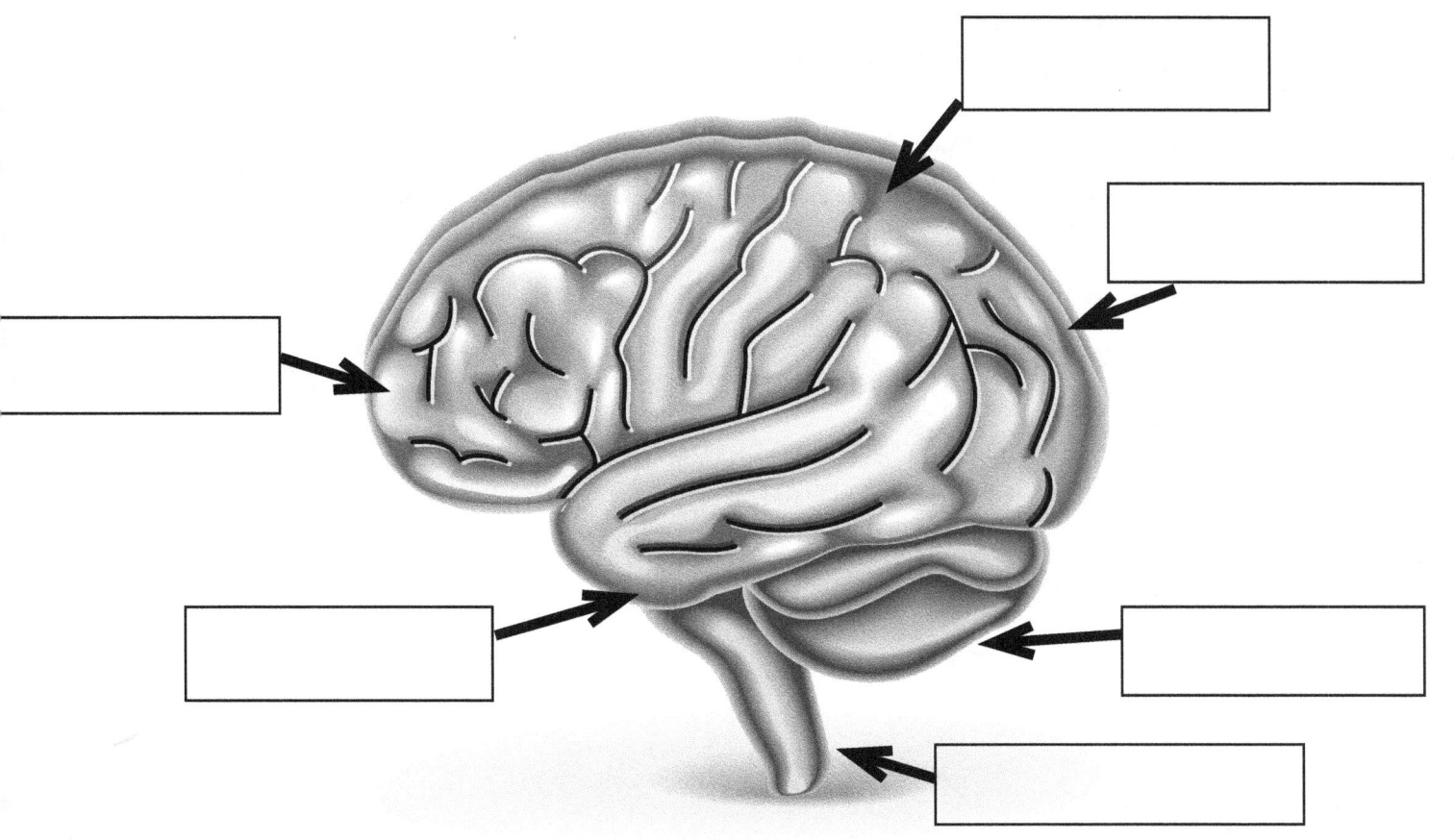

Parts of the Brain

Name	Scientific Name	Function	Color Code
Front Lobe	*Frontal Lobe*		Yellow
Side Lobe	*Temporal Lobe*		Green
Top Lobe	*Parietal Lobe*		Tan
Back Lobe	*Occiptal Lobe*		Blue
Cerebellum	*Cerebellum*		Red
Brainstem	*Brainstem*		Purple

Grade: 4
Traumatic Brain Injuries
Lesson 4: Testing Reaction Time

Lesson Time: 1 hour

References: Health A to Z: Head Injury: http://www.healthatoz.com/healthatoz/Atoz/ency/head_injury.jsp; Neuroscience for Kids: http://faculty.washington.edu/chudler/chreflex.html; The History of Measuring Reaction Time: http://chss.montclair.edu/psychology/museum/mrt.html; Reaction Time Information: http://www.science-house.org/student/bw/sports/reaction.html; Another version of the ruler lesson, with worksheets and worksheet key: http://faculty.washington.edu/chudler/bex/4rt1.pdf

Lesson objectives
- Make observations and ask questions.
- State hypotheses.
- Make predictions.
- Follow a procedure to conduct an experiment.
- Make observations and collect data.
- Draw conclusions.

Overview
The presenter discusses reaction time with the class. The students investigate the case of a young person with a head injury, and they measure their own reaction times by catching a ruler. The class analyzes data to determine if the patient's results fall within the normal range for 4th graders.

Materials

Per class:
- 1 worksheet overhead, optional
- Assorted props from previous lessons (neuron model, brain model, MRI images of normal and injured brains)

Per student:
- 1 worksheet

Per group of 4:
- 1 ruler

Key Terms

Traumatic brain injury: An injury to the brain caused by a forceful blow to the head that may result in a loss of body functioning.

Reaction time: The time it takes for the nervous system to react to an environmental cue.

Fatal: Deadly.

MRI: A machine doctors use to see the inside of a person's body or brain.

Blood clot: When blood clumps together. It can prevent oxygen flow to a certain region of the brain or body.

Bruising: An injury that occurs when blood vessels break but the skin is not broken. Bruising occurs when the brain smashes against the skull. This can cause damage to brain structures as well as to blood vessels, resulting in a breakdown of the flow of messages in the brain.

Coma: When a person can breathe and his or her heart beats, but the mind is not conscious. A person can be in this state for months or years.

Concussion: An injury resulting from a blow to the head that often results in memory loss.

Swelling: When something gets larger. Sometimes after an injury, the brain swells due to an increase in the amount of blood in the brain. This causes the brain to press against the skull.

Mode: The most common number in a set.

Mean: The average number calculated by adding up a series of numbers and dividing by the number of numbers in the set.

Median: The middle number or numbers in a set of numbers.

Range: The smallest and the largest numbers in a set of numbers.

Procedure

> **Question:**
> **How fast can your nervous system react?**

Activity: Ruler Drop

1. Pass out the worksheets.

2. Tell the students to close their eyes tightly. Ask them to clap whenever they hear a pencil. Drop a pencil at random on a desk and listen for the speed at which the students react. Repeat the activity a number of times and discuss what happened. The speed at which the students react is called the reaction time. If someone injures the brain, how will it affect the speed at which he or she can react? What else might affect reaction time? Students should suggest tiredness, medication, caffeine, alcohol, food, hunger, worry, etc.

3. Go over the case study with the class. The patient is a 4th grade girl with a head injury from a car crash. Say that a doctor has measured her reaction time, measuring how fast she catches a falling ruler. Ask for a volunteer to demonstrate the ruler drop test. Hold the ruler from the 12" end and ask the volunteer to hold his or her hand below the bottom edge of the ruler with a space between the thumb and index finger. Ask the volunteer to catch the ruler as fast as possible when you drop it. Observe the number that the volunteer's fingers hit and use the conversion chart to convert the measurement to a time.

4. Explain that you performed the test a number of times, and the patient had an average reaction time of one second. Is this normal, or has the injury affected the person's nervous system?

5. Discuss the case as a class. Ask the students to write a hypothesis as a sentence. For example: A one-second reaction time is normal. Or, a one-second reaction time is slow.

6. Discuss how the class could test their hypotheses. How many students should the class test? How will they decide what is a normal reaction time? How many trials will they perform?

7. Ask the class to make predictions. For example:
   - The average class reaction time will be less than one second
   - One second will be within the range of student reaction times.
   - One second will be outside the range of student reaction times.

8. Distribute one ruler to each pair of students and guide the students as they follow the procedures on the worksheet. The students should work in pairs, taking turns dropping and catching the rulers until each student catches the ruler 11 times. Emphasize the importance of following the procedures exactly as written. The students must record all of their measurements and they must convert the measurements into time increments.

9. Collect the rulers and discuss the results. What trends did the students observe? How can the class make sense of the data? Explain that one way to make sense of data is to organize it according to a number line. Ask the students to write their lowest reaction time to their highest reaction time in the horizontal line of boxes provided on the worksheet.

10. Show the students how to find their range of data by taking the number at either end of the number line. Does the patient's score fit within their range?

11. Show the students how to find their median score by taking the number, or numbers, at the center of the number line.

12. Show the students how to find the mode by taking the most common number from the number line.

13. Finally, show the students how to find their average reaction time. The students may require assistance to add and divide decimals. As an alternative, find the average of the students' median scores using a calculator.

14. Discuss the results. From the data analysis, it should be clear that the patient's reaction time is far slower than that of most 4th graders. This should raise suspicions that the accident severely affected the speed of her brain and nervous system.

15. Explain that doctors use the knee-jerk test to check your reflexes, which are related to reaction time, and that they use special computer programs to assess reaction time. Use the props to explain how injuries to the brain can damage neurons and thereby cause an increase in reaction time.

Key	
Distance	**Time**
2 in	0.10 sec
4 in	0.14 sec
6 in	0.17 sec
8 in	0.20 sec
10 in	0.23 sec
12 in	0.25 sec
17 in	0.30 sec
24 in	0.35 sec
31 in	0.40 sec
39 in	0.45 sec
48 in	0.50 sec
69 in	0.60 sec

Traumatic Brain Injuries
Lesson 4

TESTING REACTION TIME

CASE STUDY

Mary was in the car with her mom on the way to school one morning. The two were talking about the upcoming family vacation and had forgotten to put on their seatbelts. Mary's mom was so excited about the vacation that she barely noticed the large truck in front of her with flashing bright lights. As the cars approached an intersection, the light turned from yellow to red and the truck slammed on its brakes. Mary's mom braked as quickly as possible, but both she and Mary were thrown into the windshield.

Reaction Time Experiment

Step 1: Observations

_____

What affects the speed at which our nervous system reacts?

_____   _____

_____   _____

_____   _____

Step 2: Hypothesis

A one-second reaction time is _____
(Write: normal or slow)

Step 3: Plan Your Test

1._____

2._____

3._____

Step 4: Conduct Your Test

Trial	Distance	Time
1		
2		
3		
4		
5		
6		
7		
8		
9		
10		
11		

Distance	Time
2 in	0.10 sec
3 in	0.12 sec
4 in	0.14 sec
5 in	0.155 sec
6 in	0.17 sec
7 in	0.185 sec
8 in	0.20 sec
9 in	0.215 sec
10 in	0.23 sec
11 in	0.24 sec
12 in	0.25 sec
13 in	0.26 sec
14 in	0.27 sec
15 in	0.28 sec
16 in	0.29 sec
17 in	0.295 sec
18 in	0.30 sec

Lowest   **Highest**

Find the following:

Range: _____ Median: _____ Mode: _____

Step 5: Conclusion

_____

Share results with at least two people:

_____ _____

Grade: 4
Traumatic Brain Injuries
Lesson 5: Treating Brain Injuries

Lesson Time: 1 hour

References: NINDS Traumatic Brain Injury Information Page: http://www.wrongdiagnosis.com/artic/ninds_traumatic_brain_injury_information_page_ninds.htm; Neuroscience for Kids by Eric Chudler: http://faculty.washington.edu/chudler/injury.html

Lesson objectives
- Be exposed to cutting edge research.
- Interview a healthcare professional.
- Know that stem cells develop and differentiate into other body cells such as neurons.
- Make flipbooks showing a stem cell turning into a neuron.

Overview
The students hear a guest speaker, a healthcare professional who helps treat brain injuries. Then they learn about stem-cell research and make flipbooks showing a stem cell turning into a neuron. Finally, they review what they learned in the other lessons.

Occupation of the Day
Cell biologist: A person who studies the structure and function of the cells of living organisms.

Key Terms
Treatment: Therapy for an illness or injury.

Acute treatment: Very important treatment that must happen immediately after an injury.

Rehabilitation: Therapy that happens over a long period of time to help a patient recover lost skills.

Stem cells: Cells that can develop into any of a variety of other specialized cells.

Clinical trials: Tests of treatments that are done on human subjects.

Materials

Per class:
- 1 worksheet overhead, optional
- 1 blank writable overhead, optional
- 1 overhead or poster of stem cell turning into intestine, skin, and nerve cells
- 1 stapler

Per student:
- 1 worksheet
- 1 stem-cell booklet sheet

Per pair:
- 1 box of colored pencils
- 1 pair of scissors

Procedure

> **Questions:**
> How do doctors determine what part of a person's brain is damaged after an accident?
> How do doctors treat brain injuries?

Guest Speaker

1. Introduce the guest speaker, a healthcare professional who treats brain injuries. The guest speaker will talk for 10 to 15 minutes about his or her occupation and about brain-injury treatment and rehabilitation.
2. Remind the students to fill out their worksheets while the guest speaker talks.
3. Invite the students to ask questions.
4. Reinforce the major points that the guest speaker brought up. Remind the students that brain-injury treatment includes short-term and long-term treatment. Many different healthcare professionals are involved in treatment and rehabilitation.

Activity 1: Stem Cell Flipbook

1. Emphasize that the brain doesn't heal like other parts of the body. Once injured, it's hard to treat it. It may take years to rehabilitate someone with a brain injury, or they might not recover at all.
2. Explain that some neurons cannot grow back if they are damaged. The flipbook will demonstrate a proposed treatment where special cells called stem cells can turn into healthy neurons to replace the damaged ones. This treatment is not available yet, but many doctors and scientists hope that it will be available someday. Explain that the stem cells are cells that can turn into any cell in the body, but that most cells in our body are not stem cells. They have very specific functions. If you cut your skin, new skin will grow in: the skin cells in your finger will start making more skin cells, and your cut will go away. Stem cells are found in embryos and in bone marrow in children and adults. Show the overhead or poster of stem cells turning into specialized cells.
3. Explain that cell biologists in the San Francisco Bay Area and elsewhere are researching exciting new therapies, such as stem cell therapies. Cell biologists are scientists who study the functions of a cell. The results of these studies may lead to better treatments for human diseases.
4. Show the class a finished flipbook. Explain that the flipbook shows a cell turning into a neuron. As you flip through the book, it looks like the cell is growing a trunk, branches and a terminal. Each student will get a stem-cell sheet to use in creating his or her own booklet. The students will draw a cell body and nucleus on each page, then draw the trunk (axon) and the branches (dendrites), adding only a few details on each page.
5. Pass out the stem-cell sheets. Ask the students to cut out the 20 pages, stack them, and staple along the left hand edge.
6. Ask the students to number the pages from 1 to 19 and to draw a circle with a dot in the center of each page as shown on p. 2 of the worksheet. This represents the cell body and nucleus.
7. Hold up a worksheet or use the worksheet overhead to point out the details the students will draw.
8. Ask them to draw a trunk on the 10th page, and to draw a completed neuron on the last page. They should refer to p. 2 of the worksheet to see what to do.
9. Starting on the second page, have them draw the sequential steps from the first page to the 10th page. Next, they should draw the steps from the 11th to the 19th page, referring to the example on the worksheet.
10. Emphasize that the worksheet shows just one way that the flipbook could be done. Encourage the students to use their imagination. Not all neurons look the same. On the blank overhead or board draw examples of other neurons.
11. Allow students time to fill in the pages. When they are done, they should show their flipbook pages to the presenter. When the pages have been drawn correctly, give the students colored pencils to color in their drawings.

Review

Review the content of the last four lessons:

- How can you protect your brain?
- What are the main parts of the nervous system and the brain?
- What are some functions of the brain?
- How does the nervous system work?
- How are brain injuries diagnosed?
- What are some current and future treatments for brain injuries?

Traumatic Brain Injuries
Lesson 5

Name: _____

Teacher: _____

Date: _____

TREATING BRAIN INJURIES

Guest Speaker

Name: _____ Occupation: _____

What does the speaker do on the job? _____

How are brain injuries treated?

_____

_____

Activity: Stem Cells

Future treatments for brain injuries may involve stem cells.
Stem cells are specialized cells that can turn into other types of cells like neurons.

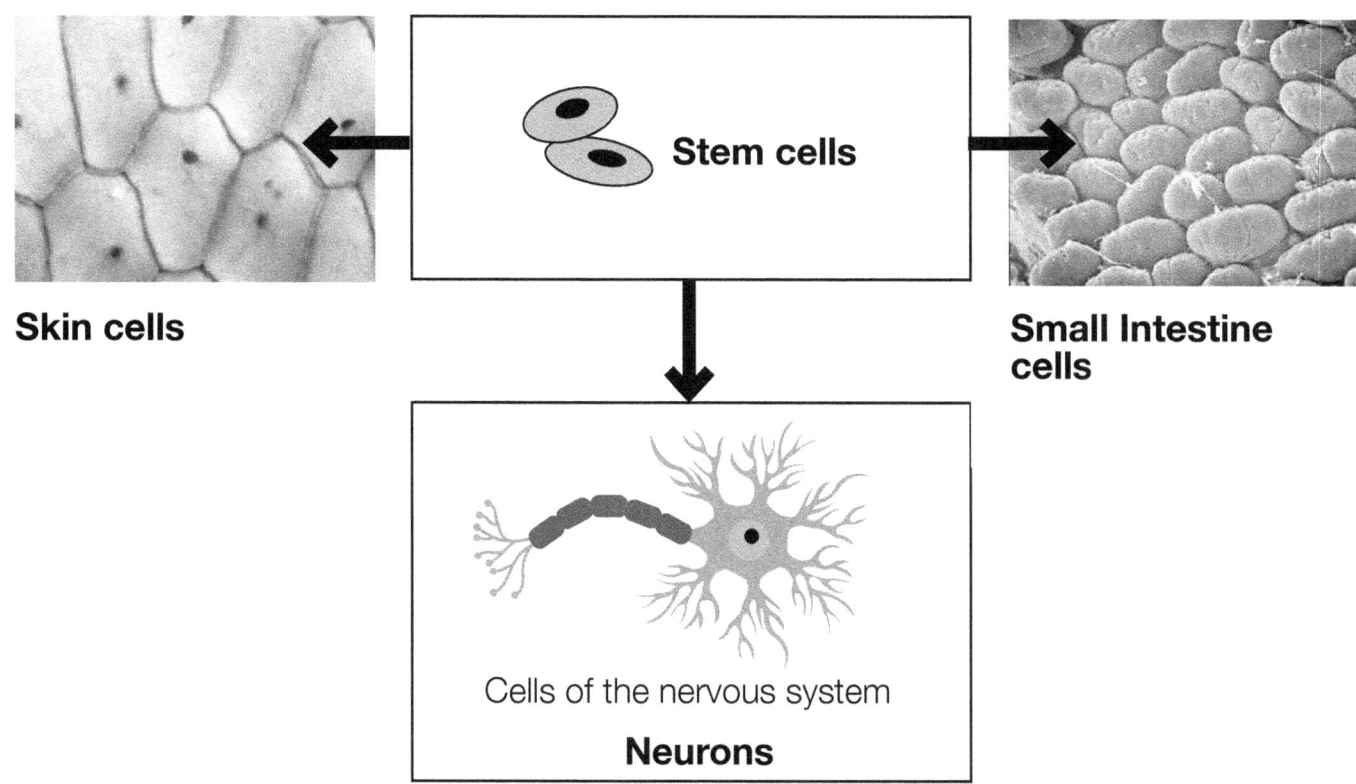

Skin cells

Stem cells

Small Intestine cells

Cells of the nervous system
Neurons

Children's Hospital Oakland Research Institute

How to make your flip book:
1. Cut out the blank pages and staple them together.
2. Number the pages.
3. Make a circle with a dot in the center of each page (cell body and nucleus).
4. Draw the finished neuron on the last page.
5. Draw a half-finished cell on the middle page, page 10.
6. Fill in the other pages, adding details slowly. Flip back to check your work.

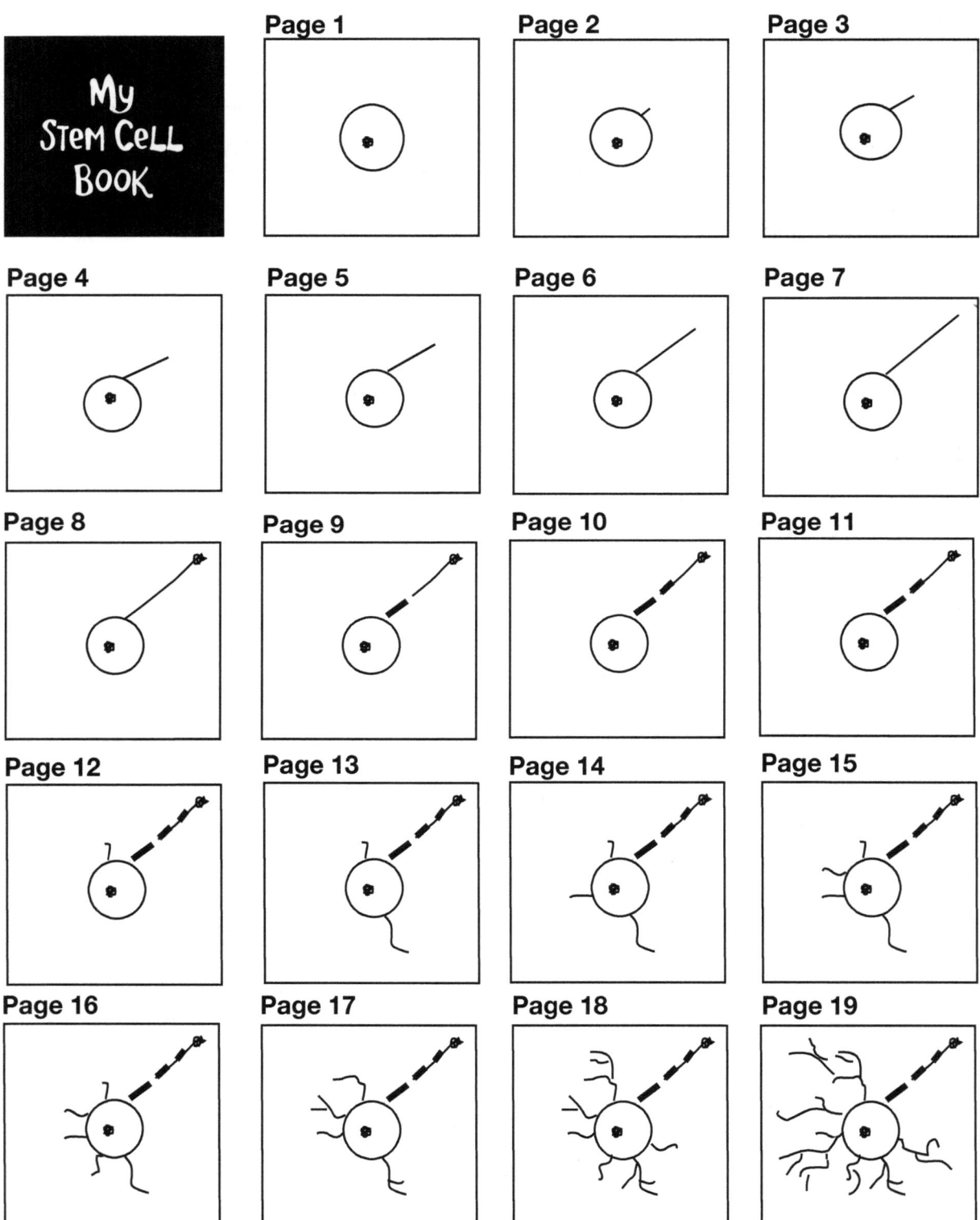

My Stem Cell Book

Grade: 4
Infectious Diseases
Lesson 1: Epidemic Outbreak

Lesson Time: 1 hour

References: Emerging and Re-emerging Infectious Diseases curricula, Master 1.2: http://science.education.nih.gov/supplements/nih1/diseases/default.htm; Ward, B. 2000. Eyewitness Book: Epidemics. New York: Doring Kindersley; Snedden, R. 2000. A World of Microorganisms. Chicago: Heinemann Library; Stalking the Mysterious Microbe http://www.microbe.org; CELLS Alive! http://www.cellsalive.com/

Lesson objectives
- Learn how infectious diseases spread.
- Know that most microorganisms do not cause disease and that many are beneficial.
- Begin a scientific investigation.

Overview
The class participates in a simulation of spreading an infectious disease. Each student receives a vial containing an unknown liquid (water or vinegar). The vial represents body fluids, and the students take turns exchanging fluids using small eyedroppers. Finally, the presenter adds a pinch of baking soda to each vial to test the students for an infectious disease. The students with reactive test tubes have the disease, and they trace back the line of transmission. The class brainstorms ways that diseases spread and how to prevent getting sick. Then the students begin investigations of the microorganisms living in the classroom.

Key Terms

Microbe: A microscopic organism that can only be seen with the aid of a microscope. Not all microbes cause diseases. Many are benign or helpful.

Germs: Microbes that cause disease.

Pathogen: A harmful microbe.

Infectious disease: A disease that is caused by a pathogen.

Epidemic: An infectious disease that spreads rapidly to a large number of people.

Colony: A group of millions of microbes growing in the same spot.

Materials

Per class:
- 1/4 cup vinegar
- 1 small box of baking soda
- 2 1/8-teaspoon measuring spoons
- 1 clean plastic fork
- 1 trash bag

Per student:
- 1 worksheet
- 1 10-ml vial with cap
- 1 eyedropper
- Before class fill all but two vials with water. Fill the last two vials with vinegar. Distribute the vials without disclosing the contents.
- 1 Petri dish containing a slice of cooked potato. Preparation: peel and boil three large potatoes the day before. Cut them into thin, round slices, about 1/4 in. thick, to fit in the Petri dishes. Store in a clean, covered container. On the day of the experiment, put one slice in each Petri dish.
- 1 cotton swab. Store swabs in Ziplock bags.
- 1 12-in. piece of masking tape

Per pair:
- 1 plastic cup
- 1/8 cup of water in the plastic cup

Procedure

Questions:
How do infectious diseases such as the flu spread?
What increases your chances of getting sick?

Activity 1: Infection Simulation

1. Show a vial and an eyedropper. Explain that the vial represents the body and all the fluid it contains. In the simulation, the students will use thin eyedroppers to exchange fluid with three other students whose names they will record on their worksheets. Then they will discover if they have been infected by a disease.

2. Pass out the vials and eyedroppers and allow time for the students to exchange body fluid and record names. These exchanges should not be reciprocal: students should not take fluid back from the same students to whom they give fluid, but from different students. They should not sniff the vials.

3. Collect the eyedroppers and add 1/16 teaspoon baking soda to each vial with the help of classroom assistants or select students. If a student has a vial that bubbles, then he or she has the infection.

4. Ask the students to deduce which students originally had the disease. To do this, the students will need to compare their list of names with one another.

5. Discuss the activity:
   - What was transmitted in the body fluid that carried the disease?
   - Why do people get sick from a cold or flu?
   - What causes diseases such as small pox, measles, and mumps?
   - If students suggest germs, what are germs?

Activity 2: Hunting Microbes

1. Explain that germs are actually microscopic organisms that are invisible to the naked eye. However, colonies of microbes can be grown if they are provided with the right environment, such as leftover food. In this activity, the students will capture microbes on cooked potato slices in Petri dishes to discover which varieties of microbes are all around us. Emphasize that most microbes are harmless or beneficial and only a small number cause infectious diseases. Give examples.

2. Explain that everything we know about microbes, we know because of scientific discoveries. Scientists follow careful procedures. A procedure is a set of instructions given in a series of steps. Pass out the investigation procedures and ask the students to read the steps out loud as you demonstrate:

   1. Take a cup with water, a Petri dish with a slice of cooked potato, a piece of masking tape, and a clean cotton swab. Be careful to keep the cotton swab clean.
   2. Open a Petri dish carefully without touching the inside of the lid.
   3. Dip one end of a cotton swab in water and rub it on a surface, such as a desk.
   4. Rub the same end of the cotton swab all over the top of the potato slice.
   5. Close the Petri dish lip and tape it shut. Write the name of the surface, the date, and your name on the masking tape and set the Petri dish aside for one week to let the microbes germinate.
   6. Throw away the cotton swab.

6. Pass out the materials to the students and lead them as they perform each step. Each student should choose a surface in the classroom. They can choose a doorknob, chair, book, bag, the floor, the sole of a shoe, their own mouth or hand, etc. Emphasize the importance of carefully labeling the dishes. Make predictions as a class.

7. Set aside one uncontaminated, cooked potato slice as a control, to use as a comparison. The control should be swabbed with plain water and sealed in a Petri dish like the other slices.

8. Store the Petri dishes in a safe place. They will be used in the next lesson. They should not be refrigerated.

Extensions

Investigate how microbes have been altered for use in biotechnology.

Diary of a Disease. Give each student an information sheet about a particular pathogen. The information may include facts like the cause of the disease, how the disease is spread, symptoms, and treatment. Have the student write a story from a disease's point of view. Some suggestions include: write a diary entry about an infectious agent entering its host, a story about how the pathogen reproduces or progresses once inside the host, a story about how the immune system fights the infectious agent, or a news article of how an infectious agent successfully infected many people.

Bacteria in the Cafeteria. This online Flash game displays different areas where bacteria grow, so it is relevant for the students. The students must distinguish between helpful and unhelpful bacteria, and this is an important concept to learn. Source: American Museum of Natural History, Infection Detection Protection—
http://www.amnh.org/nationalcenter/infection/

**Infectious Disesases
Lesson 1**

EPIDEMIC OUTBREAK

Name: _____

Teacher: _____

Date: _____

iNfectioN stimuLatioN

What does each represent?

[   ]———🧪💧———[   ]

BraiNstorm

How do colds spread? _____

What increases your chances of getting sick? _____

I gave fluid to:

　　Person #1: _____

　　Person #2: _____

　　Person #3: _____

I received fluid from (these people must be different from the three above):

　　Person #1: _____

　　Person #2: _____

　　Person #3: _____

Do you have the disease? _____

Who did you get it from? _____

What are germs? _____

INVESTIGATION: Capturing Microbes

Step 1: Observations

What surfaces have microbes? _____

Step 2: Hypothesis

Microbes will be found on _____.

Step 3: Plan your test

Variable: Various surfaces

Control: Potato swabbed with plain water

Step 4: Conduct your test

Equipment: Petri dish, slice of cooked potato, cotton swab, masking tape, plastic cup, 1/8 cup of water

Procedure:

1. Pour a small amount of water into a plastic cup.
2. Open a Petri dish carefully without touching the inside of the lid.
3. Dip one end of a cotton swab in water and rub it on a surface, such as a desk.
4. Rub the same end of the cotton swab all over the top of the potato slice.
5. Close the Petri dish lid and tape it shut. Write the name of the surface, the date, and your name on the masking tape and set it aside for one week to let the microbes germinate.
6. Throw away the cotton swab.

Bacteria

Bacteria are one-celled creatures that get their nutrients from their environment. They can live outside or inside the human body. They are much larger than viruses, but you still need a microscope to see them.

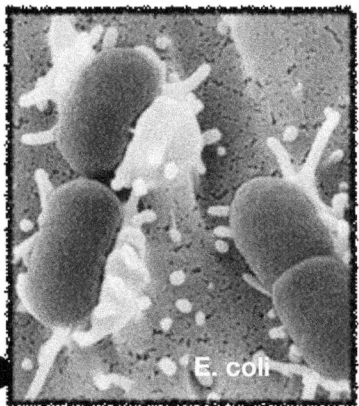
E. coli

GOOD BACTERIA

Bacillus thuringiensis - A common soil bacterium that is a natural pesticide in gardens and on crops

Escherichia coli - One of many kinds of microbes that live in your digestive system to help you digest your food every day.

Streptomyces - Bacteria in soil that make an antibiotic used to treat infections

Lactobacillus acidophilus - One of the bacteria that turn milk into yogurt

BAD BACTERIA

Bacteria can cause many health problems, including strep throat, ear infections and cavities.

Black Plague (Yersinia pestis) - In the Middle Ages (1300's) it killed 250 million people in Europe - about 1/4 of the population in just four years. Characterized by chills, fever, vomiting and boils on the skin

Spread - By fleas living on rats

Cure - Modern antibiotics have a good chance of combating the disease if diagnosed early. Health authorities may isolate the patient and destroy rodent populations responsible for the outbreak.

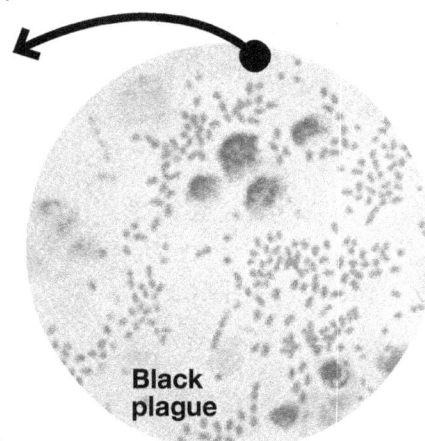
Black plague

Tuberculosis (Mycobacterium tuberculosis) - Infects the lungs causing coughing, chest pain and breathlessness

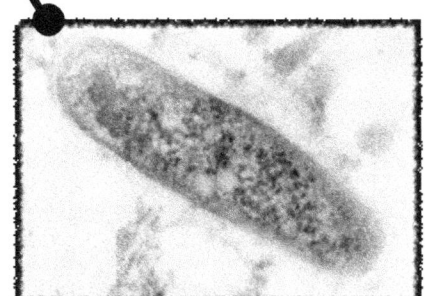
Tuberculosis

Spread - By coughing, sneezing; it is spread through the air

Cure - In 1940 a drug was found effective but now it's back - 25,000 new cases are reported every year.

Viruses

Viruses are the smallest microbes. They can only be seen with powerful microscopes. They aren't exactly alive—they need to invade another organism to multiply and survive.

GOOD VIRUSES

Tulip chlorotic blotch virus (also known as the "mosaic virus") - The stripes on a Rembrandt tulip are caused by this virus

Vaccinia virus - Virus turned into vaccine which was used in eradicating the smallpox virus

BAD VIRUSES

Smallpox virus (Variola major or Variola minor) - Shaped the history of the US. Explorers brought it to the new world after 1500 and it destroyed 1/3 of the native population

Spread - By coughing and sneezing through the air, open crusty sores

Cure - A vaccination was developed in 1872 and the disease no longer exists

Flu virus (Influenza) - Killed more people in World War I than the number of war casualties

Spread - Quickly through the air and mucus membranes by tiny droplets of a person's saliva

Cure - None, there is a vaccination which can prevent certain strains but the virus keeps changing

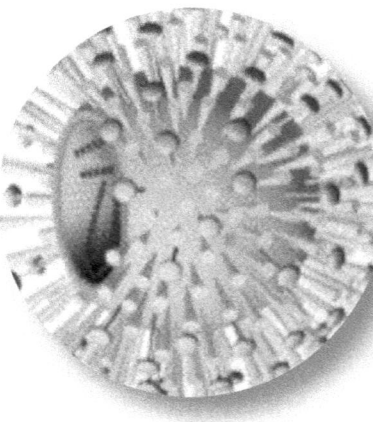
Smallpox

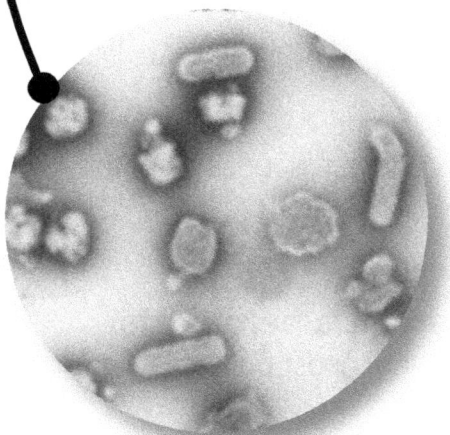
Mosaic virus

Flu virus

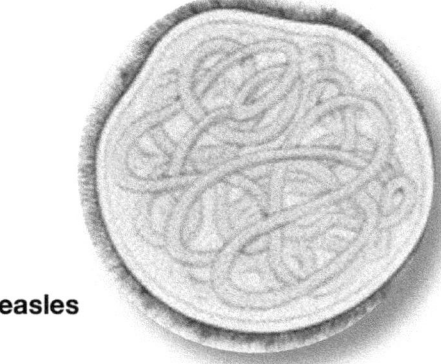
Measles

Measles (Rubella) - Also called rubeola this is a rash-based illness

Spread - Is highly contagious. Transmitted by air through coughing, sneezing and talking.

Cure - A vaccine was developed in the 1960's that can prevent 95% of measles cases for those vaccinated in time

Protozoa

Protozoa are one-celled organisms that love warm places. They are large and more complex than bacteria or viruses. They often cause tropical diseases.

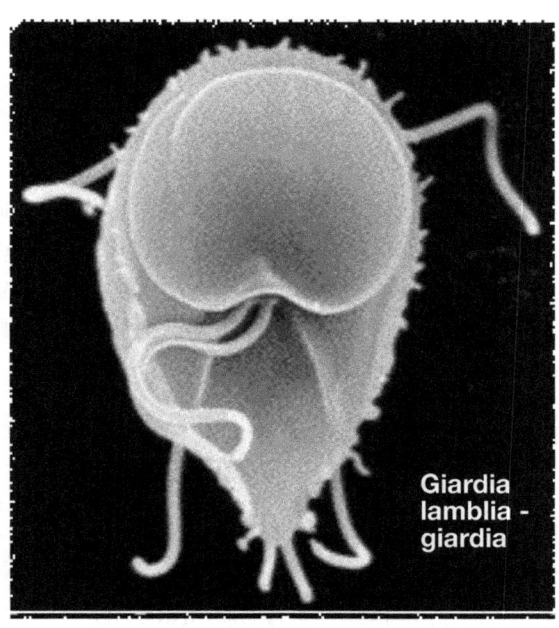

Giardia lamblia - giardia

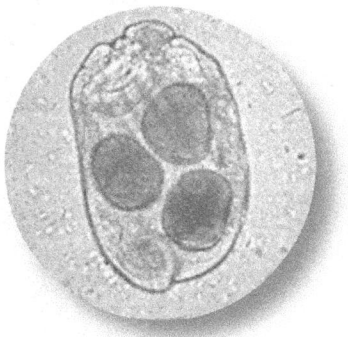

GOOD PROTOZOA

Rumen protozoa - This protozoan helps in cattle digestion. It helps cows digest plant fiber and produce fatty acids that provide around 60% to 80% of the energy needed by a cow. They live in the first stomach of cows (who have four stomachs!). Without these protozoa we wouldn't have hamburgers.

BAD PROTOZOA

Malaria (Plasmodium falciparum or Plasmodium vivax) - A deadly disease common in tropical areas. Causes headaches, fever, aches and pains all over the body.

Spread - By mosquitos

Cure - Not always possible for Plasmodium falciparum, though quinine can be used to treat it. Cure exists for Plasmodium vivax but it can return after being dormant if aggravated.

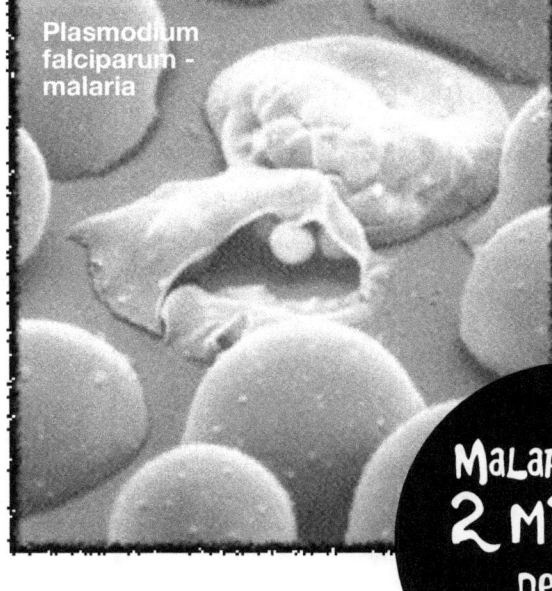

Plasmodium falciparum - malaria

Malaria kills 2 million people each year.

FUNGI

Fungi are plant-like creatures that are related to the mushrooms you'd find in the grocery store. Fungi do not make their own food from water and sunlight like other plants, so they feed on decaying plants and animals.

Penicillium

GOOD FUNGI

Soil fungus (Arbuscular mycorrhizas) - Fungus that lives in soil. It helps crops take up nutrients.

Baker's Yeast (Saccharomyces cerevisiae) - Makes bread rise

wheat bunt

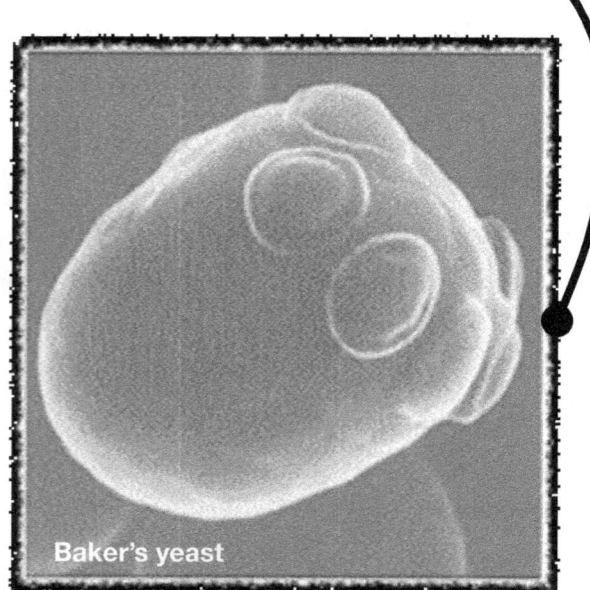
Baker's yeast

BAD FUNGI

Wheat bunt (Tilletia signifaciens) - A fungal infection of wheat kernals making them unfit for making flour

Athlete's Foot (Tinea pedis) - This fungus grows on dead skin cells between the toes and can cause itching and burning.

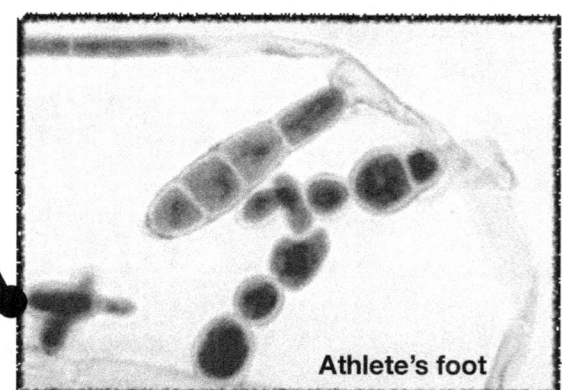
Athlete's foot

Grade: 4
Infectious Diseases
Lesson 2: Classifying Microorganisms

Lesson Time: 1 hour

References: Emerging and Re-emerging Infectious Diseases curricula, Master 1.2: http://science.education.nih.gov/supplements/nih1/diseases/default.htm

Lesson objectives
- Make observations. Differentiate between observations and inferences.
- Classify microorganisms by visual characteristics of colonies.
- Learn classifications of microbes that scientists have developed: bacteria, viruses, fungi, and protozoa.
- Know that most microorganisms do not cause disease and that many are beneficial.

Overview
The students investigate colonies of microorganisms that grew on the Petri dishes from lesson 1. They make and record careful observations, then classify colonies by color, texture, and size. Then the class learns about four types of microbes that scientists have discovered. Each student creates a paper model of a microbe.

Key Terms

Classify: To order a series of objects or things into distinct categories.

Microbe: A microscopic organism.

Germs: Microbes that cause disease.

Pathogen: A harmful microbe.

Infectious disease: A disease that is caused by a pathogen.

Bacterium (pl. bacteria): A single-celled microbe. Most are helpful, but some are harmful.

Virus: A small microbe that can cause sickness but is not considered alive because it cannot reproduce on its own.

Protozoan (pl. protozoa): A single-celled microorganism that eats bacteria. They are the most abundant animals in the world. They prefer warm, damp environments.

Fungus (pl. fungi): A plant-like organism that feeds on decaying plants and animals. It lives in warm, damp places and is related to commercially sold mushrooms.

Bacterial colony: A spot containing billions of bacteria multiplying on a surface. A bacterial colony is visible to the human eye.

Materials

Per class:
- 1 overhead of a potato slice with bacterial colonies, optional
- 4 colorful example microbes made out of construction paper: a virus, bacterium, a protozoan, and a fungus
- Assorted art supplies (to decorate microbe models)

Per student:
- 1 worksheet
- 1 sheet of colored construction paper
- scissors

Per pair:
- 1 box of colored pencils

Per group of 4:
- Handout on fungi, protozoa, bacteria, or viruses
- 1 box of colored markers
- Glue stick

Procedure

> **Question:**
> **What are microbes and what do they look like?**

Activity 1: Classification

1. Show an overhead of a potato slice covered with microbe colonies or draw one on the board using more than one color for the colonies. Ask the students how they would describe what they see. Explain that humans cannot see individual microbes with their eyes. However, they can see spots where millions of microbes have multiplied. These are called colonies.

2. Ask the students to illustrate their potato slices from lesson one. Pass out the worksheets, colored pencils, and Petri dishes. Warn that the Petri dishes must remain closed. The colonies on the potato slices are bacteria and fungi (mold). While the vast majority of bacteria and fungi are harmless, some can be harmful. The potatoes should contain a wide variety of colonies with various textures, colors, consistencies, and sizes. How many different types of colonies do the students see? What adjectives can they use? Tell the students that bacteria and fungi are responsible for decomposing our trash, that some bacteria aid our digestion or convert atmospheric nitrogen to a form that plants can use, and that some fungi produce medicine or serve as food. Imagine what the world would be like without them.

3. Ask the students to share their results in pairs and to devise a classification system. They can classify the colonies by any characteristic that seems appropriate, including size, color, texture, shape, frequency, and height. Each pair of students should come up with at least three categories. Discuss the classifications as a class.

4. Collect the Petri dishes in a sealable plastic bag. Later wash them with warm water and soap, either by hand or in a dishwasher, to use again. Sterilize them by wiping with rubbing alcohol.

Activity 2: Scientific Classifications of Microbes

1. Explain that scientists study and classify individual microorganisms with the help of powerful microscopes. Go over the four types of microbes that are described on the handouts. Show sample models of viruses, bacteria, protozoa, and fungi made from construction paper. Discuss each and the differences among them. Emphasize that microbes are everywhere and most are harmless or beneficial. Only a small number of microbes can cause disease. Ask the students to sketch each type of microbe on their worksheets.

2. Divide the class into groups of four students. Assign one type of microbe (viruses, protozoa, bacteria, or fungi) to each group, and give the students the appropriate handout. The handouts include profiles and images of good and bad microbes. Give each student a piece of construction paper, and each group a set of markers and supplies for decorating the microbes.

3. Ask each student to choose a particular microbe from their handout, to make a large drawing of it on construction paper, and to cut it out. They should then answer the following questions on the back of the cut-out:
   - What type of microbe are you making? (virus, bacterium, fungus, or protozoan)
   - What is its name?
   - Is it helpful or harmful?
   - What does it do?
   - If harmful, what kind of disease does it carry?
   - If harmful, how does it spread?
- If harmful, is there a cure?

4. Ask the students to decorate their models.

5. Have the students share their models with the class. They should hold up their models for everyone to see and explain what each microbe is and what it does.

Extension

Explain that on its surface, each microbe has a specific marker or symbol called an antigen that allows the body to recognize it for destruction. Show examples of antigens on microbe models made with construction paper. Have the students make antigens for their own microbe models.

Infectious Disesases
Lesson2

Name: _____

Teacher: _____

Date: _____

Analyze Results: Making Observations

Draw what you see in your Petri dish.
What colors, textures, shapes, and sizes do you see?

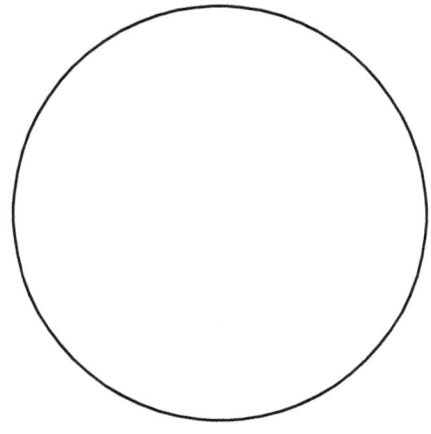

Control Petri dish

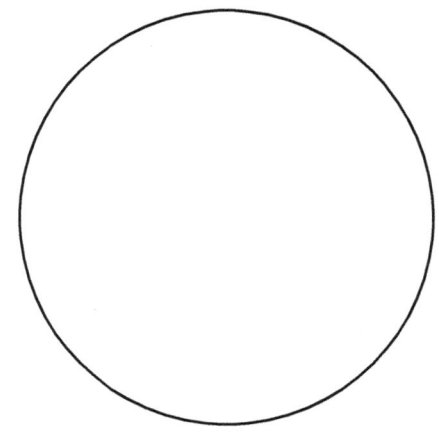

Your Petri dish

Contaminated by the surface of _____

Colors: _____
_____

Textures: _____
_____

Sizes: _____
_____

What do microbes look like under a powerful microscope?

Name	Viruses	Bacteria
Picture		

Name	Protozoa	Fungi
Picture		

My Microbe:

What type of microbe are you making? _____

What is its name? _____

Is it helpful or harmful? _____

What does it do? _____

If harmful, what kind of disease does it carry? _____

If harmful, how does it spread? _____

If harmful, is there a cure? _____

Grade: 4
Infectious Diseases
Lesson 3: Killing Microbes, Part I

Lesson Time: 1 hour

References: Medical Mysteries, a SEPA project from Rice University. Mission 2: Peril in Prokaryon, Activity 4: One Cell, Two Cell, Four Cells, Eight. http://medmyst.rice.edu/; Brown, W.E., and Williams, R.P. 1990. "Cultured Taters." Science Scope. Feb. 19-21; CELLS alive! Dividing Bacteria: http://www.cellsalive.com/; The Microbe Zoo: http://commtechlab.msu.edu/sites/dlc-me/zoo; Robert Koch: http://www.myhero.com/hero.asp?hero=robert_koch

Lesson objectives

- Know that scientific progress is made by asking meaningful questions and conducting careful investigations.
- Know that scientific investigations include hypotheses, predictions, tests, observations, and conclusions.
- Conduct an experiment.
- Learn about the conditions necessary to kill microbes.
- Formulate and justify predictions based on cause-and-effect relationships.
- Know that bacteria and fungi are living organisms and need nourishment and water to live. Viruses are not living organisms.

Overview

The class starts an experiment testing how cleaning products affect the growth of microbes. Students make predictions about the effectiveness of washing their desks with nothing, water, dish soap, alcohol, anti-bacterial soap, or baby wipes. Then they carefully follow written instructions as they attempt to kill fungi and bacteria on their desks and culture the remaining organisms on potato slices in Petri dishes. The potato slices are kept for a week and observed and analyzed during the following lesson.

Key Terms

Scientific Process: A series of steps that scientists use while doing investigations. The process includes making observations, asking questions, creating hypotheses, making predictions, planning and conducting tests, controlling variables, collecting data, and drawing conclusions.

Scientific investigation: An experiment undertaken using the scientific process.

Hygiene: Practices such as hand washing that ensure cleanliness and good health.

Bacterial colony: A spot containing billions of bacteria multiplying on a surface. A bacterial colony is visible to the human eye.

Control: An organism or item (such as a potato slice in a Petri dish) that is not treated with the experimental variable.

Variable: Something that is tested in an experiment. Something that changes or varies.

Hypothesis: A tentative explanation that can be tested by investigation.

Prediction: An educated guess concerning the outcome of an experiment.

Materials

Per class:
- 1 roll of paper towels

Per student:
- 1 worksheet

Per pair:
- 2 Petri dishes containing cooked slices of potato.
  - Preparation: peel and boil three large potatoes the day before. Cut them into thin, round slices, about 1/4 in. thick, to fit into the Petri dishes. Store in a clean, covered container.
  - On the day of the experiment, put one slice in each Petri dish and cover.
- 2 cotton swabs (store in ziplock bag)
- 1 plastic cup
- 1/8 cup water in the plastic cup
- 1 of the following cleaning products:
  - 1 baby wipe
  - 1 alcohol wipe
  - 1 small container of regular liquid soap
  - 1 small container of anti-bacterial soap
- 1 marking pen
- 1 12-in piece of masking tape

Procedure

Question:
What kills microbes?

Activity 1: Experiment

1. Begin the lesson by discussing how we know everything we know about microbes. Existing knowledge about killing microbes comes from hundreds of thousands of discoveries based on experiments done by scientists. Explain that today students will do their own tests. If harmful microbes carry dangerous diseases, how can you kill microbes?

2. The students will follow the same scientific method used by scientists to make discoveries.
   STEP 1: Observe and ask questions.
   STEP 2: State a hypothesis.
   STEP 3: Make a prediction based on the hypothesis.
   STEP 4: Plan your test.
   STEP 5: Conduct your test.
   STEP 6: Draw conclusions and share results. Investigate further.

3. Discuss observations and generate questions. What products are used to kill microbes? Have you ever used an antibacterial soap? What does your family use to clean the kitchen? How do doctors wash their hands? Did you learn anything relevant in the potato activity?

4. Show an array of common cleaning products. Ask each pair of students to come up with a hypothesis based on their previous knowledge and experience. Which cleaning method will be the most effective at killing microbes on a desk? (Or which one will not be effective?) Each student should write a hypothesis as a complete sentence. For example: "If I clean a desk with anti-bacterial soap, it will kill the microbes present," or "If I clean a desk with a baby wipe, it will not kill the microbes present." They should then state a prediction based on the hypothesis: "If a swab is rubbed on a desk that has been cleaned with anti-bacterial soap, then rubbed on a potato slice, no microbes will grow on the potato slice."

5. Review the investigative procedure on the worksheet. Discuss the following questions:
   - How many potato slices are needed to have a fair test?
   - How will the experimental potato slice be treated?
   - How will the comparison, or control, be treated?
   - Which cleaning product will be tested? How much will be used? How will it be applied to the desk?
   - What additional procedural steps are needed?
   - How will the results be compared? Will the slices be compared by the size of the colonies, the number of colonies, or both?

6. Give each pair time to complete the written procedure. Only pass out the supplies to students who have completed the procedure and answered the questions. Sample procedure:
   - Take two potato slices in Petri dishes. Carefully open the lids.
   - Take one cotton swab and dip one end in water.
   - Wipe the swab on a dirty desk and then on one potato slice (this is the control).
   - Apply soap to the surface of the desk.
   - Dip a second swab in water and wipe it on the clean desk, then on the second potato slice.
   - Close the Petri dishes and label them.
   - Leave the slices for one week.
   - Count the number of colonies.

7. Make sure that the students follow their own procedures exactly as written.

8. Collect the materials. Make sure that each pair of students labels their Petri dishes and stacks them in a corner of the room for observation the following week.

Extension

Try the experiment again on various media, including agar and bread.

Test the effects of heat on microbes. Boil one of the contaminated slices in a plastic bag. Place one contaminated slice in the fridge for a week.

Research Louis Pasteur, who discovered how microbes cause disease and invented vaccines and Pasteurization.

Research Robert Koch, who developed techniques for obtaining pure bacterial cultures.

**Infectious Disesases
Lesson 3**

KILLING MICROBES
PART 1

Name: _____

Teacher: _____

Date: _____

How do we know what we know about microbes and the immune system?

_____

Your Experiment

Step 1: Observations
How do people kill microbes or "germs"? They kill germs by...

- _____

- _____

- _____

Does _____ kill microbes?

Step 2: Hypothesis

_____ kills (or does not kill) microbes.

Step 3: Prediction

_____

Step 4: Plan your test

What product will you test? _____

What other materials do you need? _____

How will you make sure this is a fair test? _____

Step 5: Conduct your test

1. Take two Petri dishes containing potato slices.

2. Label one dish "control" and the other "experimental". Label both dishes with your names.

3. Control: Dip a swab in water and rub it on a desk, then rub it all over a potato slice. You should not touch the end of the swab with your fingers.

   Why? _____

4. Close the "control" dish and set it aside.

5. Clean the desk with _____.

6. Dip the second swab in water and rub it on the desk that has just been cleaned. Then rub it all over the second potato slice.

7. Close the "experimental" dish and set both dishes aside, taped together.

8. Observe after one week. Measure and record the size of the colonies.

Grade: 4
Infectious Diseases
Lesson 4: Killing Microbes, Part 2

Lesson Time: 1 hour

References: Medical Mysteries, a SEPA project from Rice University. MedMyst http://medmyst.rice.edu; Brown, W.E., and Williams, R.P. 1990. "Cultured Taters." Science Scope. Feb. 19-21; Collard, P. 1976.

Lesson objectives

- Know that scientific progress is made by asking meaningful questions and conducting careful investigations.
- Know that scientific investigations involve hypotheses, predictions, tests, observations, and conclusions.
- Analyze the results of an experiment on the effectiveness cleaning products in killing microbes.
- Compare results with hypotheses.
- Know that most microbes are harmless or beneficial. Only a few cause infectious diseases.
- Learn several principles of food safety.

Overview

The class participates in a simulation of spreading an infectious disease. Each student receives a vial containing an unknown liquid (water or vinegar). The vial represents body fluids, and the students take turns exchanging fluids using small eyedroppers. Finally, the presenter adds a pinch of baking soda to each vial to test the students for an infectious disease. The students with reactive test tubes have the disease, and they trace back the line of transmission. The class brainstorms ways that diseases spread and how to prevent getting sick. Then the students begin investigations of the microorganisms living in the classroom.

Occupation of the Day

Infectious Disease Researcher: A scientist who solves disease mysteries by figuring out what causes a certain disease, why some people get the disease and others do not, and how the immune system fights the disease. This information can help prevent the disease and lead to new vaccines. Some infectious disease researchers work in laboratories, where they may look for viruses or bacteria in blood samples. Others work in the cities or towns where there are illnesses. To become an infectious disease researcher, you will need college or university training. Then you, too, can become a disease detective.

Key Terms

Infection: When a harmful microbe enters and establishes itself inside a host, such as the human body.

Bacterium (pl. bacteria): A single-celled microbe that does not have a nucleus. Most are helpful, but some are harmful.

Culture: A population of microbes growing in a liquid.

Colony: A population of microbes growing on a solid surface.

Petri dish: A plate that contains a solid surface for microbes to grow on.

Fungus (pl. fungi): Fungi are organisms whose cells contain nuclei. Many of them look plant-like, but fungi do not make their own food from sunlight like plants do.

Mold: A type of fungus. Instead of seeds, molds make spores that float in the air like pollen. They are a common trigger for allergies. Molds are found in damp areas, such as the basement or bathroom, as well as outdoors in grass, leaf piles, hay, and mulch.

Materials

Per class:
- 2 plastic garbage bags for cleanup time, one for the potatoes and one for the dirty Petri dishes

Per student:
- 1 worksheet
- 1 Fight BAC coloring sheet (these can be found at www.fightbac.org/content/view/22/44/)

Per pair:
- Petri dishes with potato slices from Lesson 3
- Overhead sheet printed with grid lines for measuring colony growth.
- 1 box crayons

Procedure

> **Questions:**
> **Can cleaning products really kill microbes?**
> **How can we measure it?**

Activity 1: Interview a Researcher

1. Pass out the worksheets.
2. Introduce the guest speaker, who will talk for 15 minutes about what it is like to be a scientist who studies infectious diseases. The scientist should bring props from the lab, such as a lab coat, pipettes, Petri dishes, books, journals, and photos of his or her lab. The guest should also mention cutting edge research in his or her field.
3. Ask for questions from the class.

Activity 2: Quantitative Analysis

1. Remind the class of the steps of the scientific method. Today they will focus on the last steps, analyzing results and drawing conclusions.
2. Remind the students of the beneficial and harmless microbes they studied in Lesson 2. While the vast majority of bacteria and fungi are harmless, some can be harmful. Review that bacteria and fungi are responsible for decomposing our trash, that some bacteria aid our digestion or convert atmospheric nitrogen to a form that plants can use, and that some fungi produce medicine or serve as food.
3. Show how to analyze the results. Take two Petri dishes from the previous week. Note the cleaning product indicated on the label. Remove the tape so, that you can see the potato clearly.
4. First count the number of total squares taken up by your potato slice. Then count the number of squares taken up by the colonies. What fraction of the potato is covered by colonies? Compare the control and experimental potato slices.
5. Write your conclusion as a complete sentence: _____ kills (or does not kill) microbes living on a desk.
6. When students understand the procedure, pass out the potatoes to each group and lead them through the two parts of the analysis.
7. Discuss the results as a class. Do the results confirm the hypotheses? Which cleaning product was the most effective? Which one was least effective? Are more tests needed? What could be some sources of experimental error?
8. If time remains, think up other versions of the experiment.
9. Collect the Petri dishes.
10. Dump the potatoes into a plastic garbage bag and dispose of them.
11. Collect the Petri dishes in a sealable plastic bag. Later wash them in warm water and soap to use again. Before using again, sterilize the dishes by wiping them with rubbing alcohol.
12. IMPORTANT: Review the role of infectious disease researchers in helping us understand and prevent infectious diseases.

Activity 3: Fight BAC Coloring Sheets

1. Pass out the crayons and one Fight BAC coloring sheet to each student (use a variety of different sheets).
2. When the students have finished coloring, ask them to hold up their finished pictures and explain what the pictures show about food safety.

**Infectious Disesases
Lesson 4**

KILLING MICROBES
PART 2

Name: _____

Teacher: _____

Date: _____

Guest Speaker

1. Name: _____

2. Job Title: _____

3. What do they do? _____

_____

4. What did you learn? _____

_____

Experimental Results

What cleaning product did you use?_____

Quantitative Analysis: Potato Experiment

Step 6: Draw conclusions and share results
Describe the bacteria and fungi colonies on the following potatoes.

	EXPERIMENTAL POTATO	**CONTROL POTATO** (desk not cleaned)
Colors		
Number of colonies		

For each of your 2 potatoes, count the total number of squares taken up by the potato and count the number of squares that are discolored. Make a fraction.

What fraction of your potatoes has colonies? _____

Potato	Number of total squares taken up by the slice	Number of squares with colonies	$\dfrac{\text{SQUARES WITH COLONIES}}{\text{TOTAL SQUARES}}$
Experimental			
Control			

Conclusions

1. Write your conclusion as a complete sentence.

_____

2. Does your data support your hypothesis? Or does your hypothesis need more research?

_____

Grade: 4
Infectious Diseases
Lesson 5: The Body Fights Back

Lesson Time: 1 hour

Reference: Medical Mysteries, SEPA project from Rice University. MedMyst http://medmyst.rice.edu

Lesson objectives

- Know that the immune system is made up of specialized cells, tissues, and organs that help your body fight disease.
- Act out the three levels of the immune system that respond to invading microbes:
    - 1st level of defense: the body's exterior tissues keep germs out.
    - 2nd level of defense: white blood cells engulf invaders.
    - 3rd level of defense: special white blood cells produce antibodies to remember the invaders next time.
- Discuss ways to enhance the immune system, such as exercising, eating a healthy diet, going to regular medical exams, and taking immunizations and medications as prescribed.

Overview

The students make antigens for their microbe models from Lesson 2 and antibodies that match these antigens. Then they create skits about the immune system and perform them using their microbe models. Finally, they discuss vaccines, antibiotics, and the importance of immunizations, and they brainstorm ways to enhance the effectiveness of their immune systems.

Key Terms

Infection: A disease caused by a harmful microbe entering and establishing itself inside a host, such as the human body.

Virus: A small microbe that can cause sickness but is not considered alive because it cannot reproduce on its own. It must invade human or animal cells to reproduce more viruses.

Disease: A sickness. When something is wrong in our bodies.

Vaccine: A substance (typically in the form of a shot, pill, or nasal spray) that protects someone from a bacterial or viral infection by triggering an immune response.

Mucus: A slimy substance that coats our nasal passages and airways and traps microbes.

Immune system: A body system made of special cells, tissues, and organs that defend the body against microbes.

Lymph nodes: A structure where special cells that fight disease gather together.

Immune cells: Special cells that defend our bodies against disease. These include an army of white blood cells that patrol the body. One type of immune cell, called a phagocyte, eats invaders.

Antibiotic: Medicine that kills bacteria but not viruses.

Antigens: Chemical markers or signals on the outside of microbes. Antigens help the body identify and destroy harmful microbes.

Antibody: Antigen-recognizing molecules made by special white blood cells. Antibodies attach to antigens to mark germs for destruction.

Materials

Per class:
- Poster or overheads of photomicrographs and scientifically accurate drawings of immune-system cells, optional
- Paper props for skit:
  - Skin (pieces of pink, brown, or tan paper)
  - Eye (8 x 10-in. cutout picture of an eye)
  - Tears (6-in. blue tear drop cutout)
  - Lungs (11-in. pink cutouts)
  - Tiny Hairs (12-in. pieces of string or yarn)
  - Stomach cells (8-in. paper cutouts)
  - Eating cells, or phagocytes (white plastic platters)
  - Red Blood cells (red plastic plates)
  - Sample antigens (triangular paper cutouts)
  - Sample antibodies (Y-shaped cutouts that fit over antigens)
  - White blood cells
    - Eating cells (with activated side indicated by blue tips)
    - Helper cells (with activated side indicated by blue tips)
    - B-cells (a.k.a. antibody makers), memory cells on the back
- Construction paper for making antigens and antibodies
- Tape

Per student:
- 1 worksheet
- 1 paper microbe model from Lesson 2
- Pencil
- Scissors

Procedure

Question:
How does your body defend itself against invading microbes?

Activity 1: Antigens and Antibodies

1. Explain that on their surfaces, microbes have markers called antigens that allow the body to recognize them and mark them for destruction. Show the students how to cut out paper antigens and attach them to the surface of their microbes from Lesson 2.

2. Explain that special cells in our bodies make antibodies that recognize the antigens. When an antibody fits into the antigen, the microbe is marked for destruction. Have the students cut out antibodies that match the antigens on their microbes.

Activity 2: Immune-System Skits

1. Give a brief overview of this activity: our body's defense system is called the immune system. It has three levels of defense. Students will act out the defense system as it destroys the microbes they made in Lesson 2.

   Level 1: When germs try to get into the body, the first defense fighters work to keep them out. These defenders include skin, tears, stomach acid, and mucus and little hairs in the nose and airways.

   Level 2: Germs get inside the body, but eating cells gobble them up, and alert cell get activated. Eating cells and alert cells are special white blood cells that get activated when microbes enter the bloodstream.

   Level 3: The alert cells tell B cells, another type of white blood cell, that germs are inside the body. The B cells then make antibodies and become memory cells that remember the invader for next time.

2. Split class into three groups of 10 to 12 students. Assign each group one level of defense and give them enough props for each person. Explain the props to each group (this is much easier with an assistant). Students should use their own microbes, but should not crumple them until they are performing in front of the class.

   1st Defense: Props include: skin, tears, an eye, lungs, small hairs, and stomach cells. Microbes try to penetrate the skin but they don't get through. Microbes try to enter the lungs, but little hairs catch them. Microbes try to enter the eyes, but tears burn them and wash them away. Microbes try to enter the stomach, but stomach acid from stomach cells burns them.

   2nd Defense: Props include: red blood cells, alert cells, and eating cells. Germs enter the bloodstream but encounter alert cells and eating cells. When the alert cells and eating cells are activated, the students can turn over the props to the blue side. The activated eating cells should eat some of the microbes.

   3rd Defense: Props include: red blood cells, alert cells, B cells, and antibodies. This is the most complicated skit and needs some explaining. To show when a B cell has antibodies, antibodies that match the antigens of the groups' microbes should be taped around it. To show when the antibodies cling to a microbe, tape antibodies on the matching antigens. Then tape all the antibody-covered microbes together. In the final performance they will be crumpled. As an option, an eating cell can come by to eat them up.

3. Give the students 15 minutes to write their scripts and rehearse. What might the germs and defenders say to each other? Tell the students to think in terms of cartoons with action heroes and enemies as characters. If the class becomes too chaotic, take over and go to the next step.

4. Assist the groups as they perform in front of the class. Help them remember their lines and what to do. Direct them where to stand so everyone can see. If the class finishes all three skits in time, try the skits again with different microbes as the invaders. At the end, all of the microbes should be destroyed, good and bad.

Wrap-up

1. Show the poster or overheads of photomicrographs and scientifically accurate drawings of immune-system cells. (Optional)

2. Discuss vaccines and the importance of immunizations.

3. Ask the students how they think they could enhance the effectiveness of the immune system. Answers should include exercise and proper nutrition. Getting enough sleep is also important, as is reducing stress (e.g., by meditating, doing relaxation exercises, and/ or finding satisfactory solutions to personal problems). Research also shows that laughter increases the production of immune-system proteins!

Infectious Disesases
Lesson 5

THE BODY FIGHTS BACK

Name: _____

Teacher: _____

Date: _____

Levels of the Immune System

Level 1: When germs try to get into the body, the first defense fighters work to keep them out. These defenders include skin, tears, stomach acid, and mucus and little hairs in the nose and airways.

Level 2: Germs get inside the body, but eating cells gobble them up, and alert cell get activated. Eating cells and alert cells are special white blood cells that get activated when microbes enter the bloodstream.

Level 3: The alert cells tell B cells, another type of white blood cell, that germs are inside the body. The B cells then make antibodies and become memory cells that remember the invader for next time.

Which level will your group perform? _____

What are the characters? _____

_____

Script (Dialogue and Action):

_____

_____

_____

_____

_____

_____

_____

Grade: 4
Environmental Toxics
Lesson 1: Lead Poisoning

Lesson Time: 1 hour

References: "Kitchen Chemistry," in How to Encourage Girls in Math and Science (Dale Seymour Publications, 1982), by Joan Skolnick, Carol Langbort, and Lucille Day, pp. 137-138; Alameda County Lead Poisoning Prevention Program: The center works with local and statewide organizations to educate the community about the dangers of lead poisoning. http://www.aclppp.org

Lesson objectives
- Analyze a case study about a boy suffering from lead poisoning.
- Interview a lead expert.
- Test household objects for lead contamination using the scientific process.
- Know that scientific progress is made by asking meaningful questions and by conducting careful investigations.
- Discover that lead, a toxic heavy metal, can be found in soil, paint, old houses, pipes, pottery, folk medicine, some painted toys, jewelry, and some Mexican candy and Mexican candy wrappers.
- Learn that lead poisoning often occurs with no obvious symptoms, frequently goes unrecognized, and can affect nearly every system in the body.

Overview

Students read and analyze a case study about a child with lead poisoning. The class meets a lead expert and tests objects found in the child's house. The students make hypotheses and use cabbage indicator to simulate testing objects for lead.

Key Terms

Toxic: Poisonous.

Environmental toxics: Substances in the environment that are harmful to the health of humans. Environmental toxics can be found in air, water, soil, food, and the home.

Lead: An environmental toxic found in soil, paint, old houses, pipes, pottery, folk medicine, some painted toys, jewelry, and some Mexican candy and Mexican candy wrappers. Lead is a heavy metal element.

Materials

Per student:
- 1 worksheet
- 1 pair of latex gloves
- 1 cotton swab

Per group of 4
- 1 household object that could contain lead (but does not, because this is a simulation), such as a brightly colored ceramic bowl, a painted toy, a piece of jewelry, a piece of metal plumbing pipe, or a piece of painted wood representing a piece of a windowsill.
- 10-ml vial, capped, containing white vinegar or baking soda dissolved in water (half of the groups should have vinegar, and half should have baking soda in water)
- 10-ml vial, capped, containing cabbage indicator (made beforehand)

  Instructions for making cabbage indicator: Boil red cabbage leaves, broken into small pieces, for approximately 10 minutes or until the water turns a deep purple. Use approximately one cup of water for each cabbage leaf.
- 1 eyedropper
- 1 paper plate

Procedure

> **Questions:**
> Can cleaning products really kill microbes?
> Where is lead found?

Activity 1: Case Study

1. Distribute worksheets and read through the case study as a class.
2. Ask the students what the story is about. What are the main issues? Divide the class into groups of four to identify the main ideas of the case. Ask the groups to underline the important words or phrases. Did everyone get the same underlined words?
3. Brainstorm what the students know and need to know for 5-10 minutes. Make a chart of what they know and need to know, and discuss it. Discuss any misconceptions.

Activity 2: Expert

Introduce the lead expert who will:
- Answer questions from the class about the case study.
- Share information about his or her profession and education.
- Discuss the symptoms of lead poisoning.
- Discuss the long-term effects of lead on the human body.

  Mention the latest research in lead poisoning detection.

If no expert is present, the presenter will need to answer questions about the case study and provide background information on lead poisoning and its long-term effects, as well as on lead poisoning prevention. Lead poisoning causes learning impairment, reduced IQ, hearing loss, and other severe effects. In addition to neurological damage, it causes renal disease, cardiovascular effects, and reproductive toxicity.

Activity 3: Simulated Lead Test

1. Introduce and demonstrate the lead test. Put on a pair of latex gloves, explaining that chemicals and objects that might contain lead should not be touched with bare hands. Show a variety of items that were found in the home of the young child in the case study. Select one item. Then follow this procedure:

   a. Dip a swab into a vial containing vinegar, then rub the swab on the object.
   b. Dip the swab back into the vinegar.
   c. Use an eyedropper to add the cabbage indicator (call it lead indicator throughout the activity), one drop at a time, to the vinegar. When the solution turns pink, tell the students that the object contains lead, and that if it had not contained lead, the solution would have turned green. Explain that this is a pretend test for lead, because it would be dangerous to have objects that really contain lead in the classroom.

2. Have the students discuss which objects are the most likely sources of lead in the case study. Work with the students to come up with hypotheses. The students should write their hypotheses as complete sentences.

   Example: "The child was poisoned by lead paint in the house."

3. Pass out a pair of gloves to each student and ask them to put the gloves on.
4. Pass out 4 swabs, 1 indicator vial, 1 vinegar or baking soda vial, 1 paper plate, and 1 test object to each group of four. Each object should be placed on a paper plate.
5. Lead the students through the steps again as they do the tests. Each student should dip a swab in the clear liquid, rub it on the object, then dip it again in the clear liquid. After all four students have done this, they should take turns adding one drop of indicator with the eyedropper until the solution changes color. Ask them to record the result on their worksheets.
6. Collect the test objects and tabulate the students' findings.
7. Collect and discard the plates, gloves, and swabs.
8. Discuss the lead-containing objects in relation to the case study. Juan could have been poisoned from multiple sources.
9. Brainstorm ways to prevent lead poisoning. Discuss important sources of lead, including paint from houses built before 1978.

Environmental Toxics
Lesson 1: Lead Poisoning

Juan Moralez

Juan is a 6-year-old, Latino boy who lives in Oakland, California, with his mother, father, grandmother, and 3-year-old sister. He was a happy child who enjoyed watching TV, playing with toy cars, and eating Mexican candy. Recently, his kindergarten teacher noticed that he was acting out in class. He was having trouble learning the alphabet. In a doctor's visit, a blood test showed that he had lead in his blood, 8 times the normal level. Investigations revealed that he lived in an apartment building with old paint and old pipes. Although the family immigrated to the US six years ago, they still use Mexican pottery, but they do not use alternative medicines. Juan spends most of his time indoors. What is the source of the lead poisoning?

Guest Speaker: _____

Job: _____

Name 3 sources of lead:

1. _____

2. _____

3. _____

Lead Test

Step 1: Observations
People get sick from eating or touching things that contain lead. Juan has lead poisoning.

Step 2: Hypothesis

Juan got lead poisoning from (name of object): _____

Step 3: Plan your test

Materials: cotton swabs, gloves, paper plate, swabbing solution, indicator solution, eyedropper, object that might contain lead

Procedure:
1. Dip the swab into the swabbing solution. Rub the object with the swab.
2. Dip the used swab back into the swabbing solution.
3. Add indicator, one drop at a time, to the swabbing solution.
4. If the solution turns pink, the object contains lead. If it turns green, the object does not contain lead.

Step 4: Conduct your test

Step 5: Draw conclusions and share results

Object Name	Prediction of lead (Yes/No)	Result (color)	Contains lead? (Yes/No)

How was Juan poisoned?

_____

_____

Grade: 4
Environmental Toxics
Lesson 2: Test the Alternatives

Lesson Time: 1 hour

Reference: Teaching Toxics, (K-3 Home Tour, K-3 Warning Words)

Lesson objectives
- Formulate non-toxic cleaning products.
- Differentiate observation from inference (interpretation).
- Act like scientists, deriving explanations from observations and inferences.
- Formulate and justify predictions based on cause-and-effect relationships.
- Conduct multiple trials to test a prediction and draw conclusions about the relationship between predictions and results.
- Follow a set of written instructions for a scientific investigation.
- Measure and estimate the volume of ingredients.

Overview
Students analyze the warning labels on toxic cleaning products and discuss health consequences. They use their observations and inferences to design and test formulas for non-toxic cleaners using safe, household ingredients. The students ask their own questions and practice following written instructions with careful measurements. Groups work together to compare results from multiple trials.

Occupation of the Day
Chemist: A scientist who works with chemicals. Chemists can work for universities, research institutions, government agencies, or companies. Some chemists formulate and test chemical products such as shampoo, paint, glue, and cleaning products.

Key Terms
Observation: Something seen, or a statement made by looking at something.

Inference: A statement or conclusion based on assumed facts.

Alternative: A different choice from the usual or conventional one.

Safe: Harmless.

Hazardous: Involving or exposing one to danger, harm, or risk.

Ingredient: Something that is a part of any combination or mixture.

Substitute: A person or thing that takes the place or function of another.

Materials

Per student:
- 1 worksheet

Per group of 4
- 2 warning labels or empty containers from toxic cleaning products. It helps to enlarge labels on a photocopier. Each group can have the same labels.
- 1 measuring cup. Either 1/2 cup or 1/4 cup will do.
- 1 teaspoon
- 1 tablespoon
- 4 mixing bowls (1 for each trial). Almost any plastic container or large plastic cup will work. It should hold at least 2 cups.
- 4 stirring sticks. Coffee stirrers work well.
- 1/4 cup vinegar in a small container (buy one 12-oz. container for the class)
- 1/2 cup salt in a small container
- 1/4 cup flour in a small container
- 1/8 cup lemon juice in a small container
- 1/4 cup baking soda in a small container
- 1/4 cup vegetable oil
- 5 paper towels
- 1/2 liter water

Environmental Toxics
Lesson 2

TEST THE ALTERNATIVES

Name: _____

Teacher: _____

Date: _____

Warning Label

1. What are the health precautions?

_____

2. How could this product harm someone?

_____

3. What should someone do if he or she is poisoned? _____

4. Name at least one toxic ingredient: _____

Nontoxic Cleaner

Circle the best ingredients for a non-toxic cleaner:

Sugar   Salt

    Lemon juice   Flour

      Baking Soda   Vinegar

Pepper

   Soda   Corn Starch

    Water   Alcohol

Garlic

  Corn meal   Peppermint

Trial 1:

Amount	Ingredient

Directions:

1. _____

   _____

2. _____

   _____

3. _____

   _____

Results:

_____

What would you change?

_____

Trial 2:

Amount	Ingredient

Directions:

1. _____

   _____

2. _____

   _____

3. _____

   _____

Results:

_____

What would you change?

_____

Trial 3:

Amount	Ingredient

Directions:

1. _____

_____

2. _____

_____

3. _____

_____

Results:

_____

What would you change?

_____

Trial 4:

Amount	Ingredient

Directions:

1. _____

_____

2. _____

_____

3. _____

_____

Results:

_____

What would you change?

_____

Grade: 4
Environmental Toxics
Lesson 3: Mercury Poisoning

Lesson Time: 1 hour

Lesson objectives

- Experience the process by which scientific progress is made: ask meaningful questions and conduct careful investigations.
- Experience how doctors solve cases by asking meaningful questions and conducting careful investigations.
- Make predictions about the results of a diagnostic test.
- Simulate a test measuring the amount of mercury in blood.
- Diagnose a patient with mercury poisoning.
- Learn that mercury is an environmental toxic that can harm the brain, heart, kidneys, lungs, and immune system.
- Conclude that a diet high in fish can be a source of mercury poisoning.

Overview

The students analyze a case study about a young boy with mercury poisoning and work in teams to read profiles of other patients with similar symptoms. They use sugar solutions and urine test strips to simulate a blood mercury test, and they discover that eating fish can lead to mercury poisoning. The presenter explains how mercury travels from the smokestacks of coal burning power plants to the ocean. The students work in groups to organize marine organisms into food chains. The class then creates a pyramid representing a food web and discusses how mercury becomes more concentrated at the higher levels of the pyramid.

Occupation of the Day

Environmental scientists: Scientists who measure pollutants in the environment and develop methods for reducing pollution and solving other environmental problems. They check what is in the air, water, and soil to make sure that the environment is safe. They also give advice on how to clean the environment. For example, they might advise on how to reduce mercury levels in the environment.

Key Terms

Mercury: A silvery heavy metal found naturally in small quantities in rocks and soil in combination with other elements. Mercury mines, coal-burning power plants, and industrial factories release mercury into the air and water, where it can poison humans and other living things. It accumulates in the liver, kidneys, hair, and skin, causing a range of symptoms including learning deficits, tremors, brittle hair, stunted growth, headaches, spotted gums, and striped fingernails.

Methylmercury: The most poisonous form of mercury in the environment. When mercury is emitted into the air, it falls on soil and water where bacteria convert it into a form that causes severe health problems. The amount and toxicity of methylmercury can increase in food webs.

Environmental toxics: Substances in the environment that are harmful to the health of humans. They can be found in air, water, soil, food, and the home. Even if we cannot see or taste them, they can affect our health.

Symptoms: Signs that something is wrong with someone.

Diagnosis: The conclusion that a doctor reaches after evaluating the symptoms and test results of a patient. Typically the conclusion is the name of a medical condition. Mercury poisoning, tonsillitis, strep throat, and measles are all examples of diagnoses.

Ecosystem: A community of organisms and their physical environment.

Food chain: A sequence of organisms, each of which uses the next lower member of the sequence as a food source.

Food web: The complex interconnection of food chains in an ecosystem.

Bacteria: single-celled microorganisms found in soil, air, and water.

Part per million: The scale on which concentrations of environmental toxics are measured.

Materials

Per class:
- 1 worksheet overhead, optional
- 1 overhead table of patients and symptoms
- 3 sets of 20-ml vials of fake blood:
  - 3 vials filled with tap water. Label one of the three as the "control."
  - 5 vials with 2 Tbs. of fructose syrup. Label one of the vials as the "positive test."
  - 2 vials with moderate amounts of sugar that will test low for mercury.
- 1 pack of 100 removable orange stickers
- 1 roll of masking tape

Per student:
- 1 worksheet
- 1 handout listing various symptoms and possible diagnoses
- 1 handout table of patients and symptoms
- 1 3 x 5-in. index card

Per group of 4:
- 1 patient profile that includes the patient's name, symptoms, diet, and exercise. Four of the eight patients eat a lot of fish and have symptoms of mercury poisoning.
- 1 urine test strip
- 2 boxes of colored pencils
- 1 organism identification sheet. Each sheet pictures 4 organisms that might contain mercury, gives their names, and says what they eat.
- 1 chart showing mercury levels in sea organisms

Procedure

Activity 1: Case Study

1. Read through the case study as a whole class.
2. Ask the students to read the case again as they underline the key words. Discuss the main point of the story.
3. Fill out the "Know" side of the chart on the worksheet. Discuss Alex's symptoms and his lifestyle. Refer back to the underlined words. Did everyone get the same words? Ask if anyone has any experience that relates to the case.
4. Fill out the "Need to Know" side of the chart. What specific questions do the students have about the topic? Discuss any misconceptions.

Activity 2: Quantitative Analysis

1. Explain that Alex went to see Dr. Jane Hightower, a doctor of internal medicine at the California Pacific Medical Center in San Francisco. Ask the class to look at the handout of Alex's symptoms and possible diagnoses. Read through it with the class. Do they notice anything?
2. Explain that Dr. Hightower noticed an interesting pattern. She found other patients with similar unexplained symptoms. Pass out one profile to each group.
3. Compare the other patients to Alex on an overhead chart. The students should notice that the patients with similar symptoms had similar diets. They regularly ate seafood such as shark, mackerel, and albacore tuna.
4. Explain that Dr. Hightower looked up all the different diagnoses that matched the symptoms. Show the list of diagnoses again and explain the mercury test. Say that Dr. Hightower had a hypothesis that all of her patients with the same symptoms had mercury poisoning. Show vials of fake blood taken from the different patients. Take the control and positive test vials. First dip a test strip into the control vial and match the color to the color chart. Then do the same with the positive test vial.
5. To each group pass out one vial that matches their profile (Ali and Marjorie no mercury; Mike and Jerome low mercury; Susie, Lee, Robin, and John high mercury, i.e., mercury poisoning). Walk through the procedure with the class.
6. The tests should reveal that the patients who ate fish every day have mercury poisoning. How can that be? Discuss.
7. Explain what mercury is and how it spreads. It comes from natural and man-made sources and accumulates in ocean environments, where it is taken up by marine life. Explain how coal-burning power plants emit large quantities of mercury that end up in the sea.

Activity 3: Food Chains and Webs

1. To each group pass out colored pencils, index cards, an organism identification sheet that pictures four sea organisms, and a chart showing mercury levels in sea organisms. On the index cards, each student should make a color drawing of an organism and write its name, diet, and level of mercury. Each student in the group should draw a different organism.
2. Ask the students to place orange stickers on their cards to signify the level of mercury the organism contains:
   - HIGH = 4 stickers
   - MEDIUM = 3 stickers
   - LOW = 2 stickers
   - VERY LOW = 1 sticker (zooplankton, phytoplankton, and diatoms only)
3. Explain food chains and ask the students to arrange the organisms on their identification sheet into a food chain. Which organism has the most mercury, the one at the bottom or the one at the top?
4. Draw a pyramid on the board with four mercury levels (level 1, i.e., very low, at the bottom) and work with the students to attach the organism cards on the appropriate mercury ratings (use masking tape). The students should notice that large predators have the most mercury. What can they infer about predators? Explain that the predators have the most mercury because they eat contaminated organisms and the mercury builds up in their tissue. In general, the mercury level increases as you move up a food chain. The pyramid represents a food web, which consists of many food chains linked together in an ecosystem. Make sure that students understand that seafood is good for people; they just shouldn't eat the types of fish with high mercury levels very often.

Extension

Discuss how the class could share their conclusions. Here are some ideas:
- Write a short scientific report.
- Create a pamphlet about mercury poisoning that you can share with your family and friends.
- Create an ad urging political action.
- Create artwork such as cartoons that reveal issues about the case.
- Design a new technology that will help solve the problem.

**Environmental Toxics
Lesson 3**

Name: _____

Teacher: _____

Date: _____

CASE STUDY

aLex

"I'm worried about Alex," said his teacher. "He used to be the fastest reader in his class. Now he struggles to read simple sentences. I'm worried that he may have to repeat third grade."

"I know," said his mom. "And, I've noticed other strange things. His hair is brittle and dry and it stopped growing. He complains that his feet are numb and that his head aches. He has strange dark spots on his gums and white lines on his fingernails. I just don't understand. Until a few months ago, he was so healthy. He played soccer every day, and he ate his vegetables and tuna fish sandwiches. Now he can't play soccer anymore.

"The doctors tried CAT scans and heart tests. They found nothing."

"I would recommend Dr. Hightower," said the teacher.

1. Read the case again as a group. Underline important words or phrases.

   What is the case about? _____

2. What specific questions do you have about the topic?

What I know	What I need to know

Children's Hospital Oakland Research Institute

iNteRview with ALex

You are Dr. Hightower. Here are some questions you might ask about Alex.

How old is he? _____

How tall is he? _____   How much does he weigh? _____

What symptoms does he have? _____

How long has he had those symptoms? _____

Does he always have those symptoms or do they go away? _____

What is his diet? _____

Has he been exercising? _____

Has his school work been affected? _____

My patient

Name _____

Age _____

Symptoms _____

Diet _____

Exercise _____

Mercury Levels in Seafood		
Eat Freely	Atlantic mackerel Clams Crab Mussels	Salmon Scallops Shrimp Sole Trout
Eat in Moderation Moderate in Mercury	Anchovies Bass Cod Halibut Herring	Lobster Mahi mahi Oysters Squid
Limit High in Mercury	King mackerel Marlin Orange roughy	Rockfish Shark Swordfish Tuna

Note: Plankton (including zooplankton, phytoplankton, and diatoms) is at the bottom of the food chain and has the lowest mercury levels of sea organisms. Plankton is a food source for many animals found in the sea.

Symptoms	Possible Causes
Dry, brittle hair	• Anorexia • Thyroid disease • Malnutrition • Mercury Poisoning
Spots on gums	• Mercury poisoning • Diabetes • Vitamin deficiency • Gum disease
Trouble reading	• Attention deficit disorder • Mercury poisoning • Drug use

	Alex	John	Jerome	Marjorie	Lee	Ali	Mike	Robin	Susie
Dry, brittle hair									
White lines on fingernails									
Trouble reading									
Trouble concentrating									
Fatigue									
Plays tennis									
Swims regularly									
Eats fish									
Mercury Poisoning									

How did the patients get poisoned? _____

What do they have in common? _____

My Organism:

Organism name: _____

Diet: _____

Mercury level: _____

What types of seafood have the most mercury? _____

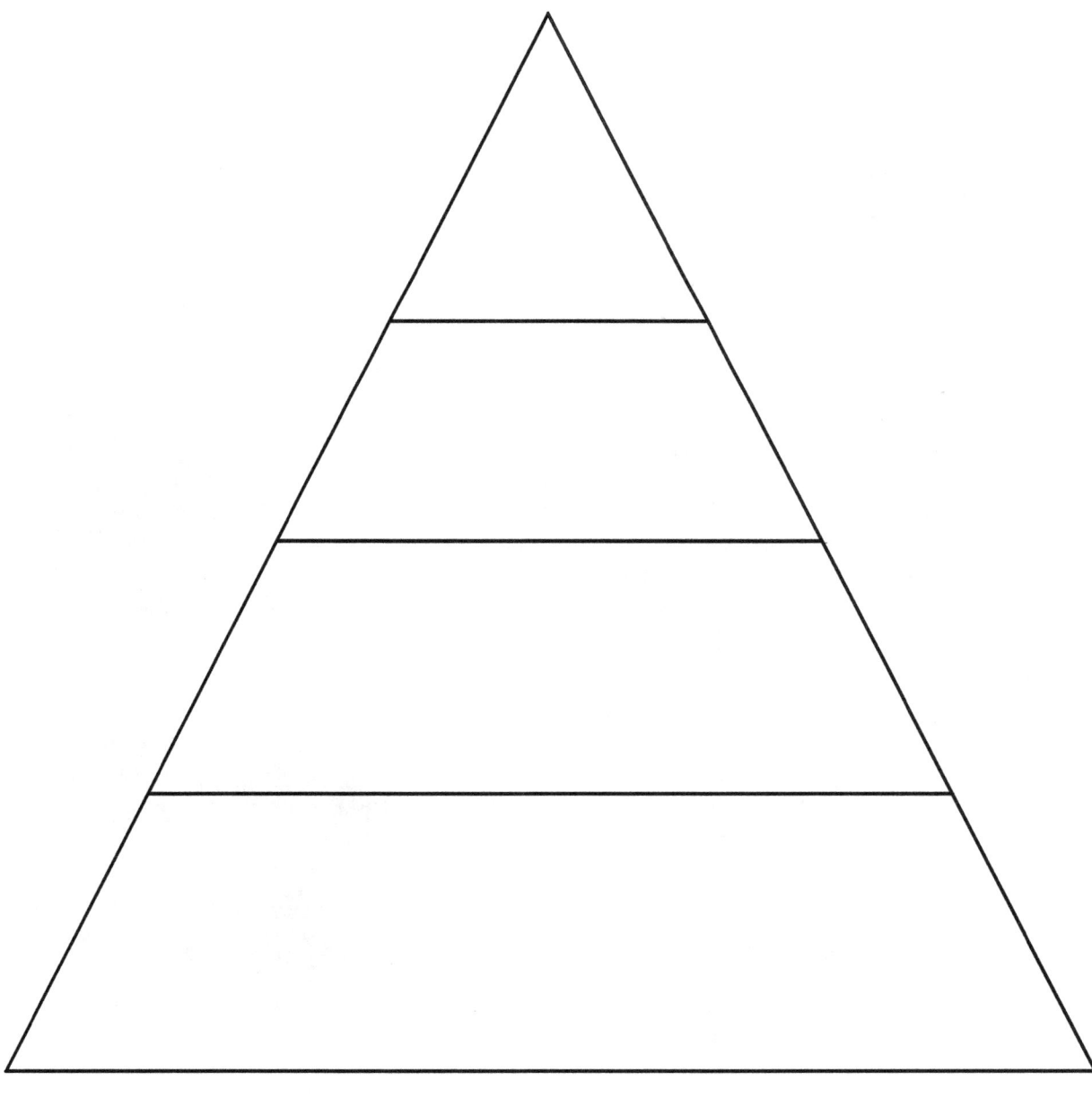

The Food Chain

_____ Blueback Herring
Herring are small fish that feed on insects, plankton, fish eggs, or other small fish such as anchovies. Like salmon, they lay their eggs in freshwater streams or lakes. This one was caught in a river in Minnesota. It weighs 15 pounds.

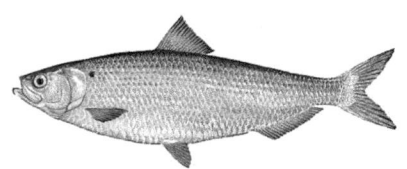

_____ Anchovies
Anchovies are fish that are about 4 inches long and have a silver stripe on them. They live in saltwater and feed on zooplankton. This one was caught in the Pacific Ocean.

_____ Zooplankton
Plankton consists of floating aquatic plants and animals. Many of them are microscopic. Zooplankton eats other plankton to survive. Plankton organisms can't move efficiently on their own, so they use the currents to move about in their habitat. This creature is less than 1 centimeter long. It is from the Pacific Ocean.

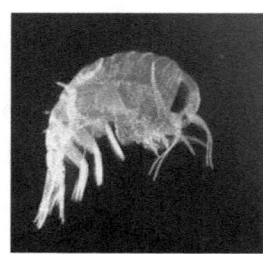

_____ Leopard Shark
The leopard shark lives all along the Pacific Coast, near the ocean floor. It eats crabs, clams, shrimp, and fish. It is heavily fished in San Francisco Bay. This shark is 4 feet long. It was caught in the bay.

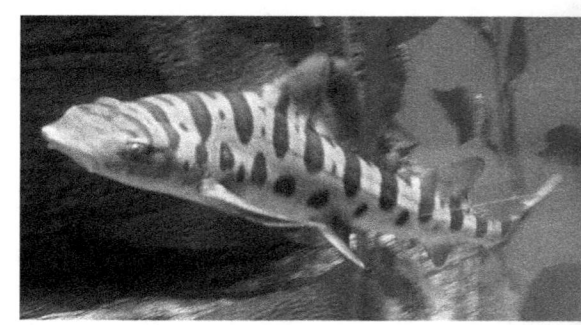

The Food Chain

Tuna
_____ These fish live in the Northwest and Pacific regions. They are heavily fished—perhaps you have eaten some yourself! They eat shellfish, some squid, and other smaller fish. This fish is about 2 feet long and was caught off the coast of San Diego.

Diatoms
_____ Diatoms are a particular type of phytoplankton. There are thousands of different species of diatoms. They use energy from the sun to make their food. They are eaten by animals and other plankton. These diatoms are microscopic. They were found in the Atlantic Ocean.

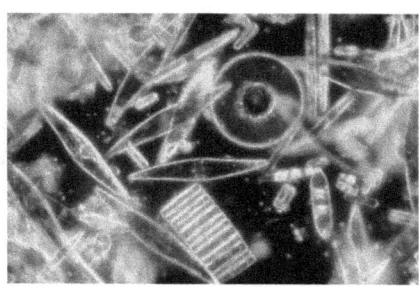

Swordfish
_____ Swordfish live in the ocean. They eat tuna and other fish, like mackerel and barracuda, and occasionally squid. They have organs that act like eye-heaters to heat their eyes to improve vision. This one is 6 feet long and was caught off the coast of Florida.

Shellfish
_____ An aquatic animal, such as a mollusk or crustacean, which has a shell or shell-like exoskeleton. They eat plankton. With the shell, this shellfish is about 3 inches long. It was caught off the coast near Santa Cruz.

The Food Chain

_____ ### SALMON
Salmon are anadromous, which means they are born in fresh water and then eventually live in the ocean. They feed on insects, sea worms, and crustaceans. This salmon is about 2 feet long and was caught in the Pacific Ocean.

_____ ### CRABS
Crabs are a type of crustacean. They eat worms, plants, and microscopic organisms. All crustaceans have hard outer shells to protect their insides. This crab is about 9 inches long and was found in San Francisco Bay.

_____ ### WORMS
A worm is an elongated, soft-bodied invertebrate animal. The most famous is the earthworm, a member of phylum Annelida, but there are hundreds of thousands of different species that live in a wide variety of habitats other than soil. They eat microscopic organisms. This worm is about 1 inch long and was found in a lake in Southern California.

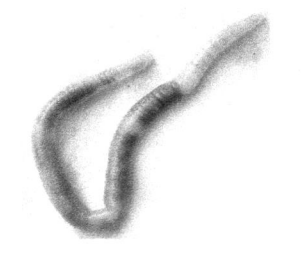

_____ ### HALIBUT
Halibut are some of the biggest fish around. Females can grow up to 500 pounds! They eat crabs, octopi, salmon, and a number of other things. This one is a large halibut that is about 5 feet long. It was found off the coast of San Diego.

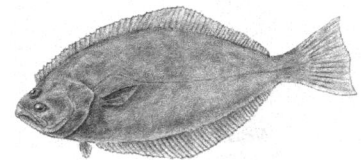

The Food Chain

____ Great White Shark
The great white shark is the world's largest predatory fish. Great white sharks eat fish, smaller sharks, turtles, dolphins, seals, and sea lions. This shark is about 15 feet long and was caught off the coast of Florida.

____ Oysters
Oysters, a type of shellfish, are mollusks. They only eat plankton and are responsible for making pearls. This oyster was found in the Pacific Ocean near Oregon. It is about 6 inches long.

____ Phytoplankton
Phytoplankton consists of microscopic plants. They get energy from sunlight. When the water is very warm, some phytoplankton species can bloom and turn the water red. This microscopic plant was found in San Francisco Bay.

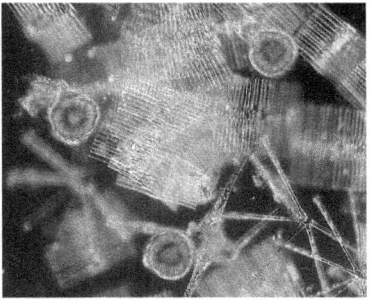

____ Mackerel
Mackerel are larger fish and extremely fast swimmers. They travel in schools and feed on clams, shellfish, and other fish. This mackerel is about 3 feet long and was found off the coast of Boston.

Investigation 2: Comparing Patients

John

John, age 30, says he's just one of San Francisco's fish lovers. "I'm a single guy. I'd have tuna fish every night for dinner when I cooked at home. It was easy to make and cheap, lean, and high in protein. When I went out, I was a big fan of ahi tuna and sea bass."

Formerly well, he began feeling ill. He started out sluggish and lethargic, then had bouts of memory loss. He had to take detailed notes of conversations.

"I had tremors so bad that I could hardly drive, and, worst of all, suffered from anxiety and panic attacks." Five doctors in five different fields couldn't find anything wrong.

He changed his diet. After a couple of months, he noticed that his energy was returning. "My memory was returning, and I could handle myself a lot better. More importantly, the anxiety began to recede. Now I'm feeling pretty close to normal."

Robin

My name is Robin, and I'm 29 years old. I love running and playing tennis. I live in California and am a hairdresser. About two years ago I wanted to lose some weight. I was using a diet that required 3 to 4 ounces of protein each day and suggested chicken or fish.

I ate tuna from a local fishmonger (3 to 4 ounces), 3 to 4 times a day for two weeks straight. I only ate chicken at lunchtime. I lost 5 lbs. the first week and 5 lbs. the second week.

I started having trouble focusing my attention at work, and it was especially noticeable while driving. On a road I've used to travel to and from work for over five years, I became disoriented. I immediately called my mother and told her where I was. I felt tingly, and I noticed I was starting to lose my hair. I had no idea what was happening, but my mother told me to stop the diet and I did. I went back to my old eating habits (which meant fish only 1 or 2 times a month). I started to feel better (clear headed and the tingling went away).

Lee

Lee, age 59, thought she had a healthy lifestyle. She was thin and active, and she ate well with lunches of tuna and fresh vegetables and dinners of halibut, sea bass, or swordfish. She loved to play tennis and swim.

Yet she spent more than a decade plagued by fatigue, stomachaches, and headaches. Her hair started falling out. Memory lapses made her think she was losing her mind.

The Sausalito, California, anthropologist and documentary filmmaker eventually ended up in the office of Dr. Jane Hightower, a San Francisco internist.

Susie

Susie, age 61, a Tiburon resident and longtime patient of Dr. Hightower's, had been complaining for years of a flu-like feeling with headaches and fatigue that she couldn't shake. She worked long hours in an office and did not get much time to play sports.

"I've been very health-conscious all my life. I read everything on the latest medical issues. I'd been eating eight or nine servings a week of tuna, swordfish, halibut, and sea bass, and loading up on mercury," said Susie, a former Pan American Airlines sales manager.

Investigation 2: Comparing Patients

Mike

My name is Mike. I'm 28 years old, and I live in San Francisco. I live a very healthy lifestyle. I eat a lot of fruits and vegetables and love to swim. I love outdoor fishing also. Although I don't eat very much fish, about twice a month we go fishing in San Francisco Bay.

Lately, I've been having slight headaches or feeling really tired. I do not always feel like this; it happens about every other week. I feel like I have the flu, and I have to go to the doctor. I do not know what is wrong.

Marjorie

My name is Marjorie. I am 55 years old. I don't feel sick, even though I don't feel that I have the healthiest lifestyle. I love chocolate and potato chips, although I do try to play tennis or go on brisk walks at least once a week.

My diet consists mainly of bread, chicken, pork, rice, and some vegetables. My favorite meal is a hamburger, and my least favorite is fish. Even as a child, I never liked fish. I have never had any illnesses, although my doctor tells me I have high blood pressure. Other than that, I feel healthy.

Jerome

My name is Jerome. I am 20 years old, and I live in Oakland. I have a very healthy lifestyle. I go running or swimming every day. On weekends, I like to play basketball.

I have a healthy diet too. I remember to eat fruits, vegetables, and dairy products every day. I do not eat red meat, because it is high in fat, so I usually eat chicken or tofu. Every once in a while, I eat fish. My favorite dish is shark soup, and I also like tuna fish sandwiches.

Sometimes, I have headaches or my gums start to bleed. It does not happen all the time, but it bothers me when it does happen. I know I don't have the flu, but sometimes I feel like I do.

Ali

My name is Ali and I am 13. I attend middle school and I will be going to high school next year. I am on my school's track team.

I feel totally healthy, even though it seems a lot of people are getting sick lately. I never get headaches or have trouble concentrating. My mom always says it is surprising I am so healthy, because I absolutely love junk food. I love chips, chocolate, French fries, and donuts.

I do not eat any meat, fish, or chicken, because I am a vegetarian. I have been a vegetarian for about three years now. I usually eat tofu or beans to get my protein.

Grade: 4
Environmental Toxics
Lesson 4: Air Pollution, Part I

Lesson Time: 1 hour

Reference: Dust catcher activity: http://www.hhmi.org:80/coolscience/forkids/airjunk/nosep2.html

Lesson objectives
- Experience the process by which scientific progress is made: ask meaningful questions and conduct careful investigations.
- Explore the causes and effects of air pollution.
- Differentiate between observations and inferences (interpretations).
- Generate hypotheses.
- Follow a set of written instructions for a scientific investigation.

Overview
The class interviews a patient whose health is affected by local air pollution. The students discuss observations and inferences about local air pollution. They conjecture about causes of air pollution around the school and follow a set of written instructions to begin an experiment. Groups of students attach pieces of clear scotch tape to particle collectors that they station around the school for one week.

Key Terms
Air pollution: Contamination of air by smoke, particulates, lead, and harmful gases, such as carbon monoxide.

Lead: A poisonous heavy metal sometimes found in paint, gasoline, imported pottery, and Mexican candy. Traces of lead can be found in soil, water, and air.

Particulate matter: Any type of solid in the air, such as smoke or dust, which can remain suspended for extended periods. Microscopic particles in the air can be breathed into the lungs and cause respiratory disease. They are also the main source of haze, which reduces visibility.

Asthma: A respiratory disease that can be aggravated by air pollution.

Materials

Per class:
- 1 Tupperware container for the control

Per student:
- 1 worksheet

Per group of 4
- 1 roll of transparent scotch tape
- 8 packaging labels with strings attached (this allows each student to make 2 particle catchers, one of which he or she can take home)
- 2 pairs of scissors
- 1 permanent marker

Procedure

> **Questions:**
> **Does air pollution cause health problems?**
> **How can you measure air pollution?**
> **What areas of the school have the most air pollution?**

Activity 1: Interview a Patient

Introduce the patient, who will talk briefly about his or her illness and how it is affected by air pollution. Encourage the students to ask questions to better understand the nature of air pollution, its sources, and how it affects the body. If a patient is not present, explain how air pollution affects people with asthma and emphysema, and invite the students to ask questions.

Activity 2: Test Air Quality

1. Discuss class observations about air pollution. What local areas seem to have the most air pollution? What parts of the school might have air pollution? How can you tell? Discuss inferences based on observations. For example, how would you interpret an observation that areas around highways look smoggy or dusty? What do you infer are sources of air pollution?

2. Challenge the students to test air pollution levels in and around their own school, so that kids suffering from respiratory problems can avoid highly polluted areas.

3. Based on student observations and inferences, work together to generate a hypothesis about the most polluted area of the school.

4. Discuss ways that environmental scientists measure air pollution. Show a simple particle catcher made out of a packaging label and a piece of clear tape. Explain that the class will be able to use microscopes the following week to observe the particles caught on the tape.

5. Before passing out the materials, work as a class to generate a series of simple steps to guide the investigation.

6. The plan should include the following:
   - Decide on locations to test.
   - Make a particle catcher:
     - Take a packaging label.
     - Cut out a ½" x 2" rectangle in the center of the label.
     - Write the name, date, and location on the particle catcher.
     - Carefully place one piece of clear tape over the rectangular opening without touching the center of the tape.
   - Hang the particle catcher at the location indicated on the label.
   - Wait one week, then collect the particle catchers without touching the tape.
   - Look at the tape under the microscope and compare the amount of particles trapped on the tape from different locations.

7. Discuss the importance of carefully following a common set of procedures to control variables. Put the control particle catcher inside a plastic container. Have the class discuss the purpose of this.

8. Pass out the materials to each group and allow them time to make four particle catchers.

9. Dispatch pairs of students to hang particle catchers around the classroom and school and to record the location and date.

10. Review the predictions that will be tested next week.

Extensions

Suggest that students make their own particle catchers to test their homes.

Connect air pollution with smog tests. Show the students pictures of 4 cars and results from 4 smog tests. Which car matches which data set?

As a class, examine the weather section of a newspaper. What is the smog level for that day?

**Environmental Toxics
Lesson 4**

AIR POLLUTION

Part 1

Guest Speaker: _____

Health Issues: _____

Symptoms:

- _____
- _____
- _____

What is... AIR POLLUTION?

OBSERVATIONS
Example: The air smells bad near Highway 580.

- _____
- _____

Inferences:
Example: Cars produce pollution.

- _____
- _____

AIR QUALITY TEST

Step 1: Observations

Observation: _____

Question: What area at our school has the most air pollution?

Step 2: State a hypothesis

The _____ will have the highest level of air pollution.

Step 3: Plan your test

Measurement: The amount of particles that collect on clear tape.

Tools: Particle catchers made with tape and packaging label with strings, handheld microscope

Time: 1 week

Procedure:

1. Take a packaging label and cut out a 1/2-in x 2-in. rectangle with scissors.
2. Write your name, the date, and the location you want to test.
3. Carefully place one piece of clear tape over the rectangular hole.
4. Hang your "particle catcher" in the desired location.
5. Set aside a particle catcher inside a plastic container as a control.
6. After one week look at the tape strips with the microscope.
7. Draw what you see and compare the amount of particles caught on different particle catchers.

Grade: 4
Environmental Toxics
Lesson 5: Air Pollution, Part 2

Lesson Time: 1 hour

Reference: Dust catcher activity: http://www.hhmi.org:80/coolscience/forkids/airjunk/nosep2.html

Lesson objectives
- Use microscopes.
- Analyze the results of a scientific investigation.
- Make and share conclusions.
- Take political action to better the health of the community.

Overview
Students observe the particle collectors from Lesson 4 under the light of small, handheld, microscopes. Groups compare results and make recommendations for school administrators. Finally, the students compose letters to government officials asking for action concerning air pollution.

Key Term
Microscope: A scientific tool that magnifies small objects, such as dust and the cells of living things.

Materials

Per student:
- 1 worksheet
- 1 white 3 x 5-in. index card
- 1 piece of paper for writing a letter
- 1 envelope

Per group of 4
- 1 handheld microscope
- 2 particle catchers from student experiments in Lesson 4
- 1 additional particle catcher: Before the lesson, leave particle catchers around town in a variety of places such as stores, rooms, or construction sites. Collect the catchers after one week and ask the students to compare them to their own results. Some students may also bring particle catchers they hung in or near their homes.

Procedure

> **Question:**
>
> **What can be done about air pollution and other environmental toxics?**

Activity 1: Analyzing Test Results

1. Review hypotheses from Lesson 4.
2. Assign students to retrieve the particle collectors from around the classroom and school.
3. Show the class how to carefully place a piece of tape from a particle collector onto one corner of an index card without adding fingerprints to the sticky side of the tape. Place the index card with the tape under the lens of a microscope, and focus the knobs. Then draw a picture of what you observed on the board.
4. Make sure that each pair of students has at least one particle catcher (some of the particle catchers may have disappeared during the week). Pass out one index card, one microscope, and two worksheets to each pair. Ask the students to draw what they see in the space provided on the worksheets. They should check the particle catcher you provided as well as their own.
5. Pass the control around for everyone to observe and draw.
6. Have the students compare their results with those of other students.

Activity 2: Sharing Results and Making a Difference

1. Discuss the results. What location had the most air pollution? What are the particles made of? Dust? Hair? Pollen? Soot? How could this air pollution impact the health of students? How could the school officials improve the air quality?
2. Emphasize that the students live in a relatively healthy environment. Talk about how regulations have improved environmental conditions over time.
3. Collect the materials from the experiment, and pass out one piece of writing paper to each student. Discuss the importance of taking political action to decrease air pollution and other environmental toxics. Read an example letter, written to the EPA or another government office. Provide addresses and names, so that the students can write their own letters. The students can write about:
   - The results of their experiments
   - What they learned about environmental toxics
   - How environmental toxics affect the lives of children and the community
   - What can be done to reduce environmental toxics in air, soil, water, and the home
4. Collect the letters and send them to the appropriate offices. Make sure that all of the letters have return addresses.

Activity 3: Fight BAC Coloring Sheets

Investigate alternative technology, such as solar cars and ovens, which could reduce local emissions.

**Environmental Toxics
Lesson 5**

AIR POLLUTION

Name: _____

Teacher: _____

Date: _____

Part 2

Step 5: Draw conclusions and share results

Control: _____

Location: _____

Experimental test: _____

Location: _____

Step 6: Further Investigation

_____
_____
_____

Grade: 5
Nutrition and Diabetes
Lesson 1: You're the Doctor!

Lesson Time: 1 hour

Reference: Sugar solution test: Program Energy, 3rd grade lesson, Sugar Regulation Part 2: http://www.programenergy.org

Lesson objectives
- Be exposed to healthcare professions involved in the diagnosis of diabetes.
- Act as physician's assistants, doctors, and lab technicians.
- Discover that diabetes is a disease in which a person cannot handle the sugar in his or her body. This results in high blood sugar.

Overview

The presenter introduces a person with diabetes, and the class tries to diagnose the patient by asking questions and using the answers as clues. Students role-play doctors, physicians assistants, and lab technicians. They work in groups of four to test fake urine and blood samples with urine strips and glucometers.

Occupations of the Day

Physician's Assistant: A physician's assistant is like a doctor, but goes to a different type of school and goes through less training than a doctor. They often work with doctors and can do a lot of the same work as a general-practice doctor, such as seeing patients and diagnosing them.

Doctor: Doctors are people who help people stay healthy. They diagnose and treat patients with diseases. There are many types of doctors. Some have general practices and see many different kinds of patients. Others are specialists, such as cardiologists, or heart doctors, who only deal with patients with heart problems.

Medical Lab Technician: Medical lab technicians perform tests in laboratories that help doctors diagnose and treat diseases. They analyze body tissues and fluids. They work with equipment such as computers and microscopes. Medical lab technicians work in many different environments such as hospitals, universities, and the military.

Phlebotomist: Phlebotomists are specialists who draw blood from patients. They have the responsibility of taking blood without hurting the patient. The blood then goes to a lab so that it can be analyzed. They work with all types of people, from children to the elderly. Phlebotomists work in hospital laboratories, private laboratories, clinics, large medical offices, and blood banks.

Children's Hospital Oakland Research Institute

Key Terms

Diabetes: A disease in which the body does not properly control the amount of sugar in the blood. As a result, the level of sugar in the blood is too high. Diabetes affects 6.5 percent of Americans.

Diagnosis: The process by which a doctor determines what disease a patient has by studying the patient's symptoms and medical history and by interpreting any tests performed (blood tests, urine tests, brain scans, etc.).

Glucose: A type of sugar. All of the sugar and other carbohydrates—as well as much of the other food—we eat is turned into glucose by our bodies.

Symptom: A sign that something is wrong with a patient. Any change in the body or its functions, noticed by the patient or doctor, which could indicate the presence of disease. Symptoms of diabetes include blurry vision, tingling feet, thirst, and frequent urination.

Long-term complications: Physical effects of a disease that develop over months or years. Long-term complications associated with diabetes include blindness, high blood pressure, kidney failure, and amputation.

Anemia: A condition where a person does not have enough red blood cells. Some of the symptoms of anemia match those of diabetes.

Acute Pancreatitis: A condition in which an organ called the pancreas becomes inflamed due to gallstones. Chemicals made by the pancreas are used to digest food in the small intestine. When gallstones prevent these chemicals from entering the intestines, the chemicals begin to digest the pancreas itself, causing severe stomachaches and nausea. Some of the symptoms match those of diabetes.

Materials

Per class:
- 1 overhead color chart for urine-strip test results
- 3 1-liter bottles filled with fake urine (one drop of yellow food coloring may be added to each liter):
- 1 liter of water labeled " low sugar"
- 1 liter of water mixed with 2.5 mg of dextrose, labeled " normal"
- 1 liter of water mixed with 15 mg of dextrose, labeled " high sugar"
- Pour the fake urine into containers for the groups following this pattern:

Cup	Urine Sample
#1	Low Sugar
#2	High Sugar
#3	Normal Sugar
#4	High Sugar

- 1 1-liter bottle filled with fake blood with high sugar level: mix 1 liter of water, 15 mg of dextrose, and 3 drops of red food coloring. Leave liquid overnight in the refrigerator and divide into small bottles.

Per student:
- 1 worksheet

Per group of 4
- 4 urine test strips
- 1-oz cup labeled "1"
- 1-oz cup labeled "2"
- 1-oz cup labeled "3"
- 1-oz cup labeled "4"
- 1 glucometer test strip
- 1 glucometer
- 1 small bottle of fake blood with high sugar level

Procedure

> **Question:**
> **How does the doctor know what is wrong with you?**

Activity 1: The Physician's Assistant

1. Introduce the diabetes patient and explain that the patient has a real disease. (Someone can role-play if a patient is not available.) Explain that students will take on the role of healthcare professionals to solve the mystery of what is wrong with their patient. The class will come up with a diagnosis, a name of a specific disease.
2. Explain that the first step in solving this mystery involves asking questions and collecting clues called symptoms. Symptoms are signs that something is wrong with the patient's body. Often physician's assistants help with the questioning.
3. Call on students to be physician's assistants who ask the patient about his or her symptoms. All of the students should fill out the patient profile on their worksheets.
4. Remind the students that physician's assistants, or nurse practitioners, also take vital signs such as blood pressure, heart rate, temperature, and weight.

Activity 2: The Doctor

1. Explain that a doctor then reviews the patient profile and meets with the patient, asking more questions and performing an examination. Doctors try to narrow down the diagnosis. Tell the students to turn to the page of their worksheets that shows the symptoms of three possible diagnoses. Ask the students to match symptoms from the patient profile with the diagnoses.
2. Ask the students to come up with their own hypotheses of a diagnosis. Most or all of the students will hypothesize that the patient has diabetes. However, it's okay for them to choose acute pancreatitis or anemia. It's okay to be wrong!
3. Tell the students that people with anemia do not have enough red blood cells, and that people with acute pancreatitis have inflammation of an organ called the pancreas.
4. Explain that diabetes is a disease. Diabetics have high blood sugar. Diabetics have a problem in that their bodies can't make enough of or use an important chemical called insulin (see Lesson 4). Insulin helps keep our blood sugar level normal.
5. Show chart of blood sugar.
6. Explain that doctors often need more information to confirm a diagnosis. Doctors order tests. Draw on the students' personal experiences visiting doctors' offices to generate a list of tests that they could order. The list should include blood tests and urine tests. Other suggestions could include vision tests, measuring height and weight, and measuring blood pressure.

Activity 3: The Lab Technician: Urine Test

1. Explain that the class will act as lab technicians testing fake urine for sugar levels. This is how they will test their hypotheses. If the patient has diabetes, then the tests will show that his/her urine contains more sugar than the urine of a normal person. People with anemia and acute pancreatitis do not have excess sugar in their urine. The class will test the urine from two people; the patient and a normal person. The urine from the normal person is called the control. The first set of samples were taken after fasting. The second set of samples were taken after drinking a glucose solution.
2. Explain that doctors nowadays usually perform blood tests instead of urine tests, because blood tests are more sensitive. Doctors usually test a person's blood twice to find out if the patient has diabetes: once after fasting, and a second time after drinking sugar water.
3. Demonstrate the urine test. Take one strip of test paper and dip it in a sample of fake urine with high sugar. Show how the paper strip turns from blue to brown.
4. Show the color chart overhead. Match the strip to a color chart showing that brown means high sugar.
5. Divide the class into groups of four. Pass out the urine test strips and the cups of fake urine to each group. Lead the groups as the group members take turns testing the four urine samples and matching the test strips to the overhead color chart.

Cup	Urine Sample	Test strip color
1. Normal person after fasting	Low Sugar	Blue
2. Patient after fasting	Normal Sugar	Green
3. Normal person, 2 hrs. after drinking glucose	Normal Sugar	Green
4. Patient, 2 hrs. after drinking glucose	High Sugar	Brown

Activity 4: The Patient and the Phlebotomist

1. Ask the students if the tests confirm the hypothesis that the patient has diabetes. Ask what the tests show about acute pancreatitis and anemia (nothing; there are different tests for these conditions).
2. Ask the patient if he/she has diabetes. Ask if he/she has anemia or acute pancreatitis. Explain that it would be possible for the patient to have both diabetes and one of the other conditions, but that the patient's symptoms do not match the other conditions, so a doctor would not order the tests for them.
3. Ask the patient to share his/her personal experience living with diabetes and how he/she was diagnosed.
4. Ask the patient to show how to test one's own blood with a glucometer.
5. Explain that when diabetics are diagnosed, healthcare professionals called phlebotomists take their blood. Show the class how to use a glucometer. Insert the black and white end of the glucometer test strip into the glucometer. Wait until a number appears on the screen. Dip the yellow end of the test strip in the fake blood. Show that the number is above 130 indicating that the diabetic has high blood sugar.
6. If time permits, pass out glucometers to each group and lead them as they test the fake blood.

Extension

Ask the students to find and interview someone in their community who has diabetes or knows someone who has diabetes. The students should ask about symptoms and treatments. The students need not report the name of the person they interview. All personal information should remain confidential.

Infectious Disesases
Lesson 5

Name: _____

Teacher: _____

Date: _____

Patient Profile

Name:_____ Age:_____

Gender (circle one): Male   Female

Symptoms

_____
_____
_____
_____
_____
_____

Diagnosis #1	Diagnosis #2	Diagnosis #3
Acute Pancreatitis	**Diabetes**	**Anemia**
• Abdominal pain • Nausea • Extreme thirst • Fever • Weight loss • Rapid pulse • More infections • Low blood pressure	• Frequent urination • Extreme thirst • Very tired • Very hungry • Weight loss • Skin problems • Foot problems • More infections	• Very tired • Pale skin • Concave and brittle nails • Big tongue • Rapid pulse • Feeling cold • Weight loss • Nausea

What is your diagnosis based on the patient's symptoms?

_____

Children's Hospital Oakland Research Institute

Procedure

Two tests will be done for each patient, one after fasting and one after swallowing 100 ml of glucose (sugar) solution.

Key for Urine Test Strips:
Blue: Low Blood Sugar
Green: Normal Blood Sugar
Brown: High Blood Sugar

Results

Test #1: After Fasting

	Subject	Color of strip	Blood sugar level
1	Normal person		
2	Patient		

Test #2: After swallowing 100 ml of glucose

	Subject	Color of strip	Blood sugar level
3	Normal person		
4	Patient		

Diagnosis: After the tests were run, did you change your diagnosis? Why or why not?

_____

_____

_____

Procedure

Two tests will be done for each patient, one after fasting and one after swallowing 100 ml of glucose (sugar) solution. Write down the result of each blood test in the correct box.

Glucometer Key:
Low blood sugar: <80 mg/dl
Normal blood sugar: 80 mg/dl - 120 mg/dl
High blood sugar: >120 mg/dl

	After fasting	Reading	Low, normal or high blood sugar?
1	Normal person		
2	Patient		

	After swallowing glucose	Reading	Low, normal or high blood sugar?
3	Normal person		
4	Patient		

Grade: 5
Nutrition and Diabetes
Lesson 2: Testing for Starch

Lesson Time: 1 hour

References: Iodine Test: http://en.wikipedia.org/wiki/Iodine_test; Diabetes Facts: Harvard School of Public Health: http://www.hsph.harvard.edu/nutritionsource/diabetes.html

Lesson objectives
- Practice investigative science skills, including asking questions, making hypotheses, following procedures, and drawing conclusions.
- Investigate foods containing carbohydrates.

Overview
Students brainstorm foods that will break down into sugar and cause sugar to enter the blood. They taste two carbohydrates, a simple sugar and a starch. Then the class uses iodine to test a variety of foods for starch. Finally, the students make recommendations of foods that diabetics should eat only in moderation.

Key Term
Carbohydrate: Foods that break down into sugar as you eat them and digest them. They include sugar and starch.

Digestion: the process by which your body breaks down and absorbs the nutrients found in your food.

Iodine: A brownish dye that indicates the presence of starch. It turns to dark purple when it touches starch.

Glucose: Sugar found in the blood.

Starch: Complex carbohydrates that are found in bread, cereal, pasta, rice, beans, and potatoes.

Sugar: A sweet substance found in fruits, dairy products, and candy. Sugar in the blood is called glucose.

Observation: What you see.

Prediction: An educated guess of what will happen.

Conclusion: What you decide after looking at evidence.

Materials

Per student:
- 1 worksheet
- 1 saltine cracker
- 1 piece of dried fruit

Per group of 4
- 1 small bottle tincture of iodine
- 1 eyedropper
- Food samples:
    - 1 piece of cooked pasta
    - 1 cooked garbanzo bean
    - 1 piece of hard-boiled egg white
    - 1 piece of cheese
    - 1 piece of raw cabbage
    - 1 teaspoon of sticky white rice
    - 1 piece of white bread
    - 1 banana chip
    - 1 piece of pear
- 1 cookie tray
- 1 sheet of wax paper
- 1 paper towel

Procedure

Question:
What foods contain starch?

Introduction

1. Review that we all have some sugar in our blood and that blood sugar comes from food. Remind the students of the blood and urine tests in lesson one. Both the normal person and the patient drank glucose before the tests. Both people had some sugar in their blood. The diabetic just had more sugar.

2. Explain that most people have bodies that can deal with blood sugar. Their cells use up the sugar for energy. In diabetics, cells have trouble using the sugar in blood, and their blood sugar level gets high.

3. Explain that carbohydrates are foods that break down into sugar in the body. Brainstorm a list of foods that might be carbohydrates. The list should include foods that taste sweet.

4. Pass out a piece of dried fruit and a saltine cracker to each student. Ask them to taste the two foods. Ask the class to vote if both the fruit and the cracker are carbohydrates.

5. Explain that there are two types of carbohydrates, or foods that break down into sugar in your body. Simple carbohydrates are obviously sweet. Complex carbohydrates aren't sweet. They break down into sugar as you digest them. They're called starch.

Activity: Iodine Test for Starch

1. Explain that you can use iodine to test if a food contains starch. Iodine is a brown liquid that changes color when it touches starch. Show a bottle of iodine. Warn the students to be very careful and keep the iodine off their hands and clothes to avoid stains!

2. Demonstrate how to test a saltine cracker for starch. Drop one small drop of iodine on the cracker. Show and explain that the color of the iodine changes from brown to purple. Explain that only one small drop of iodine is needed.

3. Explain that the class will work in groups of four using iodine to test for starch. Ask the class to look at their worksheets and tell them to make predictions about the nine foods they will test. Explain to them that it is okay for the predictions to be wrong.

4. Pass out to each group the following supplies:
   - 1 tray
   - 9 food samples
     - pasta
     - garbanzo bean
     - egg white
     - cheese
     - cabbage
     - rice
     - bread
     - banana chip
     - pear
   - 1 piece of wax paper
   - 1 small bottle tincture of iodine
   - 1 eyedropper
   - 1 paper towel

5. Lead the groups as they test the samples one at a time, in order. Ask them to write down their observations.

6. Discuss the results and ask the students to compare their results to their predictions.

7. Have the students generate a list of carbohydrates and lead them in a discussion of which ones contain starch and which ones contain sugar. Explain that starch is a complex carbohydrate and is better for diabetics than sugar.

8. Ask the students to make recommendations for foods that diabetics should eat in moderation.

Extension

Ask students to look in their kitchens and find foods high in starch. Ask them to list the items and write down how many times a day or week they eat those foods.

**Nutrition and Diabetes
Lesson 2**

TESTING FOR STARCH

Name: _____

Teacher: _____

Date: _____

Testing for Starch Using Iodine

Trial	Food	Prediction: Do you think there will be starch?	Color	Conclusion: Was there starch in the food?
1	Pasta			
2	Garbanzo			
3	Egg White			
4	Cheese			
5	Cabbage			
6	Rice			
7	Bread			
8	Banana Chip			
9	Pear			

Testing for Starch

Conclusions

Foods that can raise your blood sugar levels	Is this food a starch or a sugar?

All of these foods are called _____.

Your body uses these for _____.

Grade: 5
Nutrition and Diabetes
Lesson 3: Your Digestive System

Lesson Time: 1 hour

References: The National Digestive Diseases Clearinghouse Information Center: http://digestive.niddk.nih.gov/ddiseases/pubs/yrdd/; Discovery Kids: http://www.yucky.com/flash/body/pg000126.html

Lesson objectives

- Explore the organs of the digestive system.
- Learn how certain foods, called starches, break down into sugar as they travel through the digestive system.
- Learn that sugar and other nutrients are absorbed into the bloodstream through the small intestines.
- Learn that diabetics have a hard time dealing with sugar and foods that break down into sugar.

Overview

The students learn about the anatomy and function of the digestive system as they build a 25-ft model of the digestive tract. Then they work in groups to assemble a puzzle of the digestive system and discuss how sugar enters the bloodstream.

Occupation of the Day

Physiologist: Physiologists are scientists who study organs and how they physically work. They study all parts of the body, from tiny cells to complex systems of organs. This knowledge forms the foundation for discovering new ways to treat diseases. Physiologists can work in many different settings such as universities, pharmaceutical companies, and government laboratories.

Key Terms

Accessory digestive organs: Organs producing chemicals that help digest food. Food does not travel through these organs.

Anus: The valve through which feces exit the body.

Carbohydrates: Foods that break down into sugar as you eat them and digest them. They include sugar and starch.

Digestion: The process of transforming the food we eat into forms that we can absorb.

Digestive system: The group of organs that break down foods into chemical components that the body can absorb and use for energy and for building and repairing cells and tissues.

Esophagus: A tube leading from the mouth to the stomach.

Gallbladder: A small accessory organ that is located under the liver and helps with digestion.

Glucose: Sugar found in the blood.

Large intestine (colon): A long, 5-ft tube leading from the small intestine to the rectum. This is where excess water is taken out of the food material left over from the small intestine.

Liver: The largest glandular organ in the body. An accessory organ of the digestive system, it produces and secretes bile that helps break down fats.

Pancreas: An accessory organ that secretes chemicals that aid in digestion, it is located behind the stomach.

Rectum: A holding chamber for feces that are leaving the large intestine.

Small intestine: A long, 25-ft tube where the digestion of protein, fat, and carbohydrates is completed, and where the majority of the nutrients are absorbed.

Starch: Complex carbohydrates that are found in bread, cereal, pasta, rice, beans, and potatoes.

Stomach: The enlarged, muscular portion of the digestive tract between the esophagus and the small intestine. It has a capacity of about 1 liter.

Materials

Per class:
- A 25-ft model of the digestive system, including:
  - 1 funnel (the mouth)
  - 1 ft of plastic tubing (the esophagus)
  - 1 mortar and pestle (the stomach)
  - 20 ft of plastic tubing, 1-in diameter (the small intestine)
  - 8 sponges with spiky surfaces (the small intestine)
  - 5 ft of plastic tubing, 3-in diameter (the large intestine)
  - 6 in of plastic tubing (the rectum and anus)
  - 4 extra large plastic syringes without needles (the salivary gland, pancreas, gallbladder, and liver)

Per student:
- 1 worksheet
- 1 saltine cracker per student

Per group of 4
- 1 digestive system puzzle with outlines of the mouth, esophagus, stomach, small intestine, large intestine, and rectum/anus for the students to label, cut out, and color
- 1 poster board with an outline of a human torso per group of 4 students
- 1 box of crayons
- 2 pairs of scissors
- 1 glue stick

Procedure

> **Question:**
> How does the digestive system work?

Activity 1: Experiencing Digestion

1. Pass out a saltine cracker to each student. Ask the students to close their eyes as they smell the cracker without eating it. Are they getting hungry? What changes can they feel in their bodies? What do they feel is happening in their mouths?

2. Ask the students to begin chewing the cracker without swallowing it. What is their mouth doing? What is their tongue doing? How is the taste changing? (The taste should become sweeter as the starch begins to be broken down into sugar.) Time the students as they continue chewing for a total of at least 40 seconds. Ask the students to swallow the cracker as they feel what is happening.

3. Explain that within the next hour the cracker, a food made of something called starch, will be broken down into sugar and will enter the bloodstream. How does that happen?

Activity 2: Building the Digestive System

1. Explain that the students will assemble a digestive system that is the actual length of their own digestive systems. The students are going to act like physiologists. Physiologists are scientists who study how the parts of our body work. Ask the class to follow along on their worksheets.

2. For each organ, call on a volunteer to hold an object that represents that organ. Each volunteer should hold his or her part of the digestive system next to the proceeding part.

3. Call on a volunteer to hold a funnel representing the mouth. Explain that the mouth is the first part of the digestive system. Your teeth cut and grind your food. This is where 5% of the starch you eat breaks down.

4. Call on a volunteer to hold a 12-inch plastic tube representing the esophagus. Explain that when you swallow food it passes into the esophagus which is a tube leading from your mouth into your stomach.

5. Call on a volunteer to hold a mortar and pestle representing the stomach. Explain that from the esophagus, the food enters the stomach. The stomach is a muscular bag that churns and mixes your food. The digestion of other types of food such as protein begins here.

6. Call on two volunteers to hold 20 feet of plastic tubing representing the small intestine. Explain that in the body the small intestine is coiled, but ask the volunteers to stretch out the tubing to show how long the small intestine is. Explain that starch digestion continues in the small intestine. As the starches break down into simple sugars, the sugars are absorbed through the walls of the small intestine. The walls are like sponges with millions of small finger-like projections called villi. Pass out one spiky sponge to each group of four students so that they can feel the texture.

7. Call on two volunteers to hold 5 feet of plastic tubing stretched out to represent the large intestine. Explain that bacteria break down any remaining starches in the large intestine. As waste material travels down the large intestine, water is removed and the waste becomes denser.

8. Hold up 6 inches of plastic tubing representing the rectum. Explain that excess food material is called feces. It collects in the rectum before exiting through the anus.

9. Hold up four syringes labeled the salivary gland, the liver, the gall bladder, and the pancreas. Explain that digestion would not be possible without the digestive juices from these four organs. The accessory organs add digestive juices full of molecules called enzymes that aid in digestion. Some digestive juices break up starches, others work on fat and protein. Give the syringes to four volunteers. One volunteer should walk to the mouth, the others to the small intestine as you explain where the accessory organs add digestive juices. Salivary glands squirt saliva into the mouth. Explain that the liver is the largest glandular organ in the body. It works with the gall bladder to squirt bile into the small intestine. The liver squirts bile into the gall bladder, and the gall bladder squirts it into the small intestine. This helps to break down fat. The pancreas squirts enzymes into the small intestine to break down starch and proteins. Each volunteer should push the plunger of his or her syringe to show where digestive juices are secreted into the digestive tract.

10. Ask the students to complete page 1 of the worksheet.

Activity 3: Digestive System Puzzle

1. Explain that our 25-ft digestive system fits inside our body. The small and large intestines are coiled like snakes. Ask the students to look at page 2 of their worksheets, where they will see a more realistic diagram of the digestive system. Explain that each group of four students will assemble a poster of the digestive system with paper organs (accessory organs are not included).
2. Show the students the completed digestive system puzzle as an example.
3. Pass out the poster boards, organ outlines, scissors, and crayons. Ask the students to complete their puzzles.
4. Give glue sticks to the groups when they get the organs in the correct places.
5. Collect the posters and display them at the front of the class.
6. Ask the students to complete page 2 of the worksheet.

Extensions

As a class, read the story of digestion found at http://yucky.discovery.com/flash/body/pg000126.html

Play pin the organ on the person: ask one person from each group to come to the front of the class to tape an organ from the digestive system onto an image of a person. For each organ, the student must describe what it does, where it is found, and how it relates to digestion.

Ask students to write down observations about their own digestive systems after they eat dinner tonight. What is happening to the food while it is in the mouth? Can they feel the food traveling through their throats? What is happening to the food once it is in the stomach?

**Nutrition and Diabetes
Lesson 3**

Name: _____

Teacher: _____

Date: _____

Diagram	Name	Role in digestion of sugar	Accessory organs
(funnel)			salivary glands
(straw)			
(mortar and pestle)			
(coiled tube)			liver, pancreas, gallbladder
(curved tubes)			
(short tube)			

Children's Hospital Oakland Research Institute

Digestive System Puzzle

1. Label the following diagram.
2. Put a star by the organ where starch begins to break down into sugar.
3. Underline the name of the organ where sugar is absorbed and enters the bloodstream.
4. Arrange the puzzle pieces on your poster.

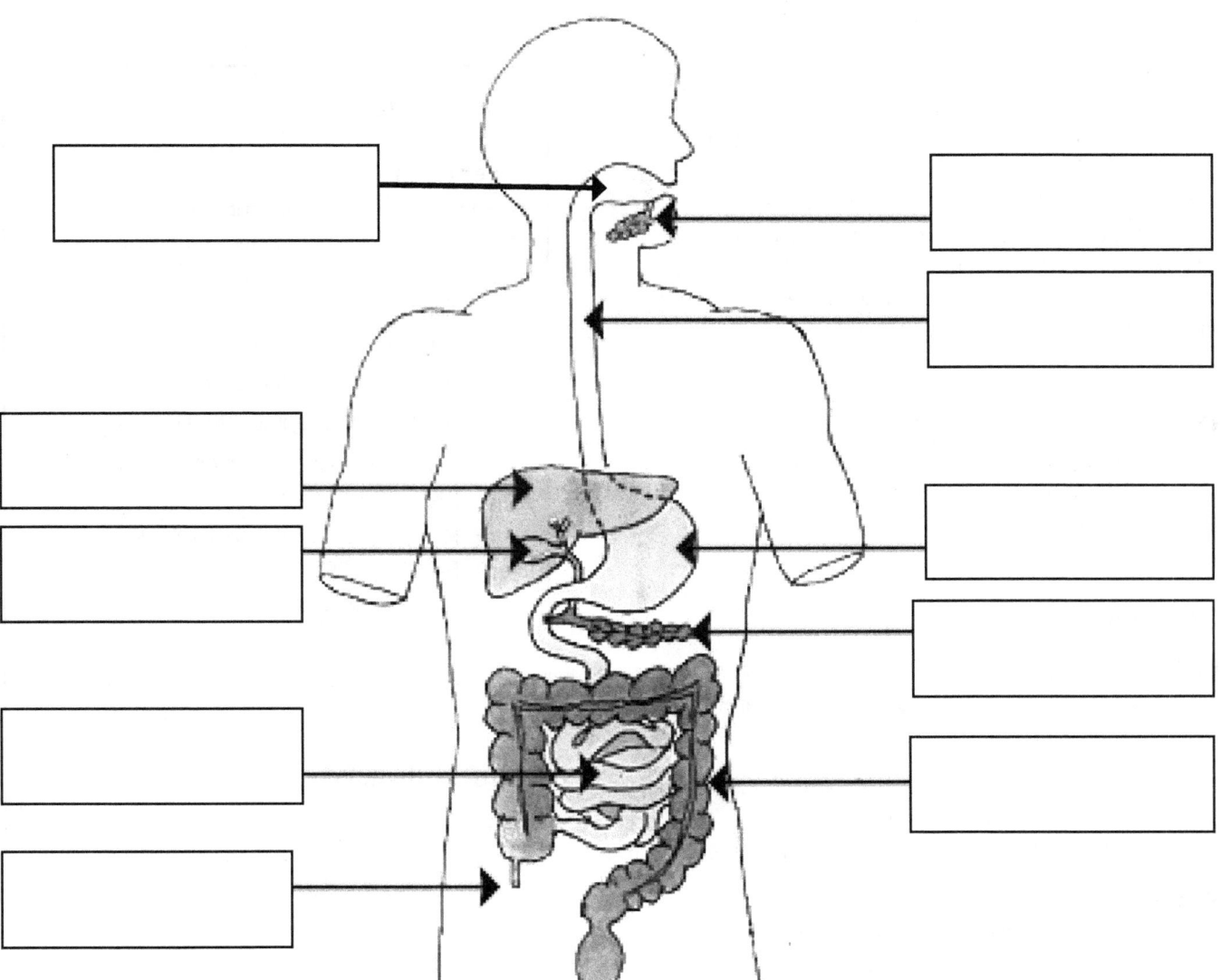

Grade: 5
Nutrition and Diabetes
Lesson 4: The Role of Insulin

Lesson Time: 1 hour

Lesson objectives
- Explore the role of insulin in regulating blood sugar.
- Meet a research scientist and hear about job opportunities in science.
- Hear about the most recent advances in diabetes treatment and prevention.

Overview
The students make antigens for their microbe models from Lesson 2 and antibodies that match these antigens. Then they create skits about the immune system and perform them using their microbe models. Finally, they discuss vaccines, antibiotics, and the importance of immunizations, and they brainstorm ways to enhance the effectiveness of their immune systems.

Occupation of the Day
Endocrinologist: A doctor who specializes in diseases dealing with the systems of the body that produce hormones, one of them being insulin.

Key Terms
Cell: The basic unit of structure and function in all living things. All of our organs and our blood are made of cells.

Insulin: A substance produced in the pancreas that allows cells to take up sugar and turn it into energy. Insulin is used as a treatment for diabetes.

Pancreas: An organ that sits between your stomach and intestines and is responsible for producing insulin and digestive enzymes.

Type I diabetes: Occurs when no insulin is being produced.

Type II diabetes: Occurs when not enough insulin is being produced, or cells reject the insulin.

Materials

Per class:
- ▶ 1 worksheet overhead, optional
- ▶ 1 poster or overhead of type I diabetes, optional
- ▶ 1 poster or overhead of type II diabetes, optional
- ▶ Materials for role-playing game:
  - 16 plastic plates representing glucose
  - 16 plastic lids representing insulin
  - 4 red-streamer sashes for blood group members
  - 1 large poster of the pancreas for the pancreas group
  - 1 large poster of cells for the body cells group
  - 1 large poster of intestines for small intestine group

Per student:
- ▶ 1 worksheet

Procedure

> **Questions:**
> After you swallow a cracker, what organs does it travel through?
> Where does the sugar from the starch in the cracker get absorbed?
> Why do diabetics have high blood sugar?

Activity 1: Insulin Role-Playing Game

1. Explain that the class will engage in a role-playing game to learn what goes wrong in diabetics' bodies. Review that everyone has blood sugar. Explain that diabetics have high blood sugar because their bodies can't use the sugar that's in their blood.

2. Before beginning the role-playing game, give the students the worksheet. As you explain the game, they should write down each role on p. 1.

3. Explain that the body is made up of billions of cells. To do their work, cells need energy from blood sugar, called glucose. They can only use glucose if they have a chemical called insulin. In this game, the job of body cells is to get insulin and sugar. Molecular diagrams of glucose and insulin appear on the worksheet. The students do not need to understand these diagrams. Tell them that these are the kinds of drawings that scientists use to represent molecules, which are very small particles of a substance.

4. Explain that the blood is the delivery service of the body. It takes nutrients from the small intestine to the body. It carries glucose all over the body. The role of blood cells in the game is to carry glucose and insulin to the body cells.

5. Explain that the pancreas is an accessory organ in the digestive system. It also has another role. It makes insulin, the key that allows the cells to use glucose. The role of the pancreas in the game is to make insulin.

6. Choose four students to be the blood, and give them red sashes. Explain that they will walk around the room carrying glucose and insulin to the cells.

7. Choose five students for the pancreas. Sit the five students in a group with the pancreas sign and give them a stack of lids labeled insulin. Explain that when you give them a signal, they will make insulin and they will give the insulin to the blood.

8. Choose five students to be the small intestine. Sit them in a group with the intestines sign and give them a stack of plastic plates representing glucose. They will give glucose to the blood.

9. Explain that the rest of the students are body cells and they can remain seated. When they get insulin from the blood they can stand up. And when they have both insulin and glucose they can clap their hands and sit down.

10. Ask the pancreas to make insulin. The blood should carry the insulin to the body cells.

11. When all of the cells have insulin, the blood should pick up glucose from the small intestine and take it to the cells. When the cells have both insulin and glucose, they should clap their hands and sit down.

12. Have students play this version of the game one more time.

13. Play the game again simulating type I diabetes. Show the poster or overhead of type I diabetes (if available) and explain that the pancreas doesn't make insulin. Ask the pancreas to sit dormant as the blood carries sugar around the room.

14. Explain that when insulin isn't being produced, too much sugar travels through the blood. The body cells have to reject the sugar, so the diabetic has high blood sugar.

15. Play the game again simulating type II diabetes. Show the poster or overhead of type II diabetes (if available) and explain that either not enough insulin is being produced or the cells are rejecting the insulin. Ask half the cells to reject the insulin. They must then also reject the glucose.

16. Review what the students learned from this game, and explain that some diabetics are given insulin to control their blood sugar. Others can control it through diet.

Guest Speaker: Researcher or Endocrinologist

1. Introduce the guest speaker (if available) and explain that the guest will elaborate on the ideas that were presented in the game.

2. Tell the students to ask any questions that were generated during the game.

Wrap-up: Ask the students to complete p. 2 of the worksheet, to review what they know about diabetes. Go over the answers with them.

Extension: Ask the students to find out if they have any family history of diabetes. Is it common in their families or has nobody in their families ever been affected?

Children's Hospital Oakland Research Institute

**Nutrition and Diabetes
Lesson 4**

THE ROLE OF INSULIN

Name: _____

Teacher: _____

Date: _____

	Role of Body Part in Game
Body Cells	
Blood	
Pancreas and the Small Intestine	
Glucose	
Insulin	

Diabetes is _____

_____

Foods diabetics can eat:

_____

_____

_____

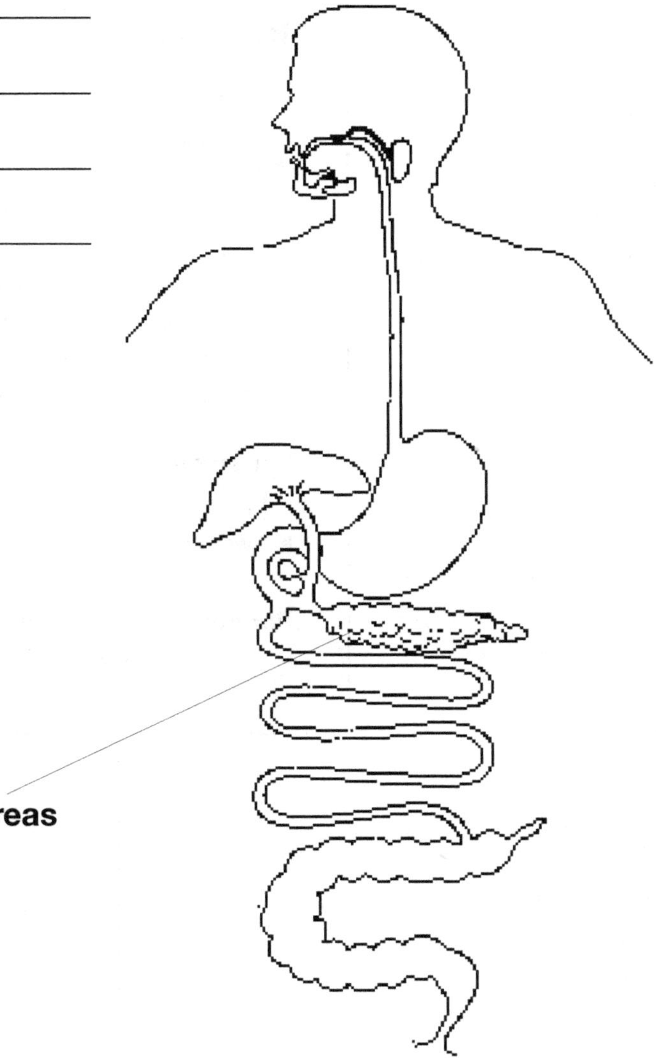

Symptoms:

_____

_____

_____

_____

Pancreas

Long-term Problems:

_____

_____

_____

_____

Grade: 5
Nutrition and Diabetes
Lesson 5: Diabetes and a Diverse Community

Lesson Time: 1 hour

References: 60 minutes TV Show: " The Fattest Americans"; http://www.cdc.gov/diabetes/news/docs/010126.htm

Lesson objectives
- Learn that diabetes affects certain ethnic groups more than others due to genetics and lifestyle factors.
- Explore how exercise and a healthy diet can help prevent diabetes.
- Create healthy menus and exercise regimens.

Overview
Students learn that diabetes affects some communities more than other communities. They watch a short video about the Pima Tribe, which has one of the highest rates of diabetes. The students use pie charts to analyze information about the disease, and they generate preventive strategies for their own community.

Key Terms

Data: Information that has been systematically gathered.

Genes: Tiny units that make up the blueprint of your body. Genes are inherited from parents.

Geneticist: A scientist who studies genes, how they are inherited, and what they do.

Health disparity: When certain populations have a higher rate of a disease than other populations.

Prevention: Taking care of oneself to keep a disease from starting.

Protein: A molecule found in food and used by the body in all of its organs. The body uses protein to fight infections and build muscles and other tissues.

Recommended daily fat intake: The amount of fat a person should eat daily. Most people should eat less than 65 grams of fat per day.

Statistics: Results of mathematical tests used on a collection of data.

Materials

Per class:
- 60 minutes video about Pima Indians and diabetes
- 1 worksheet overhead, optional
- Plastic food:
  - Carbohydrates, e.g., rice and bread
  - Proteins, e.g., fish and meat
  - Fats, e.g., butter and vegetable oil
  - Vegetables, e.g., broccoli and carrots

Per student:
- 1 paper plate
- 1 worksheet

Per pair:
- 1 box of crayons

Procedure

> **Question:**
> **Why do some ethnic groups have more diabetes than others?**

Activity 1: Pima and Pie Charts

1. Pass out the worksheet and point out the section pertaining to the video.
2. Show a 15-minute video about diabetes in the Pima Indian tribe.
3. Discuss the worksheet. What did the students learn about diabetes? Discuss how genetics and lifestyle contribute to the high rate of diabetes among the Pima. Discuss how the lifestyle, including diet, of the Pima changed over time.
4. Show a pie chart indicating that 6% of Americans are affected by diabetes. Ask the students to draw a pie chart showing the number of Pima with diabetes (50%).
5. Tell the class that 11.4% of African Americans over the age of 20, and 8.2% of Hispanics over the age of 20 have diabetes. Ask the class to draw pie charts for those two ethnic groups.
6. Pretend that the entire class is a tribe of Pima Indians. Calculate the number of students that would have diabetes and ask those kids to stand up.

Activity 2: Choices and Charts

1. Show a bar graph of how many minutes a modern Pima and a traditional Pima exercise each day. Ask the students to draw a bar showing how many minutes a typical American exercises each day (18 min), and how many minutes they spent exercising the day before. Then tell them the recommended amount of exercise for kids (30 min per day for ages 9 to 13), and ask them to draw this bar. Explain that kids who don't exercise the recommended amount may be at risk for developing diabetes later in life.
2. Show a plate of fake food that represents what an average American kid eats. Fill 50% of the plate with plastic foods that are carbohydrates, fill 40% with plastic fat, and fill 10% with plastic meat representing protein. Emphasize that each portion of the plate represents the amount of calories from carbohydrates, fat, or protein. A small amount of fat contains a large number of calories.
3. Draw a pie chart on the board showing the recommended amount of carbohydrates, protein, and fat for a 5th grader and for a diabetic (about 50% carbohydrates, 30% fat, and 20% protein for both). Ask the students to draw this pie chart on their worksheets. Discuss how the recommended plates differ from the typical American kid's plate. Discuss other important aspects of the recommended plate. For a non-diabetic, half of the carbohydrates are whole grains. The rest of the carbohydrates come from vegetables and fruit. The protein comes from lean meat and low-fat milk. For a diabetic, almost all of the carbohydrates should be complex carbohydrates found in whole grains and vegetables, with very little coming fruit, candy, and other sweets, which contain simple sugars.
4. Pass out the paper plates and ask the students to draw four equal sections indicating a balanced meal for a 5th grader. The sections are for dairy, grain, protein, and fruits or vegetables. Healthy choices will ensure that their carbohydrates, fat, and protein are in balance. Pass out crayons so the students can draw food in the four areas of the plate. Encourage them to draw ethnic foods they may eat at home. It's okay to have a food such as a sandwich or taco overlapping two or more areas. Ask them where the carbohydrates and fat come from in the meals they have drawn.
5. Discuss how people who don't eat healthy diets are at risk for diabetes. Discuss how having diabetes changes your life forever.
6. Ask the students what the school and community can do to decrease the incidence of diabetes. What physical education programs could they implement? What school lunch program should they require? What would school breakfasts look like?

Extension

Ask students to find a recipe for a food low in fat. Tell them to share the recipe with their family and help make the meal. They should eat the food and write what they thought about the food. Was it tasty? Would they recommend the food to somebody who had diabetes?

**Nutrition and Diabetes
Lesson 5**

Name: _____

Teacher: _____

DIABETES and a Diverse Community

Date: _____

Four factors that place someone at risk for getting diabetes?

1. _____   3. _____

2. _____   4. _____

Pima and Food

Traditional	Modern Times	Trying now

Pima and Exercise

Traditional	Modern Times	Trying now

If the class was the Pima tribe, how many of us would have diabetes? _____

American Adults ■ Diabetics ▪ Others

African-American Adults

Mexican-American Adults

Pima Adults

Children's Hospital Oakland Research Institute

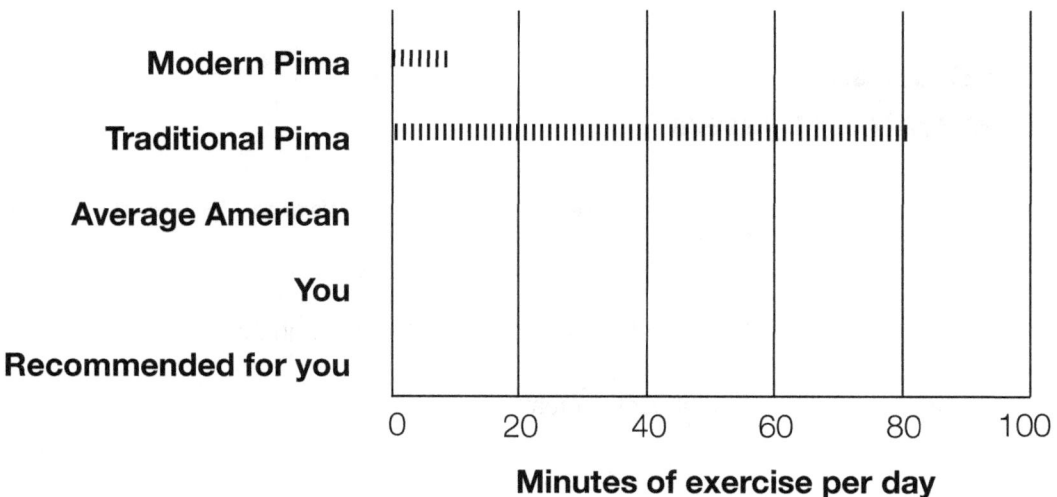

Food - Example Dinner Menu

Carbohydrate: Rice
Protein: Chicken
Veggie: Broccoli
Dairy: Milk
Fat: Butter

Typical American child's plate:

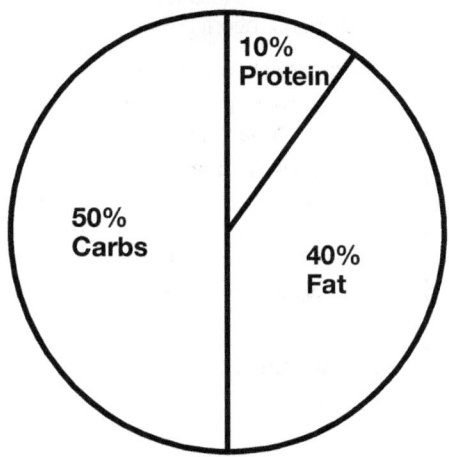

Recommended plate:

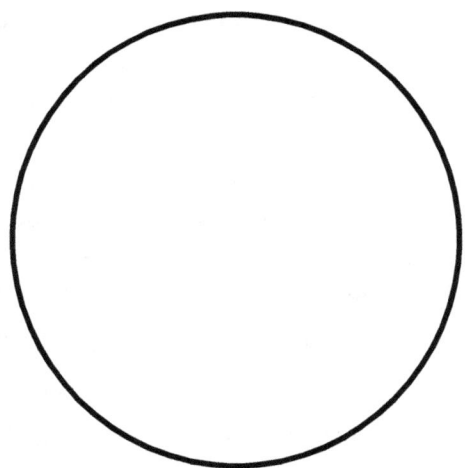

Will you be at a higher risk for diabetes as you grow older? _____

People with a family history of diabetes have a higher risk of having diabetes.
People who are from certain ethnic groups have a higher risk of having diabetes.

Why? _____

Grade: 5
Asthma and Lung Disease
Lesson 1: Your Respiratory System

Lesson Time: 1 hour

References: Science Museum of Minnesota: http://www.smm.org/heart/lessons/lesson7.htm; Background Information: The Respiratory System: http://www.lung.ca/children/grades4_6/respiratory/how_we_breathe.html

Lesson objectives
- Explore the anatomy and function of the respiratory system through the use of models and diagrams.
- Investigate the mechanisms that control breathing.

Overview
The presenter demonstrates the function of the lungs with inflatable pig lungs or a plastic lung model. The students assemble and investigate models of the lungs made out of plastic bottles and balloons. They explore how the diaphragm controls breathing, how the lungs inflate and inhale oxygen, and how the lungs deflate and exhale carbon dioxide.

Key Terms

Respiratory system: The organs and structures used to exchange air in and out of the body. It includes the nose, mouth, trachea, lungs, bronchi, and alveoli.

Lung: A spongy elastic organ that stretches and constricts as we breathe in and out.

Diaphragm: A strong muscle just below the lungs that controls the breathing process. As the diaphragm flattens, it causes the chest to expand and air is sucked into the lungs. When the diaphragm relaxes, the chest gets smaller and the air in the lungs is forced out.

Cell: The basic unit of structure and function in all living things.

Trachea: A long pipe that connects the nose and mouth to the lungs.

Bronchial tubes: Two tubes that carry air from the trachea to the lungs.

Alveoli: Tiny air sacs, located at the ends of bronchioles in the lungs, through which gases are exchanged between the lungs and the bloodstream.

Blood vessel: A tube through which blood travels in the body.

Capillaries: The smallest and thinnest blood vessels. They have very thin walls.

Mucus: A slimy substance that lines your nose and airways. Germs and dirt stick to it.

Materials

Per class:
- 1 worksheet overhead, optional
- 1 inflatable pig lung model with stand and pump. (As an alternative, a plastic, anatomically correct model can be used)
- 1-liter plastic soda bottle model of the lungs (pre-made) for demonstration
- Prepare ahead of time:
  - Collect plastic bottles (1 for each pair of students).
  - Make a slit about 1/4 of the way up from the bottom and cut off the bottom of the bottle.
  - Wash and dry the bottles.

Per student:
- 1 worksheet

Per pair:
- 1 box of crayons
- 1-liter plastic soda bottle (pre-cut) to make model of the lungs
- 1 rubber band
- 1 sandwich bag
- 1 balloon

Procedure

> **Question:**
> **What parts of our body allow us to breathe?**

Demonstration: How We Breathe

1. Demonstrate the pig lung model in front of the class. Answer questions from the students about the lung.
2. As you pump the lungs, explain that the lungs breathe in oxygen and exhale carbon dioxide.
3. Explain that the nose and mouth connect with a tube called the windpipe or the trachea. The trachea is in the front of the neck and is very hard with tough rings around it. Ask them to feel the front of their necks.
4. Identify the bronchi, lungs, and diaphragm. Our lungs are pumped by a muscle called the diaphragm, located under the lungs.

Activity 1: Plastic Lung Models

1. Demonstrate a plastic-bottle lung model. Briefly introduce the following questions that the students will answer using the models they construct:
   - What does the balloon represent? (Do not answer yet.)
   - What does the bottle represent? (Do not answer yet.)
   - What does the plastic bag represent? (Do not answer yet.)
   - Pull the bag down, away from the neck of the bottle. What happens to the balloon?
   - Push the bag into the bottle. What happens to the balloon?
   - Place the top of the bottle next to your cheek as you pull the bag in and out. What do you feel?
   - If the bottle was a real respiratory system, what would it breathe in?
   - What would it exhale?
   - What is one thing that you would change about this model to make it a more accurate representation of the lungs? (Do not answer yet.)
2. Pass out the plastic bottles, balloons, sandwich bags, and rubber bands. Ask students to do the following:
   - Put a balloon over the mouth of the bottle and stuff the balloon inside the neck of the bottle.
   - Cover the base of the bottle with a sandwich bag.
   - Secure the sandwich bag with a rubber band.
3. Instruct the students on proper use of the lung models. The models should be used carefully and gently. The rubber bands break easily and the bags pop with excessive use.
4. Hand out the worksheet. Give the students time to explore the models and answer the questions on the worksheet.
5. Collect the lung models and go over the answers to the worksheet.
6. Explain that the lungs are located inside the rib cage, which is represented by the bottle. The diaphragm, represented by the plastic bag, lines the bottom of the rib cage. Explain that when we breathe in, the diaphragm pulls itself down, so the space inside our rib cage increases. Since there is more space, the lungs expand. As the lungs get bigger, air comes into the lungs. When we breathe out, the diaphragm pushes itself upwards, going back to its dome shape. This creates less space for the lungs, so they get smaller. The lungs push the air out.

Activity 2: Coloring Sheet

1. Pass out one box of crayons to each pair of students. Discuss the function of the parts of the respiratory system as the class locates, labels, and colors each part on the second page of the worksheet.
2. Ask the students to label and color the mouth, nose, throat, and lungs.
3. Explain that the trachea is a long tube that divides into two parts called the bronchi just before it enters the lungs. Air travels from the trachea to the bronchi. Ask the students to label and color the trachea and bronchi.
4. As the bronchi enter the lungs, they divide into even smaller tubes, called bronchioles. Air keeps moving from the bronchi to the bronchioles. Ask the students to label and color the bronchioles.
5. Explain that finally, the smallest tubes end at small bubble-like structures called alveoli. The alveoli are small air sacs that are covered with very small blood vessels. The alveoli deliver the oxygen to the blood vessels and exchange it with carbon dioxide. We exhale carbon dioxide. Ask the students to label and color the alveoli.

Asthma and Lung Disesase
Lesson 1

YOUR RESPIRATORY SYSTEM

Name: _____

Teacher: _____

Date: _____

chest cavity
rib cage
trachea
mouth
diaphragm
lung

1. What do the following represent?

    Balloon = _____

    Bottle = _____

    Plastic bag = _____

2. Pull the bag down, away from the neck of the bottle. What happens to the balloon?
   _____

3. Push the bag into the bottle. What happens to the balloon? _____

4. Place the top of the bottle next to your cheek as you pull the bag in and out. What do you feel?
   _____

5. If the bottle was a real respiratory system, what would it breathe in? _____

6. What would it exhale? _____

7. How could you make the model more accurate? _____

Find and label the following parts of the respiratory system:

Lung   Bronchus   Trachea   Mouth
Nose   Throat   Alveoli   Bronchioles

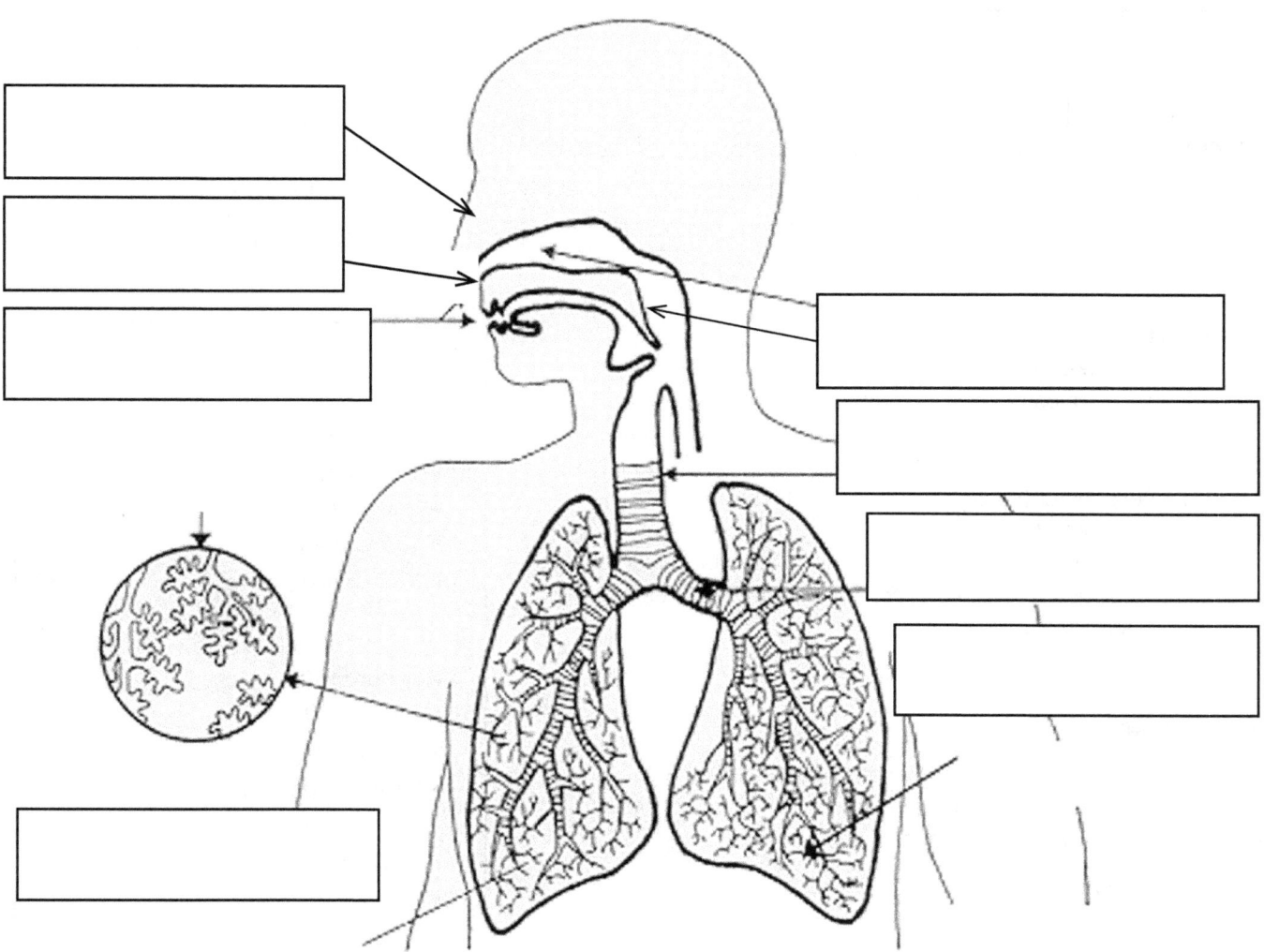

Grade: 5
Asthma and Lung Disease
Lesson 2: Do You Have Asthma?

Lesson Time: 1 hour

References: Peak Flow Ranges: http://parenting.ivillage.com/tweens/twhealth/0,,3qk5,00.html
Habits of the Heart: Lessons: Catch Your Breath: http://www.smm.org/heart/lessons/lesson9.htm
Inside the Human Body: The Respiratory System: Grades 4-6: How Smoking Affects Your Lungs: http://www.lung.ca/children/grades4_6/tobacco/how_tobacco_affects_lungs.html

Lesson objectives
- Learn about asthma.
- Learn how to become a healthcare worker who treats patients with asthma.
- Use a peak flow meter to measure their ability to force air out of their lungs.
- Make and test predictions using peak flow meters.

Overview

A healthcare worker talks to the class about his or her occupation. The guest speaker describes asthma, how common it is, and what the symptoms are. The guest speaker demonstrates how to use a peak flow meter. Then the students perform an experiment testing the health of their lungs. The students use a peak flow meter to determine how well they can blow air out of their lungs. They analyze the results, linking peak flow readings to variables such as family history of asthma, exposure to smoking, and height.

Key Terms

Asthma: Asthma is a disease of the lungs that causes tightened airways, swollen tissue inside the airways and excess mucus. These problems make it difficult to breathe.

Asthma triggers: Substances that can cause excess mucus production and airway restriction in an asthma patient. These triggers often include dust, pollen, cigarette smoke, cold air, strong fumes, pollution, mold and exercise. Each person with asthma has his or her own set of triggers.

Peak flow meter: A device that measures how much air a person can blow out of his or her lungs when blowing fast.

Lung capacity: The total amount of air in the lungs when a person has inhaled as deeply as possible.

Symptoms: Physical signs of a disease or condition.

Variable: Something that affects the result of an experiment. Variables such as age, gender, and health can affect someone's peak flow readings.

Materials

Per class:
- 1 overhead of worksheet, optional
- 3 large poster papers for graphs
- 100 round stickers
- 5 measuring tapes to measure the height of students

Per student:
- 1 worksheet
- 1 data collection sheet
- 1 cardboard mouthpiece

Per pair:
- 1 peak flow meter

Procedure

> **Questions:**
> What could affect the health of your lungs?
> How could you measure the health of your lungs?

Guest Speaker

1. Pass out the worksheet.
2. Introduce the healthcare worker, who will talk for 15 minutes. The talk should cover (if a guest is not available, the presenter should cover c, d, and e):
   a. What he or she does for a living
   b. How he or she helps people
   c. What is asthma?
   d. How common is asthma (5% of adults and 8% of children)?
   e. What are some asthma triggers?
3. Invite the students to ask questions.

Activity 1: Quantitative Analysis

1. Show a peak flow meter. Healthcare workers such as the guest speaker use peak flow meters to diagnose asthma. Peak flow meters measure how much air you can blow out in one fast blast. People with asthma can't breathe out as much as people who don't have asthma because mucus and swelling obstructs their lungs.
2. Demonstrate the proper use of a peak flow meter. Place a cardboard mouthpiece on the mouth part. Move the red arrow down to the base. Stand up straight and take a deep breath. Blow into the mouthpiece as hard and as long as you can. Read the number next to the red arrow and write this number on the board. Remind the class to keep their hands off the back of the instrument. Also remind them that each person has his or her own mouthpiece.
3. Explain that today the students will test their lungs using the peak flow meters. The higher the peak flow reading that they get, the more air they can force out of their lungs. Explain the difference between lung capacity and peak flow readings.
4. Ask students for reasons why people might have different peak flow readings. These factors are called variables. Write the word "variable" on the board. Explain that a variable is something that affects something else. For example, one variable affecting how much air you can exhale might be age. People who are older might have larger lungs, so they can force out more air. The students should suggest other variables such as:
   - Athletic ability
   - Gender
   - Height
   - Having a family history of asthma
   - Having asthma
   - Living with smokers or smoking itself
   - Weight

   Discuss which variables are controllable in one's life (athletic ability, living with smokers, weight) and which are uncontrollable (height, age, gender, family history of asthma, etc.) This use of "controllable" and "uncontrollable" should not be confused with "control of variables" in an experiment. All of the preceding variables can be controlled in an experiment. Also make sure that the students understand the difference between these variables, which might affect peak flow readings, and asthma triggers, which cause asthma attacks.

5. Ask the class how they would design an experiment to see if one of these variables could affect peak flow readings and thus lung health. Work with students to come up with a plan. Generate hypotheses. Each pair of students will get one peak flow meter and two mouth pieces. Each student should take a minimum of three readings.

   Reading #1 _____
   Reading #2 _____
   Reading #3 _____

6. Emphasize that the exercise is not a competition for the highest reading. There is a range of healthy readings.
7. Pass out the peak flow meters.
8. Count to three. Tell students to blow at the count of three and record their readings.

9. Repeat step 8 two more times, and then ask students to pass the peak flow meters to their partners.
10. Have the partners take three peak flow readings (step 8).
11. Collect the peak flow meters.

Activity 2: Data Collection

1. Pass out a data collection sheet to each student and show an overhead of the sheet. Demonstrate how to fill in the sheet. Students should write their highest reading and their height. Students should not write their names, to keep the data anonymous.

   Example:

   Highest Reading: 500

   Height: 4'5"

Normal Predicted Average Peak Expiratory Flow for Children (in liters/minute)

Height (in.)	Peak Flow	Height (in.)	Peak Flow	Height (in.)	Peak Flow
43	147	51	254	59	360
44	160	52	267	60	373
45	173	53	280	61	387
46	187	54	293	62	400
47	200	55	307	63	413
48	214	56	320	64	427
49	227	57	334	65	440
50	240	58	347	66	454

2. Collect the data sheets.
3. Mix the data sheets up and then pass them out randomly to the students.
4. Tape a large piece of poster paper to the board. Create a large graph on the paper that matches the graph on the worksheet with peak flow readings along the y-axis and height along the x-axis.
5. One at a time, call each student up to place a removable sticker on the spot that matches the height and reading on the data sheet that they are holding.
6. The students should see a pattern on the graph that height is correlated with peak flow readings. Taller people tend to have higher readings.
7. Discuss the results and how errors could have happened. For example, students could misread the peak flow meters. Explain that readings from hundreds of people would be needed to draw firm conclusions about the impacts of the variables.
8. Remind the students that low peak flow readings do not always indicate asthma. Only a trained healthcare worker like your doctor can diagnose asthma.
9. If time permits, look at the students' peak flow readings with respect to other variables such as age, gender, family history of asthma, and exposure to secondhand smoke. Make a class line graph or bar graph as appropriate to display the results for each variable.
10. Note: If any of the readings are abnormally low, consult the school nurse.

**Asthma and Lung Disesase
Lesson 2**

Name: _____

Teacher: _____

Date: _____

Guest Speaker

Name: _____ Occupation: _____

What is asthma? _____

How common is asthma? _____

What do Peak Flow Meters measure? _____

What VARIABLES could affect Peak Flow Meter readings?

1. Having asthma
2. Age
3. _____
4. _____
5. _____

Experiment

Hypothesis _____

_____

Plan Your Test

_____

_____

Conducting Your Test

Peak Flow Readings:

Reading #1_____

Reading #2_____

Reading #3_____

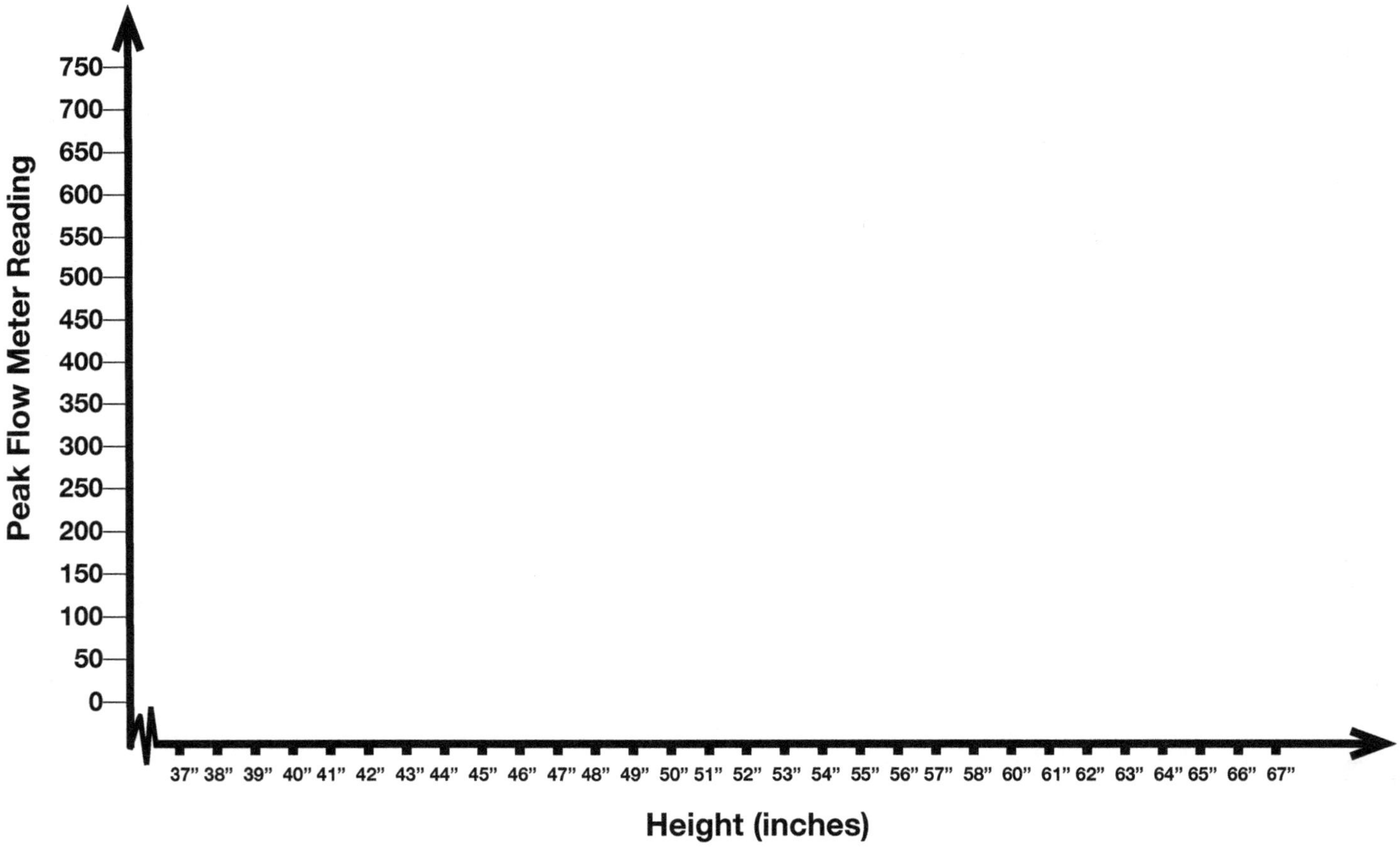

Peak Flow Meter Reading (y-axis: 0 to 750 in increments of 50)

Height (inches) (x-axis: 37" to 67")

Conclusion:

_____

_____

_____

Data Collection Sheet

Highest Reading:
Height: _____feet _____inches = _____Total inches (Multiply feet by 12 and add inches to get total inches.)

Grade: 5
Asthma and Lung Disease
Lesson 3: LeapFrog Asthma Books

Lesson Time: 1 hour

References: LeapFrog Enterprises http://www.leapfrog.com; Harcourt Science 5th Grade, Unit A, page A18; The American Lung Association: http://www.lung.ca/diseases-maladies/asthma-asthme/treatment-traitement/index_e.php

Lesson objectives
- Learn how asthma is treated.
- Meet a patient with asthma.
- Solve a case study about a young boy with asthma.
- Create an asthma action plan.

Overview
Students breathe through straws to simulate the experience of having asthma. They meet a patient with asthma who talks about his or her symptoms, medications, and medical history. Then they read a case study about a child with asthma and use an interactive storybook from LeapFrog Enterprises to solve the case and to create an asthma action plan.

Key Terms

Asthma action plan: A set of instructions made with a doctor, it gives details about how a person with asthma should manage his or her asthma outside the hospital.

Asthma flare: Also called an asthma attack or asthma episode. An episode during which the symptoms of asthma are triggered.

Bronchioles: Tiny air tubes that branch from the bronchi inside the lungs.

Controller: Medicine taken everyday to help prevent asthma symptoms.

Nebulizer: A piece of equipment that turns liquid medication into a mist that can be inhaled.

Peak flow meter: A device that measures how much air a person can blow out of his or her lungs when blowing fast.

Reliever: Medicine that is taken to relieve the symptoms of asthma. Sometimes taken before exercise.

Spacer: Also called a holding chamber. A piece of equipment that is used with an inhaler to make the inhaler easier to use.

Symptoms: Signs that show that something is wrong with the body.

Materials

Per class:
▶ 1 worksheet overhead, optional

Per student:
▶ 1 worksheet
▶ 1 straw

Per pair:
▶ 1 LeapFrog Quantum Pad
▶ 1 *Meet the Amazing Broncholis* book
▶ 1 *Meet the Amazing Broncholis* cartridge
▶ 2 headphones
▶ 1 headphone splitter

Procedure

> **Question:**
> **What is asthma and how is it treated?**

Activity 1: Breathing Through Straw

1. Ask the students to feel what it is like breathe normally for a moment.
2. Pass out one straw to each student. Ask the students to breathe through the straws. Explain that this is what it feels like when the airways constrict in an asthma attack.
3. Ask the students to breathe through the straws while pinching them gently.
4. Ask the students to imagine how it would feel to breathe though the straw if it were filled with mucus as thick as a milk shake.
5. Discuss what the students experienced.

Activity 2: Interview an Asthma Patient

1. Pass out the worksheets.
2. Introduce the guest speaker (if available). Ask the guest speaker to talk about what it is like to live with asthma, at what age his or her asthma was diagnosed, and what kind of medications he or she uses.
3. Invite the students to ask questions of the guest speaker.

Activity 3: LeapFrog Asthma Books

1. Read over the case study as a class.

   Case Study:
   "Hello nurse, this is Barry's mom. Yes, I'm very concerned. His teacher called me while his class was on a field trip to the circus. Barry began wheezing and coughing uncontrollably. Outside the circus tent he still had trouble breathing. This isn't the first time that I've noticed something was wrong. He wakes up in the middle of the night coughing. I'm worried that it might be something serious. What's the matter with him and what should we do?"

2. Explain to the class that they will be using an interactive book to solve this case study and will also be able to ask more questions of the guest speaker.
3. Show the Quantum Pad with the Meet the Amazing Broncholis book in place. Demonstrate the proper use of the device by showing how to attach the headphones to the headphone splitters. Explain that the students can slide the pen over certain words and the Quantum Pad will define the words for them.
4. Demonstrate how to turn the Quantum Pad on and how to touch the "Go" buttons to start a new page.
5. Explain that there are games inside the book that the students can find by using the pen to touch the pictures on each page.
6. Briefly go over the worksheet questions.
7. Pass out the Quantum Pads for 30 minutes and let the students use them to answer the questions on the worksheet.
8. Encourage the students to ask questions to finish the case study.
9. Discuss the case study as a class.

Extension

Ask students to look around in their environment for potential triggers for people with asthma. They should make a list of the ones that are most common. Then ask them to identify a way to decrease their exposure to each one.

**Asthma and Lung Disesase
Lesson 3**

LEAPFROG ASTHMA BOOKS

Name: _____

Teacher: _____

Date: _____

Guest Speaker

Guest Speaker Name _____

The guest speaker was diagnosed with asthma at age _____

Some of the medications the guest speaker takes are:
_____
_____

Case Study: Barry

"Hello nurse, this is Barry's mom. Yes, I'm very concerned. His teacher called me while his class was on a field trip to the circus. Barry began wheezing and coughing uncontrollably. Outside the circus tent he still had trouble breathing. This isn't the first time that I've noticed something was wrong. He wakes up in the middle of the night coughing. I'm worried that it might be something serious. What's the matter with him and what should we do?"

Barry at the doctor's office

1. What is the device called that measures your breathing?

_____

2. What medicine should be taken at the same time every day?

_____

3. True or false? Only you and your doctor should be on your asthma team._____

Barry in his room

4. What do Barry's parents do at home to prevent Barry from having an asthma flare at home?

_____

Barry's neighborhood

5. Name 3 things that trigger people's asthma:

_____   _____   _____

Barry at his soccer game

6. What does Taylor use before her soccer games? _____

Barry outside his house

7. Why do Barry's peak flow readings slip? _____

8. What does C.L.U.B. stand for?

    C = _____

    L = _____

    U = _____

    B = _____

After Case Study

Know	Need To Know

Grade: 5
Asthma and Lung Disease
Lesson 4: Lung Disease and Cigarette Ads

Lesson Time: 1 hour

Reference: NIH: Chemicals and You: http://science.education.nih.gov/supplements/nih2/chemicals/other/glossary/glossary1.htm

Lesson objectives
- Identify harmful chemicals found in cigarettes.
- Calculate the lifetime cost of smoking.
- Analyze misleading information in cigarette advertisements.

Overview
The presenter shows harmful chemicals that are found in cigarettes and uses plastic lung models from the first lesson to demonstrate how cigarette smoke contributes to lung disease. The students solve word problems, calculating the cost of smoking cigarettes for a lifetime. They brainstorm the negative effects of cigarette smoke and identify misleading information in cigarette ads, then design their own anti-smoking ads.

Occupation of the Day
Oncologist: A doctor who specializes in the study of cancer. A lung cancer patient's oncologist will diagnose his or her cancer, determine how much it has spread, and perform (or advise on) appropriate treatment.

Key Terms

Addiction: When a person cannot stop doing something.

Nicotine: An addictive chemical found in cigarettes.

Carcinogens: Chemicals that cause cancer.

Emphysema: A disease a person can get from smoking. It is characterized by damaged or torn alveoli.

Lung cancer: A disease that makes the lung cells multiply abnormally, causing damage to lung function.

Bronchitis: A disease characterized by the lining of the bronchi being infected or inflamed.

Tar: The black sticky substance used to pave roads.

Acetone: A chemical common in paint and nail polish remover.

Ammonia: A chemical used in many cleaning solvents.

Arsenic: A main ingredient in rat poison.

Carbon monoxide: A chemical emitted in car exhaust.

Formaldehyde: A chemical used to preserve dead animals.

Lead: A poison found in old paint.

Vinyl chloride: A chemical used to make plastic bags.

Chemical: Any substance having a defined molecular composition.

Materials

Per class:
- 1 worksheet overhead, optional
- 1 empty bottle of nail polish remover
- 1 empty can of paint
- 1 empty box of plastic trash bags
- 1 empty bottle of window cleaning spray
- 1 empty box of rat poison that contained arsenic
- 2 used batteries
- 1 half pint jar filled with black molasses and labeled "tar"
- 3 plastic lung models from Lesson 1. Prepare them ahead of time to represent three lung diseases:
  - Wrap a pipe cleaner around the balloon lung to represent muscles tightening around the airways in asthma.
  - Cut holes in the balloon lung to show how emphysema enlarges and distorts the alveoli leaving large air pockets in the lungs.
  - Stuff a small ball of foil or paper into the balloon lung to represent a tumor growing in the lung.
- Overheads or posters of various cigarette advertisements (for free images see http://tobaccofreekids.org/adgallery)

Assorted overheads or posters showing the effects of smoking, such as lung cancer, emphysema, wrinkles and stained fingertips (for items to purchase see http://healthedco.com)

Per student:
- 1 worksheet
- Materials for creating an anti-smoking poster
  - Paper
  - Crayons
  - Scissors, optional
  - Magazines from which pictures can be cut out, optional
  - Glue, optional

Procedure

Question:
How might cigarette smoke affect the health of your lungs?

Introduction

1. Discuss question above.
2. Show a smoking ad. Explain that the class will be learning about smoking, lung diseases, and misrepresentations in cigarette advertising. By the end of the lesson the students will be able to spot lies that are hidden in cigarette ads.
3. Show products that contain chemicals found in cigarettes: plastic bags, nail polish remover, tar, batteries, window cleaner, and rat poison.
4. As you show each product, ask if the students would want to eat the chemicals in that product and ask if that chemical is good for you. Explain that all of these chemicals are found in cigarettes. If you smoke cigarettes or breathe cigarette smoke from someone else, you are ingesting these chemicals. Over time, the chemicals poison your body and cause serious health problems.

Demonstration: Smoking and Lung Diseases

1. Take out the three pre-prepared lung models from lesson one that demonstrate lung diseases.
2. Show the lung representing asthma. Explain that cigarette smoking aggravates asthma and can trigger asthma attacks. Ask the students what happens to the lungs in an asthma attack. Explain that the pipe cleaner represents the muscles tightening around the airways. Try to pump the lungs. Show that you can't push air out of the lungs.
3. Show the lung model representing emphysema. Show that there are holes in the balloon. Explain that dangerous tobacco chemicals destroy the alveoli. They expand and pop. With fewer alveoli, your lungs do not get enough oxygen. Show images of healthy lung tissue and lung tissue affected by emphysema. Try to pump the lung. Show that the lungs won't inflate properly.
4. Show the lung model representing lung cancer. Explain that cigarette chemicals called carcinogens cause cancer. Lung cells grow out of control into lumps called tumors. Show the lump in the lung model. People with lung cancer often go through a treatment called chemotherapy and lose their hair. Oncologists are people that study and treat cancer. Show images of lungs with tumors. Try to pump the lung. Show that the lung doesn't work properly.
5. Explain that the chemicals from tobacco build up in a smoker's lungs, blocking or thinning the airways. This makes it difficult to breathe and get oxygen into the lungs.
6. Smokers lungs are sometimes so diseased that they have to breathe through holes in their neck that connect to their trachea or need pure oxygen attached to their face to help them breathe while doing normal activities, such as walking in the house or climbing stairs.
7. Smokers are at higher risk for other diseases and conditions such as bronchitis, heart disease, and high blood pressure.
8. Show various images illustrating other effects of smoking, including stained teeth, stained fingernails and wrinkles.

Activity 1: The Real Cost of Smoking

Work with the students on the following word problems to determine the cost of smoking.

Bob smokes one pack a day, all year. Each pack costs $4. How much did he spend in a year?

4 x 365 = $1,460 in one year

Jamal smokes one pack a day for 30 years, and each pack is $4. How much did he spend?

$1,460 x 30 = $43,800

Maria was a chain smoker. She started smoking three packs a day when she was 12 and continued until she died of lung cancer at 70. Each pack costs $4. How much did she spend on cigarettes in her lifetime?

70 – 12 = 58

58 years x 365 days x 3 packs a day x $4 a pack = $ 254,040

Ask the students to solve the following individually:

Crystal smokes two packs a day. Each pack costs $4. How much does she spend on smoking in a year? Flying to New York and spending the weekend in a 5 star hotel costs $1,200. What costs more: Crystal's cigarettes for a year or a trip to New York?

2 x $4= $8

$8 x 365 = $2,920

Her smoking habit costs more.

After the students determine the amount that each person wasted on cigarettes, ask them to think of things that they could buy instead. The worksheet includes a list of prices for various things that the students might like.

Activity 2: Hidden Lies in Advertising

1. Work with the students to brainstorm a list of all the problems associated with smoking cigarettes. The list should include the following:
   - Cigarettes contain dangerous chemicals that can hurt you.
   - Smoking causes lung diseases like emphysema and lung cancer.
   - Smoking triggers asthma.
   - Smoking is addictive.
   - Smoking is an expensive habit.

People who smoke have:
- More wrinkles
- Less money to spend
- Dry grayish skin
- Hollow cheeks
- Bad breath
- Bad smell in clothes, hair and skin
- Stained fingertips
- Stained teeth
- Decreased ability to play sports
- Sleeping problems
- Higher risk of bone fractures.
- Higher risk of heart disease and stroke
- Higher risk or emphysema
- Higher risk of cancer of the mouth, esophagus, skin, and lungs.

2. Show several cigarette ads, and work with the students to identify how the ads mislead people: cigarette ads attempt to link smoking to good looks, wealth, romance, popularity, and prowess in sports. The truth is that smoking is detrimental to all of these things.

3. Have the students design their own anti-smoking ads.

Extensions

Tell students to share the dangers of smoking with their family members.

Tell students that if their family members want to quit, they can use resources such as 1-800-NO BUTTS, which helps people quit.

Asthma and Lung Disesase
Lesson 4

Lung Disease & Cigarette Ads

Name: _____

Teacher: _____

Date: _____

Chemicals in Cigarettes

Name one dangerous chemical that is in cigarettes_____

Smoking and Lung Disease:

Name three diseases that you could get if you smoke

1._____ 2._____ 3._____

What type of doctor works with people with cancer? _____

Why are cigarettes addictive?

_____

_____

What happens to people who smoke?

_____

_____

_____

_____

Costs of Various Items

iPod Nano	$200.00
Playstation 2	$200.00
Round trip plane tickets to Australia	$1,500.00
1 year tuition at a public university	$5,000.00
New BMW	$35,000.00

The Real Cost of Smoking

1. Bob smokes one pack a day, all year. Each pack costs $4. How much did he spend in a year?

   _____

2. Jamal smokes one pack a day for 30 years, and each pack is $4. How much did he spend?

   _____

3. Maria is a chain smoker. She started smoking three packs a day when she was 12 and continued until she died of lung cancer at age 70. Each pack costs $4. How much did she spend on cigarettes in her lifetime?

   _____

4. Crystal smokes two packs a day. Each pack costs $4. How much does she spend on smoking in a year? Flying to New York and spending the weekend in a 5-star hotel costs $1,200. What costs more: Crystal's cigarettes for a year or a trip to New York?

   _____

Grade: 5
Asthma and Lung Disease
Lesson 5: Preventing Lung Disease

Lesson Time: 1 hour

References: BADvertising Institute: www.badvertising.org; PBS Kids Go! http://pbskids.org/itsmylife/body/smoking/article4.html

Lesson objectives
- Become empowered to say no to cigarettes and other drugs.
- Write persuasively to discourage people from smoking.
- Encourage others to make healthy choices.

Overview
The class watches a video about smoking. The students write letters either urging a friend or a family member to quit smoking, or praising them for not smoking. Then the class tries out strategies for saying "no" to smoking.

Key Terms

Peer pressure: When your friends try to make you do something. You could feel peer pressure to dress a certain way, to play with certain kids, or to act out.

Advertising: A technique used to convince people to buy a product.

Surgeon General's warning: A statement that tobacco companies have to put on their cigarette ads and cigarette cartons warning people about the dangers of smoking.

Materials

Per class:
- 1 worksheet overhead, optional
- 10-minute video on cigarette advertising
  - "The Truth About Tobacco" or
  - "Finding the Power"
- 1 large poster paper for brainstorming health effects of smoking
- 1 roll of masking tape
- Various images of health effects from Lesson 4

Per student:
- 1 worksheet
- 1 piece of paper for writing a letter
- 1 envelope

Per pair:
- 1 die per pair of students

Procedure

> **Questions:**
> Why should people quit smoking?
> How can you say "no" to smoking?

Activity 1: Video
1. Briefly go over the questions on the worksheet that relate to the video.
2. Show a short video about cigarette advertising.
3. Give the students time to complete the worksheet. Discuss their answers. Discuss how cigarette ads mislead consumers.

Activity 2: Write a Letter
1. Ask the class if they know anyone who smokes. Explain that the students will write real letters to those people. Instead, they may write a letter praising someone for not smoking.
2. Tape a large piece of paper to the board.
3. Brainstorm all the reasons why someone should quit or not start. Reasons might include those below. People who smoke have:
   - More wrinkles
   - Dry grayish skin
   - Hollow cheeks
   - Bad breath
   - Bad smell in clothes, hair and skin
   - Stained fingertips
   - Stained teeth
   - Decreased ability to play sports
   - Sleeping problems
   - Higher risk of bone fractures.
   - Higher risk of heart disease and stroke
   - Higher risk of cancer of the mouth, esophagus, skin, and lungs
   - Increased risk of emphysema
4. Write down guidelines for the letter. Give students two options for writing the letter: they can either write to somebody who does smoke or somebody who does not.
   - Tell the person that you care about him or her, and that you want him or her to be healthy.
   - If the person does not smoke, tell the person why you are glad about this.
   - If the person does smoke, tell the person how smoking affects the body.
5. Start an example letter on the board:
   Dear Friend,
   I care about you and I want you to feel good. I'm also worried about you. When you smoke, I worry that you will get lung cancer or emphysema. I want to support you as you quit smoking.
   Sincerely,
   Friend
6. Allow 15 to 20 minutes for letter writing.
7. Ask a few students to share their letters in front of the class.

Activity 3: Peer Pressure
1. Ask the students if they have ever felt pressured to do something.
2. Explain that peer pressure is when your friends try to make you do something. You could feel peer pressure to dress a certain way, to play with certain kids, to act out, or to smoke.
3. Write six strategies for refusing peer pressure on the board and number them:
   1. Be a broken record (repeat the same refusal, no matter what the other person says).
   2. Walk away.
   3. Ignore the offer.
   4. Suggest an alternative.
   5. Give an excuse.
   6. Say "No."
4. Show a die. The class will work in pairs. One student will try to pressure the other student to smoke. The other student will roll the die. He or she will use the strategy that corresponds with the number rolled.
5. Demonstrate the six strategies with volunteers from the class. Explain that it's best not to enter into an argument with people trying to pressure you to smoke, because this might encourage them to give their own arguments and keep up the pressure.
6. Pass out the dice to each pair.
7. If time permits, call on students to act out their scenarios and strategies for rejecting peer pressure in front of the class.

Extensions
- Tell students to make a list on butcher paper of reasons why they want to protect their respiratory systems and of ways they are going to take care of their respiratory systems. Find a place to hang it in class or somewhere else at the school, so that others can see it.
- Discuss how smoking is detrimental to good looks, popularity, and prowess in sports.

**Asthma and Lung Disesase
Lesson 5**

Name: _____

Teacher: _____

Date: _____

Questions: Thumbs Up Thumbs Down

1. How do tobacco companies advertise in movies?

_____

_____

2. Give one example of tobacco incidence.

_____

_____

3. What percent of movies got a poor rating for tobacco incidence? _____%

4. The article in People magazine was about women and _____.

5. Is smoking cigars healthier than smoking cigarettes? Why or why not?

_____

_____

6. What is the problem with the Surgeon General's warnings on billboards?

_____

_____

How can smoking affect your health?

_____

_____

Strategies for saying "No" to cigarettes

What are the 6 ways to say NO to cigarettes?

1. _____

2. _____

3. _____

4. _____

5. _____

6. _____

Date_____

Dear_____,

_____
_____
_____
_____
_____
_____
_____
_____
_____
_____
_____
_____
_____

Sincerely,

_____

Grade: 5
Heart Disease
Lesson 1: The Heart As a Pump

Lesson Time: 1 hour

References: CardioHEADS: www.colorado.edu/Outreach/BSI/CardioHEADS; The Science Museum of Minnesota: www.smm.org/heart/lessons/lesson4a.htm

Lesson objectives

- Know that the circulatory system consists of specialized structures for transporting materials around the body via the blood.
- Discover that the heart is a muscular organ, is made up of chambers and valves, and pumps blood.
- Use models and animal hearts to explore the basic structure and function of the heart and its location in the body.

Overview

The presenter dissects a real sheep heart and the students investigate heart models and animal hearts. Then the presenter shows various objects and demonstrates various household pumps to show how the heart works.

Key Terms

Heart: A muscular organ that pumps blood.

Cell: The basic unit of life.

Tissue: Parts of the body made up of groups of cells that have similar functions.

Muscle: Tissues that contract and relax to move internal organs or the skeletomuscular system.

Organ: A structure made of specialized tissues that work together for a common purpose.

Cardiovascular system: All the tissues and organs involved in moving blood around the body to bring nutrients and O2 to the cells and take CO_2 and other waste products away from the cells. It includes the heart, blood vessels, and blood, and is also known as the circulatory system.

Blood: A liquid that is pumped by the heart. It carries oxygen and nutrients to the body cells.

Blood vessel: A flexible tube that carries blood throughout the body

Chamber: Another word for "room." The heart has four chambers.

Valve: A device for regulating the flow of a liquid or gas by covering and uncovering an opening. Examples of valves include faucets, garden hose nozzles, and soap dispensers. Heart valves are "one way doors" made of tissue; they control blood flow through the heart, only allowing the blood to flow in one direction.

Pump: A device for moving a liquid or gas from one place to another. Examples of pumps: bike pumps, balloon pumps, squirt guns, turkey basters, eyedroppers, squirt bottles (cleaning products, Windex), and gas pumps. The heart is a biological pump.

Materials

Per class:
- 1 VHS tape or Cardiovascular DVD (optional) from HEADS-UP, a SEPA project based in Texas. The tape includes two segments. The first mini-lecture is about the cardiovascular system and the sheep heart dissection.
- 1 sheep heart
  - Cut the heart in half with a butcher knife before class and store in a sealed plastic bag.
- 1 dissection kit:
  - 1 tweezers
  - 1 scalpel
  - 1 probe
- 1 pair of latex gloves for the presenter
- 1 overhead document reader machine so students can see dissection, optional
- 1 balance, protected with plastic, to weigh hearts
- 1 valentine
- 1 muscle model
- 1 turkey baster
- 1 squirt bottle with adjustable nozzle (to demonstrate a valve)
- 1 metronome
- 1 bicycle pump or balloon pump
- 1 1-L bottle of water (if the classroom has no sink)
- 2 500-ml clear plastic cups.
- 1 roll of paper towels

Per student:
- 1 worksheet
- 1 pair of latex gloves

Per pair:
- 1 plastic human heart model
- 1 fresh animal heart from a butcher shop (chicken, pig, or other)
- Several toothpicks
- 1 tongue depressor
- 1 plastic knife

Procedure

Question:
How does the heart work?

Introduction
Show a clip of the HEADS-UP video about the heart, pausing to discuss the animation of the heart pumping blood around the body. The video should give the class a good overview of the heart and the circulatory system.

Activity 1: Sheep Heart Demonstration
Dissect the sheep heart, either following the dissection video or on your own. Point out interesting heart parts:
- Specific blood vessels: aorta
- Specific chambers: right and left atria and ventricles
- The fat around the sheep heart
- The point or apex of the heart
- Valves

Activity 2: Human Heart Models

Heart Part	Function
Thick muscular walls	Squeeze the heart to pump blood around the body
Blood vessels	Take blood into and out of the heart
Chambers	Collect, hold and then squeeze blood as heart pumps
Valves	Close and open the chambers

1. Explain the activity. Each pair of students will get one heart model and worksheets that match the model. They will review the sheep heart dissection again and identify the parts on the worksheet. The parts include valves, chambers, veins and arteries.
2. Pass out the heart models and worksheets. Lead the class as they dissect their models. Allow time for the students to find all the parts on the worksheet.
3. Discuss and compare results. Does the form and structure of the heart match its function?
4. How can you take care of your heart?

Activity 3: Animal Hearts
1. Pass out latex gloves to each student. Each pair of students should also be given several toothpicks, a tongue depressor, and a plastic knife to use in their dissection.
2. Give one animal heart (chicken, pig, or other) to each pair of students.
3. Ask the students to estimate and compare the dimensions of the sheep heart and the fresh animal heart.
4. Weigh the sheep heart.
5. Allow each pair of students to weigh their animal heart.
6. Write the typical weight of each type of heart on the board.
7. Ask the students to dissect their animal heart and compare its structure to that of the sheep and human hearts.

Activity 4: Worksheet and Wrap-up
1. Show the various items found on the worksheet, including the valentine, the muscle model, the turkey baster, the squirt bottle, and the metronome. Discuss how they are like and unlike the heart.
2. Demonstrate and discuss the household pumps.
    a. What are the devices?
    b. What are they doing and where is the liquid going and how is it moving?
    c. How are the pumps like or unlike the heart?
3. Discuss what the students have learned about the heart.
4. Discuss how real hearts compare to the models and the pumps.

Extensions
Bring extra, pre-cut sheep hearts, so each group of students can see the heart. Give each group a pie pan, gloves, and tongue depressors or toothpicks to use as probes.

Obtain other animal hearts from a science supply store and compare the size, mass, volume, and structure of the various hearts.

Online sheep heart anatomy: www.gwc.maricopa.edu/class/bio202/heart/anthrt.htm

"The Heart: An Online Investigation" from the Franklin Institute Online: http://sln.fi.edu/biosci/heart.html

Amazing heart facts from PBS NOVA episode "Cut to the Heart" - www.pbs.org/wgbh/nova/heart/heartfacts.html

Excellent animation of heart valves working: www.smm.org/heart/heart/pumping.htm

**Heart Disease
Lesson 1**

THE HEART AS A PUMP

Name: _____

Teacher: _____

Date: _____

Label the heart parts

Write words from the list to label the parts of the heart.

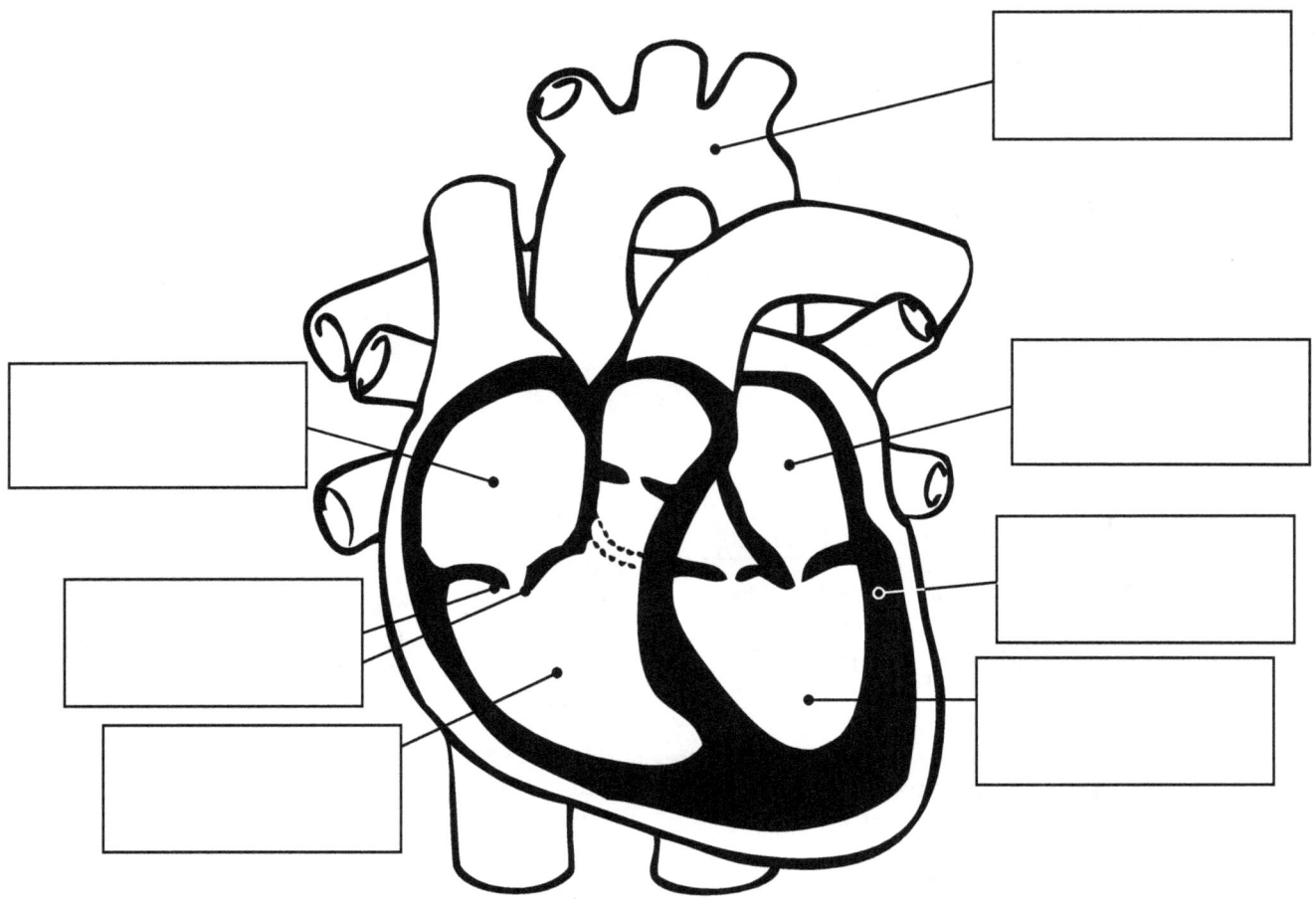

Word list

- aorta
- valves
- heart muscle
- left ventricle
- left atrium
- right ventricle
- right atrium

Activity 2: Demo

How are the following items like or unlike a heart?

Item	Like	Unlike
valentine		
muscle		
turkey baster		
squirt bottle		
metronome		

What is the special job of the heart?

_____

FORM FOLLOWS FUNCTION

How do the following structures help the heart to do its job?

Structure	Function
Heart muscle	
Blood vessels	
Chambers	
Valves	

What is the job of the circulatory system?

_____

_____

_____

Grade: 5
Heart Disease
Lesson 2: The Circulatory System

Lesson Time: 1 hour

References: Online video demonstrating path of blood in body: www.pbs.org/wnet/redgold/journey/phase2_a1.html
How Blood Works: www.howstuffworks.com/blood.htm; www.funsci.com/fun3_en/blood/blood.htm
Animated demonstrations of the circulatory system and the heart: www.becomehealthynow.com/article/bodycardio/699/
Tracing procedure: www.smm.org/heart/lessons/lesson6.htm; Heart Game: CardioHEADS www.colorado.edu/outreach/BSI/CardioHEADS

Lesson objectives
- Know that the circulatory system consists of specialized structures for transporting materials around the body via the blood.
- Experience how blood circulates through the heart chambers, lungs, and body.
- Know the importance of carbon dioxide (CO_2) and oxygen (O_2) in cellular respiration.
- Know that carbon dioxide and oxygen are exchanged in the lungs and tissues.
- Know that blood carries carbon dioxide from the body cells to the lungs.
- Know that blood carries oxygen from the lungs to the body cells.

Overview
Students walk around a large map of the heart and deliver oxygen to the body and carbon dioxide to the lungs as they learn the names of blood vessels and heart parts. They trace the path of blood through the circulatory system and the heart using red and blue crayons on a series of schematic diagrams.

Key Terms
Vein: A blood vessel carrying blood towards the heart.

Artery: A blood vessel carrying blood away from the heart.

Circulatory system: A system including the heart and the blood vessels that transport blood to and from every cell of the body. Also known as the cardiovascular system.

Capillary: The smallest type of blood vessel, the location where oxygen enters cells and carbon dioxide leaves cells. Capillaries connect the arteries and the veins and are found all over the body.

Red blood cells: Disk-shaped cells that carry oxygen and carbon dioxide in the blood.

Oxygen: A gas (O_2) in the atmosphere that humans need for survival. When oxygen enters the lungs, it is transferred into the blood.

Carbon dioxide: A gas (CO_2) that is produced in cells when sugars are broken down to produce energy. Cells release carbon dioxide as a waste product, and the blood carries it to the lungs. It leaves the body when we exhale.

Periodic table: A chart of the chemical elements. The periodic table is organized into periods and groups according to the properties of the elements.

Materials

Per class:
- 10 green balls labeled "O_2"
- 10 orange balls labeled "CO_2"
- 1 8-ft x 12-ft heart map with latex paint on canvas
- 2 sets of heart anatomy labels
- 2 12-in diameter, paper disks with red on one side and blue on the other
- 2 overheads
  - 1 overhead of the simplified circulatory system on the front of the worksheet
  - 1 overhead of the heart map on the back of the worksheet
- 1 red overhead pen
- 1 blue overhead pen

Per student:
- 1 worksheet
- 1 red crayon
- 1 blue crayon

Procedure

> **Question:**
> **What does the blood carry?**

Introduction

1. Review the previous lesson and give an overview of today's lesson.
2. Pass out the worksheets and one red crayon and one blue crayon to each student. The red crayon represents oxygenated blood and the blue crayon represents oxygen-poor blood.
3. Trace through the simplified circuit of the circulatory system on the first overhead with a blue and red overhead pen as the students trace their own worksheets. Explain how oxygen and carbon dioxide are exchanged in the circulatory system. All cells need oxygen to have energy, and they produce carbon dioxide as a waste product. The blood cells carry oxygen from the lungs to the cells and remove carbon dioxide from the cells and carry it back to the lungs. The red crayon is oxygen-rich blood that your cells need so they can turn your food into energy. The blue crayon is oxygen-poor blood that has the waste products from the cells. Begin in the lungs with a red crayon, trace through the heart to the body tissue. Switch to a blue crayon and trace from the body tissue, through the heart to the lungs.

Activity 1: The Heart Game

1. Clear the desks out of the way and place the heart map on the floor. Place 10 oxygen balls in the capillaries of the lung tissue and 10 carbon dioxide balls in capillaries of the body tissue.
2. Explain the game as you walk through the heart map. The class will work in teams. One team will sit along the edge of the lung tissue with the oxygen balls, and the other team will sit along the edge of the body tissue with the carbon dioxide balls. One person at a time will travel through the heart map, delivering oxygen to the cells and delivering carbon dioxide to the lungs as the team explains what is happening.
3. Demonstrate how to walk through the heart. Students must remove their shoes and walk carefully between the lines following this order:
   - START in the capillaries of lungs with a blood cell disk. Take oxygen from the lungs and turn the disk red side up.
   - TRAVEL through the pulmonary vein to the left atrium, then the left ventricle, then out the aorta to the arteries leading to the capillaries in the body tissue.
   - EXCHANGE: Give the body tissue the oxygen and get one carbon dioxide. Turn the disk over to the blue side.
   - TRAVEL through the vena cava vein to the right atrium, then the right ventricle, then out the pulmonary artery to the capillaries of the lungs.
   - EXCHANGE the carbon dioxide for oxygen. Turn the disk over to the red side.
   - END your turn. Ask a teammate to take your place as they continue another circuit.
4. Mention common health conditions that can affect the circulatory system. Fat build up can slow down and restrict blood flow. Heart disease is the number one cause of death in the US. Tell the students during the next class they will learn about blood pressure.
5. Play the game until 20 minutes remain in the class time. To review what the students have learned, follow the instructions for activity 2.

Activity 2: Tracing the Circulatory System

1. Show the second overhead and trace the image at the same time as the class. This time go into more detail about the parts of the circulatory system. Start again in the capillaries of the lungs with a red pen. Talk about specific blood vessels and heart chambers and move your pen to capillaries of the body tissue. Ask the students to name the parts of the heart and circulatory system as you work.
2. Switch from a red overhead pen to a blue overhead pen. In the capillaries, oxygen leaves the blood and enters cells that need oxygen to break down sugar for energy. The cells unload carbon dioxide and other waste products into the blood. Red blood cells are the carriers of both oxygen and carbon dioxide. They carry only one of these gases at a time.
3. Trace with the blue pen back towards the heart. The blood is now oxygen-poor and travels into larger and larger veins that lead back to the heart.

4. Trace from the body into the right atrium. Oxygen-poor blood from the body enters this chamber where it is pumped into the right ventricle, then out to the lungs to be replenished with more oxygen. Trace through the right ventricle to the lungs.
5. Finish in the lungs, reviewing that carbon dioxide is released into the lungs and expelled as you exhale.

Extension

Have the students play the heart game assuming that this is the heart of a smoker. The blood vessels will be narrower, and carbon monoxide will be permanently bound to some of the red blood cells. The heart will have to work harder to get oxygen to the tissues. Some of the red blood cells will pass through the lungs without picking up any oxygen. The students will have to move faster to get enough oxygen to the tissues. Ask them what effect this has on the heart (it will beat faster and have to exert more pressure to get the blood through the narrowed arteries; it will not always get as much oxygen as it needs for its own functioning, and the person may have a heart attack).

**Heart Disesase
Lesson 2**

THE CIRCULATORY SYSTEM

Name: _____

Teacher: _____

Date: _____

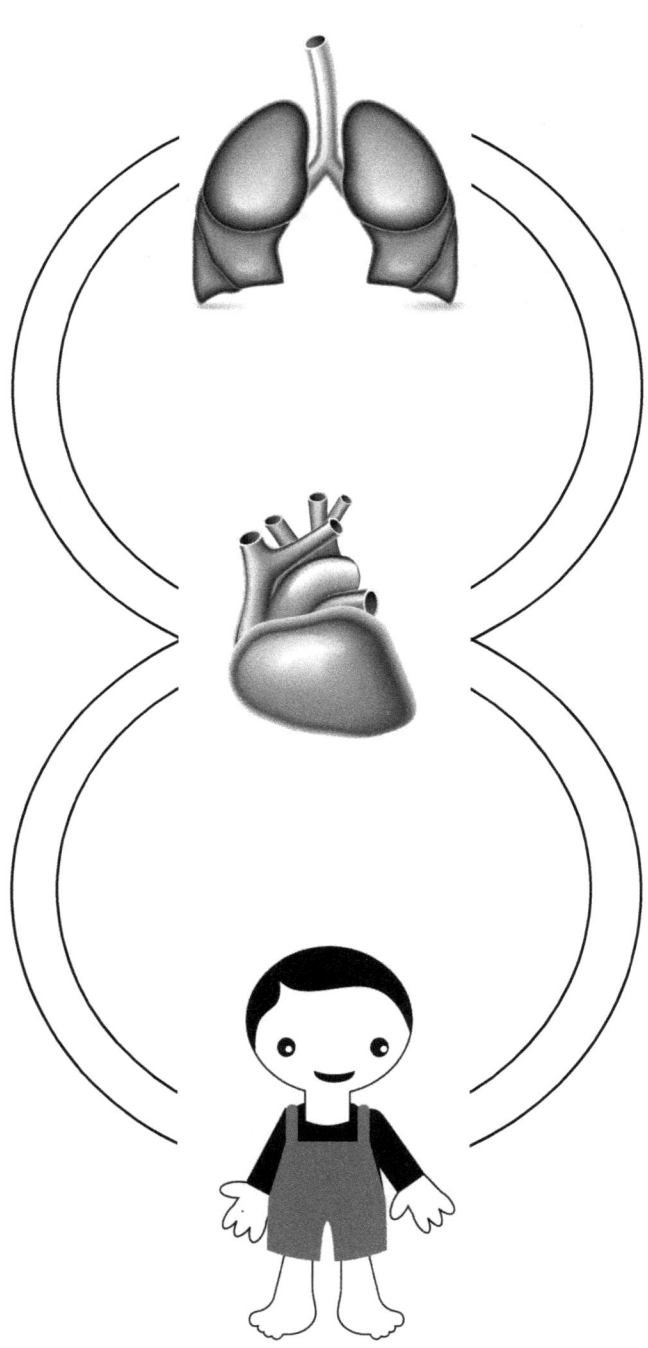

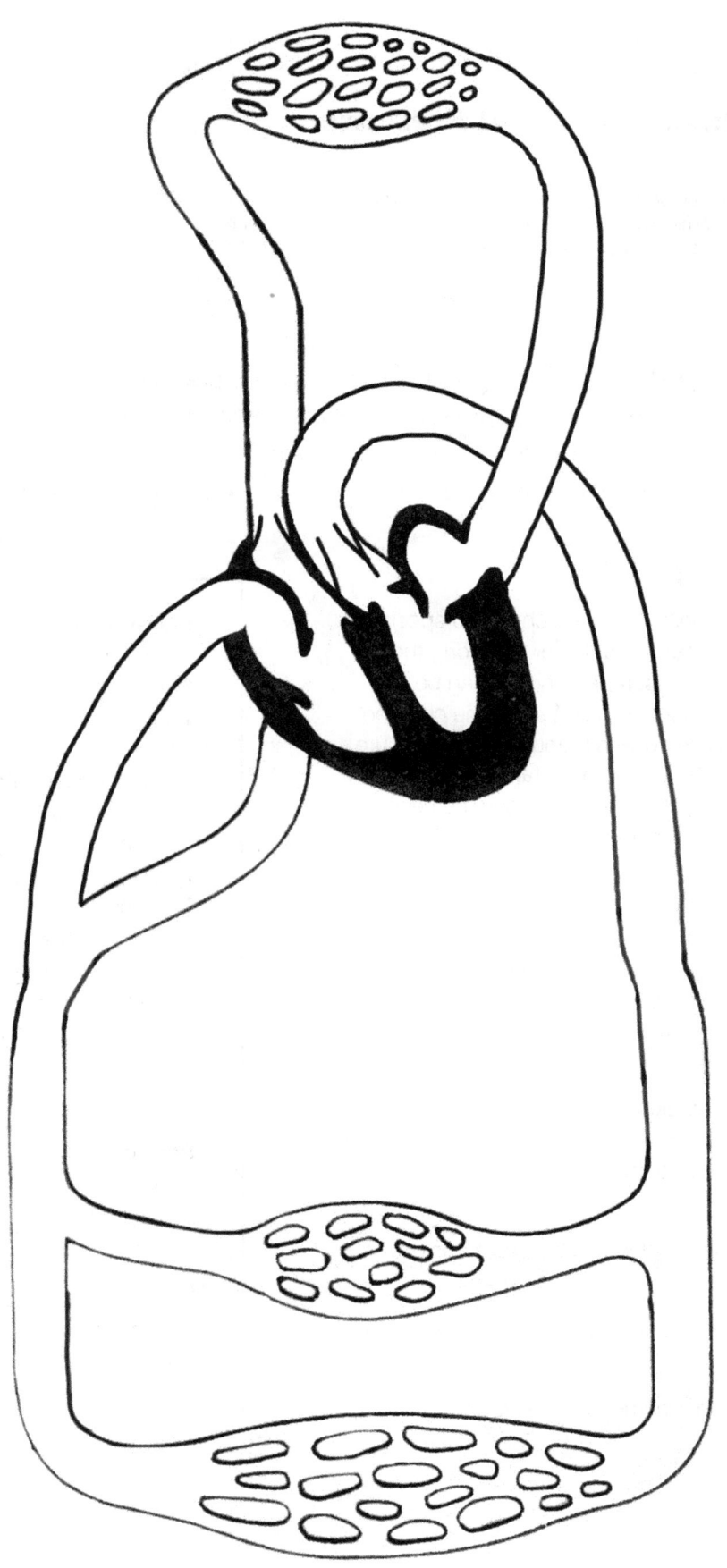

Grade: 5
Heart Disease
Lesson 3: Exploring Blood Pressure

Lesson Time: 1 hour

References: Chart of age-appropriate blood pressure ranges: www.smm.org/heart/lessons/lesson3.htm
Your guide to lowering high blood pressure: http://www.nhlbi.nih.gov/hbp/bp/bp.htm
How to take blood pressure: http://www.madsci.org/experiments/archive/859422898.Bi.html

Lesson objectives
- Meet a healthcare worker or a researcher who specializes in the heart.
- Measure blood pressure with manual blood pressure monitors.
- Know that blood pressure is an important health measurement.
- Know the implications of blood pressure.
- Be able to identify health behaviors that lead to high blood pressure.

Overview
A healthcare professional or a researcher who specializes in the heart tells the class about his or her work, the danger of high blood pressure, and how it can be prevented. The presenter and guest show the class how to measure blood pressure with manual blood pressure monitors. The students work in pairs taking each other's blood pressure. Finally, the class discusses the health effects of high blood pressure.

Key Terms
Pressure: The force of something pushing against something else. The stronger the force that is pushing on something, the higher the pressure.

Blood Pressure: The pressure of blood pressing against the walls of the blood vessels. Blood pressure is measured with two numbers that represent the pressure in the blood vessels when the heart is relaxed and when it is squeezing.

Diastolic: Blood pressure when the heart muscle is relaxed.

Systolic: Blood pressure when the heart muscle is squeezing.

Hypertension: Another name for high blood pressure.

Materials

Per class:
- 1 squirt bottle with adjustable nozzle from Lesson 1
- 1 empty quart container
- 500 mL of tap water (if the classroom has no sink)
- 1 overhead of the circulatory system from Lesson 2
- Additional overhead:
  - 1 illustration of systolic and diastolic blood pressure
  - 1 image of two people: Who has hypertension?
  - 1 illustration of clogged arteries

Per student:
- 1 worksheet
- 1 heart-map worksheet from Lesson 2

Per pair:
- 1 blood pressure monitor
- 1 stethoscope

Procedure

**Question:
What is blood pressure?**

Introduction

Ask a volunteer to use the squirt bottle with the valve in the open position. The water should be squirted into the empty container. Close the aperture of the valve until only a thin fast stream shoots out. Ask the volunteer to use the squirt bottle again. What changed? Does it take more or less force to squirt the same amount of water? Our circulatory system works like the squirt bottle. If the blood vessels get smaller, it takes more force and pressure to move the same amount of blood through the system. The pressure of blood in the blood vessels is called blood pressure. Everyone has some blood pressure, and it can be measured. As your heart pumps, the blood presses against the walls of the blood vessels and the pressure goes up. As your heart relaxes, the pressure goes down.

Introduce the guest speaker, who will tell the class about his or her work related to heart disease and explain the importance of blood pressure as an indicator of heart health. The guest speaker will also discuss how lifestyle affects blood pressure. The following points should be made by the presenter if a guest speaker is not available: (1) high blood pressure is an indicator of risk for heart disease, (2) people who exercise regularly have lower blood pressure, (3) eating too much salt raises blood pressure, 4) fatty foods clog arteries, which increases blood pressure (remind students of the squirt bottle demonstration), and (5) being overweight increases risk of high blood pressure.

Activity 1: Blood Pressure Monitor Demonstration

1. Demonstrate how to use the blood pressure monitor on a student:
   a. Place the cuff on the upper arm of the person whose blood pressure you want to measure so that the arrow or circle lines up with the inside of the elbow.
   b. Insert the head of the stethoscope just under the arrow or circle and place the earpieces in your ears. Make sure that the valve (knob) is turned all the way clockwise.
   c. Pump the gauge up to 150 for a child.
   d. Slowly release the valve until you hear a clear tapping sound.
   e. When you first hear the tapping, note the number on the gauge as the systolic pressure.
   f. Continue slowly releasing the valve and stop when you can't hear the tapping sound or when the needle stops vibrating. This is the diastolic pressure.
2. Put the higher number on the board first. Draw a slash beside it and put the lower number to the right of the slash.
3. The higher number or systolic pressure is the pressure when the heart is contracting or beating (pumping blood), and the lower number is the diastolic pressure, when the heart is at rest or between beats (filling with blood). Ask students whether they think the higher number measures the heart beating or the heart at rest.
4. Show the overhead of systolic and diastolic pressure.

Activity 2: Students Measure Blood Pressur

1. Write the average blood pressure of infants (70/40), children (100/60), and adults (120/80) on the board. Make sure that the students understand that everyone has blood pressure and that blood pressure only becomes a problem when it is too high or too low for a given age group. Also, taking blood pressure accurately takes practice, so the students shouldn't jump to conclusions if their measurements are outside the normal range for their age group.
2. Distribute a stethoscope to each pair of students. Before trying to take blood pressure, each student should listen to his or her own heart to become familiar with the stethoscope and get a sense of how loud heart sounds are. In general, students who cannot hear a heartbeat when the stethoscope is directly over the heart cannot hear the pulsing artery in the arm to measure blood pressure, either.
3. Before the pairs of students take each other's blood pressure, ask for a volunteer to demonstrate the correct way to use a blood pressure monitor.
4. Note: In a loud classroom, it might be easier for

students to watch the pulsing movement of the needle on the pressure gauge than to listen for heartbeats.

Activity 3: Discussion

1. Put away the blood pressure monitors.

2. Discuss the results of the blood pressure activity. What does pressure mean? Did anyone have high blood pressure? If you were using a pump to move water, what would happen if you decreased the size of the nozzle opening? What would happen if the heart were pumping blood through clogged vessels? Would the heart have to beat harder and faster to get the blood through the vessel? Could this cause high blood pressure?

3. Show the overhead of clogged arteries. Brainstorm factors that could affect high blood pressure—such as exercise, a high salt diet, and a high fat diet—and discuss.

4. Show the overhead of the two people with hypertension and discuss how hypertension is the silent killer. Point to each person and ask the students if they think that person has high blood pressure. The answer will be yes in both cases. Emphasize that someone can look healthy, but still have hypertension. Discuss the health implications of hypertension, and say that a healthy diet and exercise can help prevent it.

Activity 4: Review

1. Use the squirt bottle pump and the heart-map worksheet to review the following points:
   - The circulatory system consists of specialized structures for transport of materials.
   - Blood circulates through the heart chambers, lungs, and body.
   - Blood takes (O_2) from the lungs to the body.
   - Blood takes (CO_2) from the body to the lungs.
   - Carbon dioxide (CO_2) and oxygen (O_2) are exchanged in the capillaries of the lungs and body tissue.

2. Read over the case study on the worksheet as a class. Ask the students to make recommendations for Mona, the patient.

Extensions

Look at the food labels on foods you eat for one week and record the amount of sodium per item. Total this list at the end of one week. What do you think about the amount of salt eaten during the week? Do this for the listings of total fat and cholesterol. Make a list of the foods with the most sodium, fat, and cholesterol.

**Heart Disesase
Lesson 3**

EXPLORING BLOOD PRESSURE

Name: _____

Teacher: _____

Date: _____

Understanding Blood Pressure

1. What is blood pressure? _____

2. What is diastolic blood pressure? _____

3. What is systolic blood pressure? _____

4. What is your blood pressure? _____ / _____

Case Study: Mona

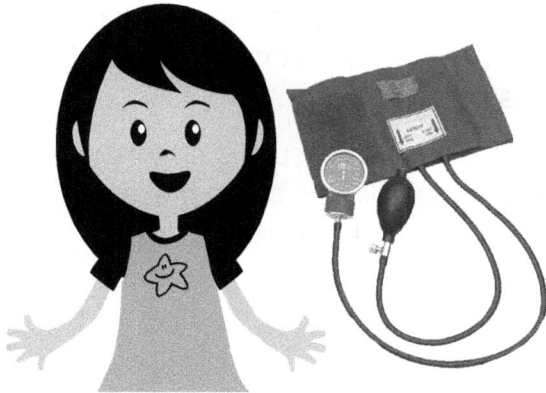

Mona had no symptoms. She did not know anything was wrong with her until she went for a routine checkup. After measuring her height, weight and temperature, the nurse took her blood pressure and remarked that it was too high. Most adults have blood pressure readings of about 120 over 80, but Mona had a reading of 150 over 100. Her doctor had a serious talk with her: Blood pressure is a health measurement that shows how forcefully your blood is pushing against your blood vessels. Over time, high blood pressure can lead to serious problems, including heart disease and stroke. Mona would need to drastically change her diet and lifestyle if she wanted to live to a ripe old age.

What are three things Mona should do to live longer?

- _____
- _____
- _____

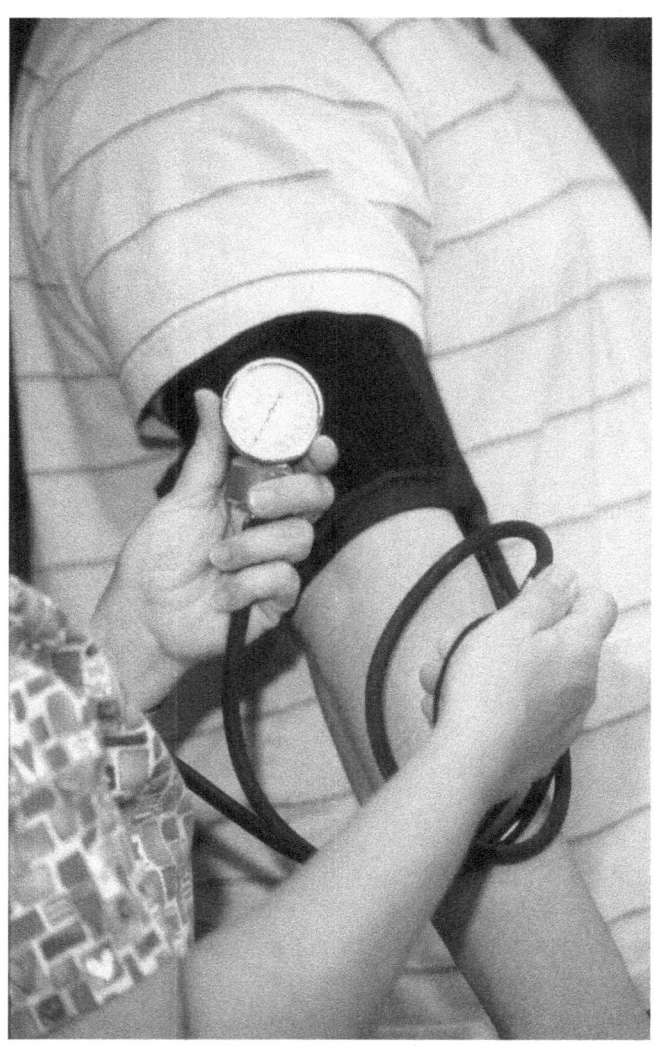

Blood pressure range:
Age: 5 to 12 years
Systolic (mm Hg): 90-110
Diastolic (mm Hg): 60-80

How to use a manual blood pressure monitor:

1. Place the cuff on your partners arm just above the elbow with the air tubes coming out over the inside of your elbow, where there is a large artery.

2. Place the round end of the stethoscope over the artery and just under the cuff. Place the other two ends in your ears.

3. Hold the bulb of the pump in your hand. Make sure that the knob is turned all the way to the right.

4. Pump the gauge up to about 140 for a child or 200 for an adult.

5. Slowly release pressure by turning the knob to the left. Stop when you hear the heartbeat and record the number. This is the systolic pressure.

6. Continue to release pressure by turning the knob to the left. Stop when you can't hear the heartbeat anymore. Record this number as the diastolic pressure.

7. Don't worry if your pressure isn't within the normal range. Taking blood pressure requires training and practice.

Who has hypertension?

Systolic:
When heart is contracting

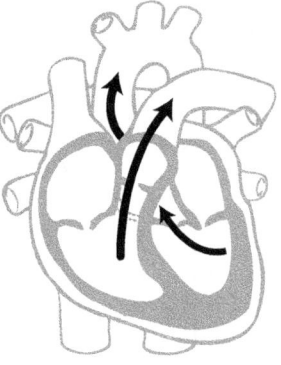

Diastolic:
When heart is at rest

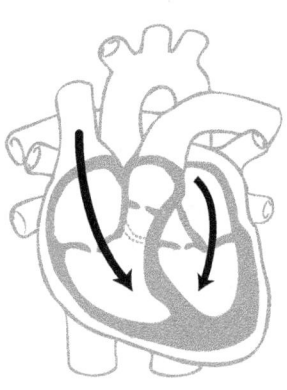

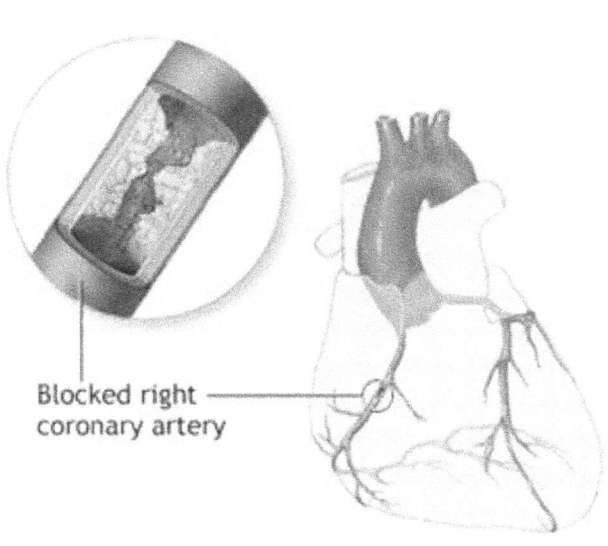

Blocked right coronary artery

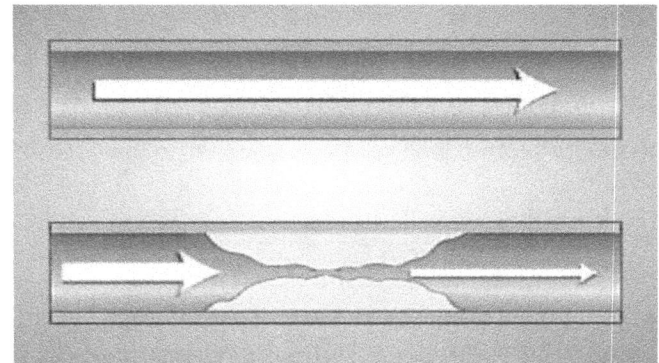

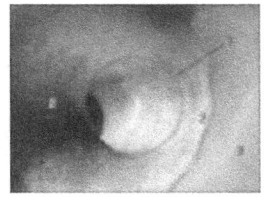

Grade: 5
Heart Disease
Lesson 4: Heart Rate and Exercise

Lesson Time: 1 hour

Reference: "Heart Rate," in How to Encourage Girls in Math and Science (Dale Seymour Publications, 1982), by Joan Skolnick, Carol Langbort, and Lucille Day, pp. 167-168.

Lesson objectives
- Know that scientific progress is made by asking meaningful questions and by conducting careful investigations.
- Identify testable questions.
- Generate hypotheses.
- Identify controlled, independent, and dependent variables.
- Plan an experiment.
- Write a procedure.

Overview
The students learn how to meaure heart rate, then do a controlled experiment testing the effect of exercise on heart rate. The presenter leads the students through each step of the scientific process. The students then plan their own experiments that they will conduct the following week.

Key Terms

Scientific method: The process by which scientific progress is made. It involves making observations, asking meaningful questions, creating hypotheses, making predictions, identifying variables, designing a procedure, collecting data, analyzing data, and drawing conclusions.

Hypothesis: A tentative explanation that can be tested.

Prediction: An educated guess concerning the outcome of an experiment.

Variables: Something that changes. Anything that can affect the results of an experiment.

Independent variable: The condition in the experiment that the experimenter will change. The condition in the experiment that differs between the control and the experimental subject.

Dependent variable: The variable that will be measured.

Subject: The person being tested.

Control: The subject that has no special treatment. Measure this subject before and after without making any changes. For example if you were testing the effects of fertilizer on plant growth, the control plants would be the plants that didn't have any fertilizer.

Heart rate: The number of times the heart beats in a given amount of time. Heart rate is usually measured in beats per minute.

Materials

Per class:
- 1 worksheet overhead, optional
- 1 poster of the scientific process to be left in the classroom. Points include:
  - Step 1: Observe and ask questions.
  - Step 2: State a hypothesis.
  - Step 3: Make a prediction based on the hypothesis.
  - Step 4: Plan your test.
  - Step 5: Conduct your test.
  - Step 6: Draw conclusions and share results.

Per student:
- 1 worksheet
- 1 sheet of graph paper

Procedure

> **Question:**
> **What affects heart rate?**

Activity 1: Measuring Heart Rate

1. Pass out the worksheets.
2. Ask the students what they've learned about the heart. Remind them that scientists are responsible for discovering everything we know about the heart. Scientists come up with questions, and they carefully investigate these questions with a special process called the scientific method. Refer to the worksheet.
3. Lead the students as they take their own heart rates. Show that you can use two fingers against your neck, just below the jaw line, or on your wrist. Ask the students to carefully count their heartbeats as you watch a clock or watch for 15 seconds. Ask the students to write down the number of beats that they counted and to multiply that number by 4 to get the beats per minute.
4. Explain that you will go through a plan for a simple experiment with the entire class and then give them time to develop their own variations on the experiment.

Activity 2: How to Plan an Experiment

1. STEP 1: Observe and ask questions. Discuss student observations and questions from the heart rate activity. If the students don't have many questions, discuss the following:
   - Did everyone have the same heart rate or were there differences?
   - What is a heart beat?
   - What does it represent?
   - What might affect heart rate? What would speed up or slow down your heart rate?
   - Does exercise, sleeping, emotions, temperature, spicy food, or caffeine change heart rate?

   Help the students to narrow down the questions to things they can test in the classroom. For the example experiment, choose the following: "How does exercise affect heart rate?"

2. STEP 2: State a hypothesis. A hypothesis is a tentative explanation that can be tested. For example: "Exercise makes the heart beat faster," "Exercise has no effect on heart rate," or "Exercise makes the heart beat slower."

3. STEP 3: Make a prediction based on the hypothesis. Ask the students to make a prediction in a complete sentence formulated as an "if, then" statement. They can choose one of the following (depending on their hypothesis):
   - "If a person exercises, then his or her heart rate will increase."
   - "If a person exercises, then his or her heart rate will stay the same."
   - "If a person exercises, then his or her heart rate will decrease."

4. STEP 4: Plan your test.
   - Think about what tools you will need.
   - Write down the steps you will follow to do your test:
     a. Measure heart rate and record.
     b. Exercise for 3 minutes.
     c. Measure heart rate and record.
   - Decide how to conduct a fair test by controlling variables. Testing only one subject (person) doesn't give you an accurate result. The subject's heart rate could have increased because they got excited, got scared, drank coffee that morning, or have a heart condition that speeds up the heart. All of these other factors that could affect the results are called variables. To make a fair test you need to make sure that the change in heart rate was only caused by one variable, exercise. To improve the test, have a number of subjects who are as similar as possible. For example, they could be the same age, height, grade, and gender, and they could have similar diets and general health conditions. Also, set aside an equal number of subjects that will not participate in the exercise, and call them the controls.
   - Decide how you will gather and record your data. The variable you will measure is called the dependent variable. In this experiment, heart rate is the dependent variable. It depends on exercise, which is called the independent variable.
   - Write your procedure in more detailed steps:
     a. Choose two similar subjects. Call one the control subject and the other the experimental subject.

b. Measure the heart rate of both subjects.

   c. Ask the experimental subject to exercise for 3 minutes by doing jumping jacks.

   d. Measure the heart rate of both subjects again.

   e. Compare the first and second heart rate of subjects. Find the change in the heart rate of each subject.

5. STEP 5: Conduct your test. Follow the steps of the procedure as a class. The students should work in pairs. One member of each pair should be the experimental subject, and the other member should be the control. Make sure that the students make observations and measure their heart rates carefully. The students should record everything that happens. Afterwards they should organize their data so that they can study it carefully.

6. STEP 6: Share results and draw conclusions. Pool the results for the class. Ask all the experimental subjects to report their change in heart rate. Calculate the class average. Then ask the control subjects to report their change in heart rate, and again calculate the class average. Analyze the data that the class has gathered. Draw a graph on the board. Students can graph the results on graph paper. Come up with a conclusion as a class.

6. Review that the heart is a muscle, and like all muscles it gets stronger and healthier with exercise. Any exercise that increases heart rate exercises the heart!

Activity 3: Further Investigation

1. Ask the pairs of students to come up with variations on the experiment. Here are just a few examples:
   - Try other exercises and activities such as reading, lying down, running in place, walking, sit ups, pushups, jumping, or dancing.
   - Ask the experimental subject to exercise for a longer period of time.
   - Take additional measurements: 3 minutes, 5 minutes, and 10 minutes after exercise.
   - Measure blood pressure before and after exercise.

2. Ask the students to work in pairs to fill out a procedure that they will try during the next class period.

Extensions

Enter the class data into a spreadsheet and create graphs on Excel.

Measure heart rates immediately after exercise, one minute after exercise, and two minutes after exercise.

Have the students keep a record of their heart rate for a week, measuring their heart rate daily at the same time.

Have the students collect pulse rates from various adults and list this on another graph. How does the average adult heart rate compare to the student's average rate?

The amount of time the heart takes to return to a normal, at-rest rate after exercise is called recovery time. This is a measure of the body's general fitness. The shorter the recovery time, the higher the fitness level. Determine recovery rate by first measuring and recording the pulse rate at rest. Next, run in place for two minutes. Now measure the pulse rate every minute until it reaches the at-rest rate. How long did it take to return to the normal rate?

**Heart Disease
Lesson 4**

Name: _____

Teacher: _____

Date: _____

Steps

1. Question: _____

2. Hypothesis: _____

3. Prediction: _____

4. Independent Variable: _____

   Dependent Vaiable: _____

5. Procedure: _____

6. Experimental Subject:_____

   Control Subject: _____

7. Graph

8. Conclusion: _____.

Word Bank

Dependent variable: The thing you are measuring.

Procedure: A set of steps that explain how you are going to do something.

Independent variable: The thing you are purposefully changing.

Conclusion: Your final result, stated in a sentence. How did the independent variable affect the dependent variable?

Hypothesis: A tentative explanation that can be tested.

Prediction: An educated guess concerning the outcome of an experiment.

Variables: Things that change in the experiment. For example, if you are testing to see if heat affects plant growth, then heat is a variable and the height of the plants is a variable.

Control: A subject that you set aside to compare with your experimental subject.

My Experiment

My observation: _____

My question: _____

My hypothesis: _____

My prediction: _____

My variables: _____

    Dependent variable: _____

    Independent variable: _____

Number of control subjects _____ Number of experimental subjects _____

I will only change one thing in my experiment. To keep other things the same (constant) in our experiment, I will _____ the variables.

My Procedure

1. _____
2. _____
3. _____
4. _____
5. _____
6. _____
7. _____
8. _____
9. _____

Grade: 5
Heart Disease
Lesson 5: Conducting a Heart Experiment

Lesson Time: 1 hour

Reference: "Heart Rate," in How to Encourage Girls in Math and Science (Dale Seymour Publications, 1982), by Joan Skolnick, Carol Langbort, and Lucille Day, pp. 167-168.

Lesson objectives
- Know that scientific progress is made by asking meaningful questions and by conducting careful investigations via the scientific method.
- Conduct an experiment based on questions generated by students.
- Draw conclusions from scientific evidence and state whether more information is needed to support a specific conclusion.

Overview
Students conduct experiments that they planned during the previous class.

Key Terms
(See previous 4 lessons)

Materials

Per student:
- 1 worksheet
- 1 experiment worksheet completed during Lesson 4
- 1 blank experiment worksheet from Lesson 4

Per pair:
- 1 stopwatch
- 1 stethoscope (for students measuring blood pressure)
- 1 blood pressure monitor (for students measuring blood pressure)

Procedure

> **Question:**
> **Why is heart research important?**

Activity: Student Experiments

1. Review the scientific process and the following science terms: **control subject** and **experimental subject, independent** and **dependent variable**.

2. Return the students' experiment worksheets from Lesson 4. Ask them to share the experiments they've planned. It is not possible to do a good experiment with only two subjects, so organize students working on similar experiments into teams that will pool their data.

3. Some students may need to modify their plans from the previous class in order to be part of a team. Ask students who need to do so to fill out new Lesson 4 experiment worksheets. Go around the room and to check that everyone's papers are complete.

4. Pass out the Lesson 5 worksheet. Allow time for students to conduct their experiments and complete the first page of the worksheet.

5. Show the students how to make bar graphs to display their data on the second page of the worksheet.

6. Discuss results and draw conclusions. Ask the students to write their conclusions on their worksheets. Discuss ways to share their results with their family members and the community.

**Heart Disesase
Lesson 5**

CONDUCTING A HEART EXPERIMENT

Name: _____

Teacher: _____

Date: _____

Collect and analyze data

Independent variable (the thing you're changing): _____

Dependent variable (the thing you're measuring): _____

Subject	Activity	Beginning heart rate	Ending heart rate	Difference
Control Subject				
Experimental Subject				

Word Bank:

Dependent variable: The thing you are measuring.

Procedure: A set of steps that explain how you are going to do something.

Independent variable: The thing you are purposefully changing.

Conclusion: Your final result, stated in a sentence. How did the independent variable affect the dependent variable?

Hypothesis: A tentative explanation that can be tested.

Prediction: An educated guess concerning the outcome of an experiment.

Variables: Things that change in the experiment. For example, if you are testing to see if heat affects plant growth, then heat is a variable and the height of the plants is a variable.

Control: A subject that you set aside to compare with your experimental subject.

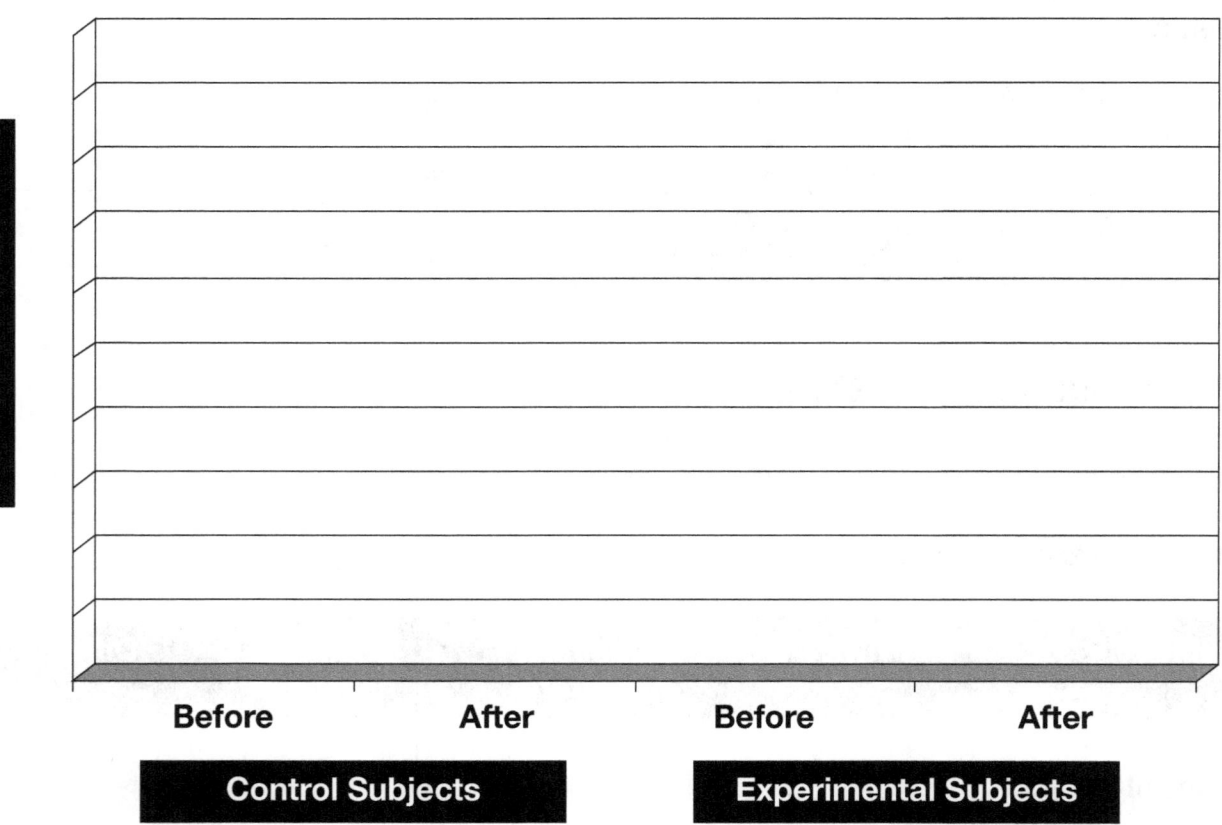

Grade: 5
Genetics and Sickle Cell Anemia
Lesson 1: DNA and Your Cells

Lesson Time: 1 hour

Reference: Harcourt Science, Grade 5: A4, A5, A14, A15

Lesson objectives
- Classify acquired and inherited traits.
- Know that inherited traits pass from one generation to the next.
- Know that information about our traits is coded in DNA within the nucleus of each cell. (Note: Red blood cells do not have nuclei.)
- Observe and compare plant and animal cells. Locate the nucleus.

Overview

Students explore and describe physical characteristics of people. They differentiate between traits that have been inherited from parents and traits acquired by accident or on purpose. Then they work in pairs to prepare and examine slides of onion skin and animal tissue using handheld microscopes. The students find the nucleus of cells, where DNA is stored.

Key Terms

Trait: A characteristic of someone or something such as eye color or ear shape.

Characteristic: Any quality or property of someone or something. For humans, characteristics can include hair color, height, intelligence, music preferences, way of laughing, etc.

Genetic inheritance: The passing down of traits from parents to their children.

Acquired trait: A trait that you weren't born with, but you learned it or got it. For example, knowledge about butterflies, a scar from an accident, and your haircut would be acquired traits.

DNA: A molecule containing code that determines how a person will look and how their body will function.

Cell: The basic building block of life.

Organelles: Small structures that are found in cells and have particular functions in the life process of cells.

Nucleus: An organelle that is found in the center of a cell and controls all of the cell's activities and the production of new cells. The nucleus contains DNA. Almost all cells have nuclei except for red blood cells.

Materials

Per class:
- 1 plastic DNA model or picture of a DNA model
- 5 overheads, optional:
  - illustrations traits mentioned in the inventory
  - onion cells with nuclei (light microscope image)
  - animal cells with nuclei (light microscope image)
  - normal and sickled red blood cells (light microscope image)
  - animal and plant cells with organelles (electron microscope images)

Per student:
- 1 worksheet

Per pair:
- 1 bottle of iodine with dropper
- 1 handheld microscope with batteries
- 1 blank slide
- 1 slide coverslip
- 1 animal tissue slide
- 1 box of colored pencils
- 1 roll of transparent tape and dispenser

Procedure

> **Question:**
> **Why do you think you look the way you do?**

Activity 1: Trait Inventory

1. Pass out the worksheets and show the overhead (optional) with examples of the traits as the students complete the trait inventory.

2. Tally the results on the board and discuss the differences between acquired and inherited traits. What are traits? How do you acquire traits? People acquire traits through personal experiences. For example, an accident may leave a scar. People inherit genetic traits from their parents. Inherited traits pass from one generation to the next through DNA found in the center of each body cell. The following traits on the inventory are NOT genetic: playing a musical instrument, running fast, holding your breath a long time, being good at video games, being good at basketball, and liking chocolate. However, acquired traits are influenced by our genes. For example, having long legs and a muscular body type (both inherited traits) will influence running ability. Similarly, although playing a musical instrument is an acquired trait, musical ability is partly genetic and partly acquired through learning and practice.

Activity 2: The Location of Genetic Information

1. Show the DNA model (or a picture if a model is not available). Explain that traits are passed from one generation to the next through a code found in the center of cells. The code is contained in a molecule called DNA. Each cell in the human body contains a complete copy of this code. Note: Red blood cells and some reproductive cells are exceptions.

2. Show how you can see a cell nucleus, where DNA is stored. Demonstrate proper procedures for making and observing slides. Place one small piece of onion skin in the center of a slide. Drop one drop of iodine in the center. Place a coverslip over the onion skin and tape the coverslip down. Place the entire slide in the microscope and focus the microscope until you can see individual cells.

3. Pass out the supplies and lead the pairs of students as they prepare their slides. Warn the students about proper laboratory safety procedures. Iodine can stain skin, clothing, desks, or carpeting if spilled.

4. Collect the iodine as soon as each pair has made a slide.

Activity 3: Observing Cells

1. Pass out one microscope and one box of colored pencils to each pair of students.

2. Ask the students to observe the cells and draw a picture of them on the worksheet. Ask the students what the picture reminds them of.

3. Show the overhead of onion skin cells and discuss what the students can see on the slides. Explain that we can only see a few parts of the cells. In onion skin, we can see cell walls, the cytoplasm and the nucleus. Discuss these cell parts. Explain that the cell is bounded by a membrane inside the cell wall.

4. When the students are done looking at the onion skin, distribute the animal tissue slides so that they can compare. Have them draw what they see. Compare the students' drawings to the drawings on the overhead images (if available). Point out the nuclei, cytoplasm, and cell membranes in the animal cells. Show the overhead of red blood cells and explain that red blood cells do not have nuclei. Then show the overhead with the electron micrographs and explain that plant and animal cells have many other parts, called organelles, which have particular functions. These are too small to see with an ordinary microscope. We can only see them with an electron microscope.

5. Discuss the similarities and differences between different types of cells. Make sure that the students can identify the nucleus of the cells. Make schematic drawings of two large cells on the board. Label one "Animal Cell" and the other circle "Plant Cell." Label the nuclei, cell membrane, and cytoplasm. Then label the cell wall of the plant cell and review that only plant cells have cell walls.

6. Ask the students to share their drawings with the class. They should describe what they observed, including the nuclei, and say what is found in the nucleus. Students should understand that all living organisms have cells with nuclei that contain DNA.

Extension

For a homework assignment, ask the students to make lists of traits they think are controlled by genes and ones they think are controlled by the environment or come about as a result of education or upbringing.

Genetics and Sickle Cell Anemia
Lesson 1

DNA AND YOUR CELLS

Name: _____

Teacher: _____

Date: _____

AN INVENTORY OF MY TRAITS AND TALENTS

Directions: Answer each question with a yes or no. Then vote if you think the feature is an inherited trait (something that got passed to you from your parents) or just about you.

Feature	Yes	No	Check if you think it's genetically inherited
Are you right handed?			
Can you play a musical instrument?			
Do you have long legs?			
Do you clasp your hands with your right thumb on top?			
Can you run fast?			
Do you have dimples?			
Can you roll your tongue into a U?			
Can you hold your breath for a long time?			
Are you good at video games?			
Do your earlobes attach at the ends of your ears?			
Are you good at basketball?			
Do you like chocolate?			
Do you have a cleft chin?			

Children's Hospital Oakland Research Institute

1. Observe the onion skin and record your observations below. Use a colored pencil to make the drawing.

2. Observe and draw the animal cells that you see in the microscope.

3. How do the plant and animal (round) cells below compare to your drawings? They were made with more powerful microscopes, so they show more detail than you were able to see.

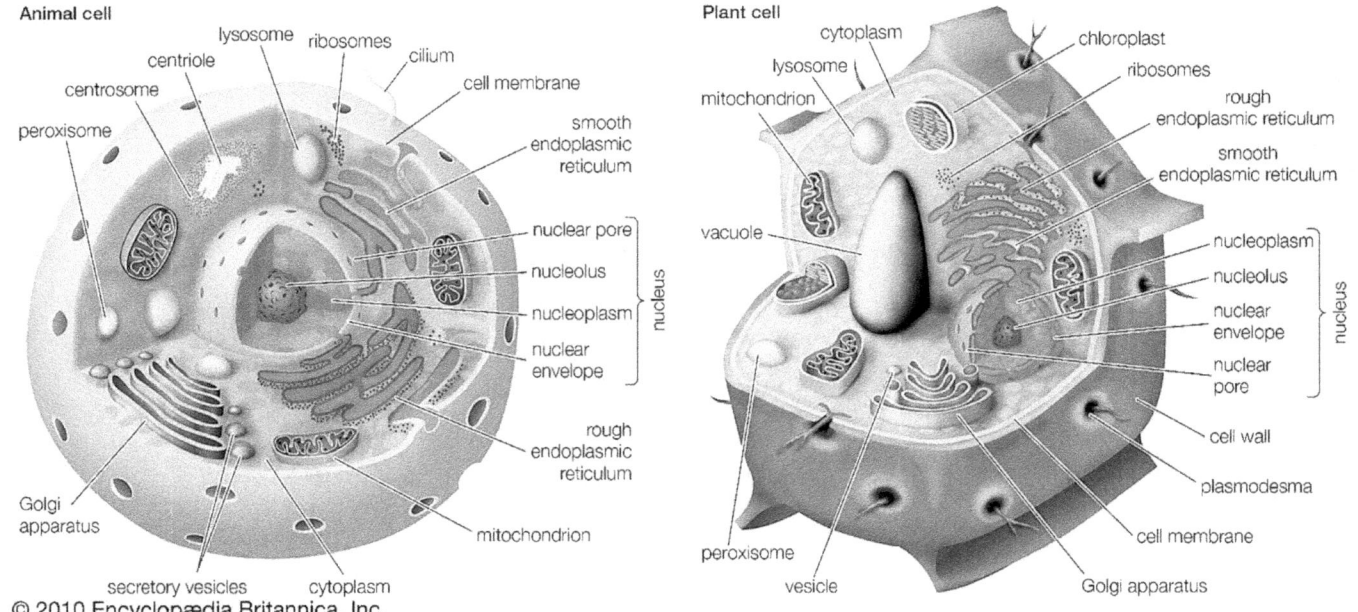

Grade: 5
Genetics and Sickle Cell Anemia
Lesson 2: See Your DNA

Lesson Time: 1 hour

Reference: Extraction of DNA from cheek cells adapted from: http://www.pbs.org/wgbh/nova/teachers/activities/2809_genome.html; DNA extraction from wheat germ developed by the Science Museum of Minnesota, Susan Fleming

Lesson objectives
- Know that DNA is a molecule found in the nucleus of cells and that it looks like a twisted ladder.
- Know that sections of DNA are called genes and code for specific traits.
- Know that genes are sets of instructions that determine how your body works and what you look like.
- Learn that scientific progress is made by asking meaningful questions and conducting careful investigations.
- Follow a written scientific procedure.
- Measure the volume of liquids.
- Make a DNA model.

Overview

Students extract and observe DNA from their own cheek cells in a procedure that involves careful measurements. Each student combines a mixture of water and saliva in a test tube with dish detergent, then ethanol. The soap breaks apart the cheek cells in the mixture and the ethanol precipitates strands of DNA to the top of the test tube. The students discuss their results and assemble strings of beads that represent strands of DNA. Then they compare their strands of beads with a molecular model of DNA.

Key Terms

Genes: Sections of DNA strands that code for specific traits. Genes are instructions, found in cells, that direct how your body looks and functions.

Chromosomes: Threadlike structures that are found inside the nucleus of a cell and contain genes made of DNA.

Helix: A spiral form or structure. The double helix of a DNA molecule resembles a twisting ladder.

Materials

Per class:
- 1 stopwatch
- 500 ml of detergent solution, 25% mild detergent or dishwashing soap (1 volume detergent or soap + 3 volumes water)
- 500 ml of ethanol or isopropyl alcohol (rubbing alcohol)
- 1 plastic DNA model (from Lesson 1), or a picture of a DNA model
- Short article about Watson and Crick

Per student:
- 1 worksheet
- 1 string
- 1 set of green, yellow, blue, and orange beads representing A, T, G, and C nucleotides

Per group of 4:
- 1 test tube rack
- 1 cup for water
- 1 cup for detergent
- 1 cup for ethanol
- 1 10-ml graduated cylinder
- 4 50-ml test tubes with caps
- 4 5-ml eyedroppers or small pipettes
- 4 disposable paper or plastic cups (labeled by each student with his/her name or initials)
- 4 stirring rods

Procedure

> **Question:**
> How can you see your DNA?

Introduction

1. Review the last lesson:
   - What gives your body directions?
   - What determines your eye color?

   The students should remember that it's DNA! Review that DNA is found inside the nucleus in just about every single cell of the body. In the experiment today, they will break away the membranes around cheek cells and the nuclei so that they can see their very own DNA!

2. Ask the students to read the activity instructions as you demonstrate each step. Remind them that scientific progress is made by asking meaningful questions and by conducting careful investigations. Every step in a scientific investigation must be done exactly as it is written to ensure the best results.

Activity 1: DNA Extraction Demonstration

1. Measure 10 milliliters (ml) of water with a graduated cylinder. Add the water to a cup.
   (5 ml = approximately 1 tsp)

2. Measure 5 ml of the detergent solution with the graduated cylinder and add this to the 50-ml test tube.

3. Swish the water from the cup in your mouth for 60 seconds. The swishing action removes dead skin cells from inside the cheeks.

4. Spit the water back into the cup. Pour this into the test tube that already contains the 5 ml of detergent solution.

5. Twist the cap onto the test tube and gently rock it on its side for 2-3 minutes. In this step, the detergent breaks the cell membrane to release the DNA. It is important to gently rock the test tube. If you shake too hard, the DNA will be broken up into very small pieces.

6. Use an eyedropper or small pipette to add 5 ml of 95% ethanol to the graduated cylinder.

7. Open and slightly tilt the 50-ml test tube. Carefully add the 5 ml of ethanol down the side of the test tube. The ethanol forms a layer on top of the soapy solution.

8. Allow the test tube and solution to stand for 1 minute in the test tube rack.

9. White, stringy material should appear at the top of the liquid in the test tube. Take the blue stirring rod. Place the circle end of the rod into the tube and twirl it. This will wind the DNA strands around the rod. Be careful not to mix the ethanol and soapy layers.

Activity 2: DNA Extraction by Students

1. Pass out the materials to each group and help them as they follow the procedure described above.

2. After the students isolate their DNA, discuss the activity. What happened? When the cells are placed in the detergent solution, the detergent dissolves the fat in the cell membrane (just like it dissolves grease on your dishes). Now that the membrane is gone, the DNA is released. When the ethanol is added, the DNA clumps together and gathers at the top of the solution just underneath the ethanol layer, because the DNA is not soluble in ethanol. Each "glob" of material contains millions of DNA strands clumped together. But what would the strings of DNA look like if we could see them with a powerful microscope?

Activity 3: DNA Structure

1. If time permits, read the short article about Watson and Crick, which describes the history of the discovery of the DNA double helix and the scientists involved in this discovery. The year 2003 was the 50th anniversary of the discovery of the DNA double helix! Watson and Crick solved the riddle of DNA's structure by constructing a molecular model.

2. Distribute string and green, yellow, blue, and orange beads to each student. Tell them that the beads represent the building blocks of DNA: green is adenine (A), yellow is thymine (T), blue is guanine (G), and orange is cytosine (C). Each student will assemble a strand of DNA that "matches" his or her partner's strand: A bonds to T, and G bonds to C. What colors match together? Ask the students to place the matched strands side by side.

3. Use the plastic DNA model or photo of a DNA model to explain what the beads and string represent.

4. Discuss: What does the model resemble? What is a helix? What part of the DNA molecule contains the genetic code that determines traits? (Answer: the A, T, G, and C nucleotides).

Extension

Have students compare their DNA to that of their classmates as well as to DNA from an onion and kiwi fruit. Students should identify any differences and similarities.

Allow the students to take their DNA home. After they isolate their DNA and twist it around a stirring rod, have them transfer it to a 1.5-ml microfuge tube containing 95% ethanol. The DNA will stay solid in this solution.

Genetics and Sickle Cell Anemia
Lesson 2

Name: _____

Teacher: _____

Date: _____

SEE YOUR DNA

Procedure for extracting chromosomes (DNA):

1. Put 10 ml of water into your cup.

2. Put 5 ml of detergent into your test tube.

3. Swish the water in your mouth for 60 seconds.

4. Spit the water back into your cup. Pour this into your test tube.

5. Place the cap on the test tube and rock it back and forth gently for 2 to 3 minutes.

6. Carefully add 5 ml of ethanol to the test tube.

Observations

What happened to your solution when you added ethanol?

_____

_____

_____

_____

_____

_____

_____

Watson and Crick

James D. Watson is one of the most famous scientists of the twentieth century. He is recognized as a discoverer of the structure of DNA and was a recipient of the 1962 Nobel Prize in medicine for his work in genetics.

James Dewey Watson.

Watson was born in Chicago, Illinois, in 1928. He was an extremely intelligent child and used his photographic memory to his advantage. By age ten he was a regular contestant on a popular radio show called The Quiz Kids. He studied zoology at the University of Chicago when he was only 15 years old. By age 19 he was conducting research on viruses at the University of Indiana, where he earned his doctoral degree. He continued his virus work in Denmark for a short period of time before several scientists convinced him to concentrate on genetics and molecular biology. This new direction led him to Cavendish Laboratory at Cambridge University in 1951. It was here that he first met Francis Harry Compton Crick, who was born in 1916.

Watson Meets Crick

A friendship soon developed between Watson and Crick. It didn't take long before Watson, who had an enthusiastic approach to genetic research, persuaded Crick to assist him in developing a DNA model. During this time, DNA research was not a high priority for most scientists. Watson and Crick entered the race to find the structure of DNA rather late.

With the odds stacked against them, Watson and Crick proceeded to develop their own hypothesis. They believed the DNA structure was actually made of two parallel strands. They obtained structural working models and attempted to fit the pieces together using proven chemical laws and prior studies. Many times the model, which resembled a large tinker-toy ladder, fell apart or simply did not fit previously established evidence. The researchers' tedious task was somewhat like trying to put together a model airplane with only a small portion of the instruction sheet and no picture of how the assembled plane should look.

Finally, two major clues fell into place. Watson and Crick knew that the amounts of the nitrogenous bases adenine (A) and thymine (T) in a DNA molecule were equal, and that the amounts of the bases guanine (G) and cytosine (C) were equal. Information from the research of Maurice Wilkins and Rosalind Elsie Franklin suggested that the sugar-phosphate part of the DNA molecule was on the outside of the structure. Watson noticed that base pairs (A/T and C/G) fit neatly into a twisted ladder or double helix form without any distortion. This also meant that each side of the ladder fit into the other and explained how DNA could be precisely copied each time a cell divides. The completed model consisted of a double backbone of sugar and phosphate molecules arranged in repeating units. Between these, like the rungs of a ladder, were the flat pairs of bases.

A Discovery Is Announced

In 1953, when Watson was only 25 years old, he and Crick announced their discovery. Almost ten years later, after numerous tests confirmed their results, the research team shared the Nobel Prize with Maurice Wilkins.

Today we know that DNA is the molecule that contains the essential set of directions that each cell needs to perform vital life functions. The details of the DNA molecule are so precise that differences in the microscopic structure could mean the difference between a man and a mouse, or between life and death

A Busy Man

Since the DNA discovery, Watson has published numerous papers, written several genetics textbooks, and taught at the California Institute of Technology and Harvard University. He has held two demanding administrative positions: he was director of the prestigious Cold Spring Harbor Laboratory in New York (an institution involved in genetic and cancer research), and he was a director of the Human Genome Project, which involved sequencing the base pairs of all of the human genes. Watson believes that the findings of the Human Genome Project will make it easier to identify individuals who are at risk of developing a variety of genetically caused diseases.

Source: http://www.discoveriesinmedicine.com/General-Information-and-Biographies/Watson-James-Dewey.html

Grade: 5
Genetics and Sickle Cell Anemia
Lesson 3: Plant Parenthood

Lesson Time: 1 hour

Reference: "Plant Parenthood," by Lucille Day, in SPACES: Solving Problems of Access to Careers in Science and Engineering (Lawrence Hall of Science, University of California, 1982). pp. 112-116.

Lesson objectives
- Know that individual sections of DNA, called genes, contain the instructions for traits.
- Learn that some visible traits depend on one gene and other traits depend on a combination of genes.
- Conduct a careful investigation simulating a plant genetics experiment.
- Decide if genes are dominant or recessive.
- Ask meaningful questions.
- Make hypotheses and draw conclusions.

Overview

Students simulate a plant experiment using cards to represent dominant and recessive traits in flowering plants. They count the number of offspring with given traits and determine the probability of inheritance.

Key Terms

Dominant: A type of gene that is expressed even when an individual only has one copy of it.

Recessive: A type of gene that is expressed only when an individual has two copies.

Genes: Sets of instructions that code for traits. They are found in the nucleus of each cell in a coiled molecule called DNA.

Traits: Characteristics such as eye color, ear shape, or sickled red blood cells. In plants, traits include things like flower color, seed shape, and plant height.

Materials

Per class:
- 1 poster or overhead showing plant mitosis and meiosis, optional
- 1 overhead of the labeling directions, optional
- 1 worksheet overhead, optional

Per student:
- 1 worksheet

Per pair:
- 1 pair of scissors
- 1 ruler
- 2 half 3-in x 5-in cards:
  - Half of a yellow card
  - Half of a white card
- 1 paper bag

Procedure

> **Question:**
> **Why don't offspring look exactly like their parents?**

Introduction

1. Tell the class about Gregor Mendel (1822 –1884): Mendel was a German priest and scientist who discovered patterns in how traits are inherited from one generation to the next. He bred thousands of pea plants and carefully recorded the traits of the offspring plants. Over time he could predict the probability that offspring would have specific traits such as height, seed shape, and color. The significance of Mendel's work was not recognized until the turn of the 20th century. Its rediscovery prompted the founding of genetics. Mendel is now known as the "father of genetics."
2. Tell the students that today they will simulate some of Mendel's experiments with pea plants.
3. Explain the similarities and differences between human and plant genetics. The plant traits the students will study today depend on only one gene. Some human traits also depend on one gene, but others depend on combinations of genes. Say that plants have long been used as a model for understanding genetics.

Activity 1: Preparation of Gene Cards

1. Give each pair of students half of a white card (to make Gene Cards for Plant 1) and half of a yellow card (to make Gene Cards for Plant 2), a pair of scissors, and a ruler.
2. Students cut three, 1-in x 2.5-in strips from each card. Using the strips, each pair of students makes the Gene Cards according to the diagram on their worksheets. Each Gene Card represents the two genes or traits for a particular characteristic in a pea plant. The gene on the front of the cards comes from one of the plant's parents, and the one on the back from the other parent. Be careful to write the "Front" label on each strip, then turn it over and write the matching "Back" label.
3. Every plant has three gene cards in this activity: one for height, one for flower color, and one for seed shape. Each characteristic has two types of genes or traits: TALL and short; RED and white; ROUND and wrinkled. Make sure to emphasize dominant genes are in ALL CAPITAL letters and recessive genes are all lowercase letters. This is very important or else their trials will not be correct:

PLANT 1:	Front of card	Back of card
Flower color:	RED FLOWER	white flower
Seed shape:	ROUND SEED	ROUND SEED
Plant height:	TALL PLANT	short plant

PLANT 2:	Front of card	Back of card
Flower color:	RED FLOWER	white flower
Seed shape:	wrinkled seed	wrinkled seed
Plant height:	short plant	short plant

4. Tell students the following rules of heredity:
   - A pea plant receives genes for each characteristic at random from each parent.
   - A pea plant needs only one copy of a dominant gene (uppercase letters) in order to show the trait.
   - A pea plant needs two copies of a recessive gene (lowercase) in order to show the trait.
   - These rules will be used for the rest of the activity.
5. Ask the students to describe plants 1 and 2. (Plant 1 is TALL with RED flowers and ROUND seeds. Plant 2 is short and RED flowers and wrinkled seeds.)
6. Apply these rules to see what one characteristic (say flower color) might look like in one offspring of Plants 1 and 2. Shake the two flower color cards in a paper bag, and pour them onto the table. Look at the traits that are face up. Decide what trait will show in the offspring. Point to the example on the worksheet.

Activity 2: Plant Parenthood

1. Before they begin with the simulation, ask the students to describe a plant they think will result from the crosses. Each prediction should have a trait for plant height, flower color, and seed shape. Ask the students to write their predictions on the worksheet.

2. Have each pair of students place one set of white and yellow gene cards (6 cards) in a paper bag. Shake the bag thoroughly and dump the gene cards onto the table. The genes that land face up will determine the traits of the offspring.

3. Match the traits that are showing for each characteristic, using a white one from plant 1 and a yellow one from Plant 2.

4. Using the rules of heredity (above) determine the appearance of this offspring. For example, if you turn up: RED /white, ROUND/wrinkled, short/short, then the offspring will be short with red flowers and round seeds.

5. Record these characteristics on the chart on the worksheet. List the plant height first, then the flower color and seed shape.

6. Repeat this simulation until the appearances of 10 offspring have been determined. Have each pair of students find the percent of the plant offspring with each trait: TALL, short, RED, white, ROUND, wrinkled. Then record these percentages. Compare the results of the simulation with the predictions.

7. Discuss why the results might have occurred.

8. What is the probability of a short offspring (50%)? Of a white-flowered offspring (25%)? Of an offspring with wrinkled seeds (0%)? How do these probabilities compare with the simulated results?

9. If time permits, show a poster or overhead of plant reproduction with diagrams of mitosis and meiosis. Each parent plant passes down one copy of a gene to the offspring. The visible traits of the offspring depend on the combination of genes they receive from their parents.

10. Discuss what the students learned from the activity and how it relates to humans.

**Genetics and Sickle Cell Anemia
Lesson 3**

Name: _____

Teacher: _____

Date: _____

PLANT 1

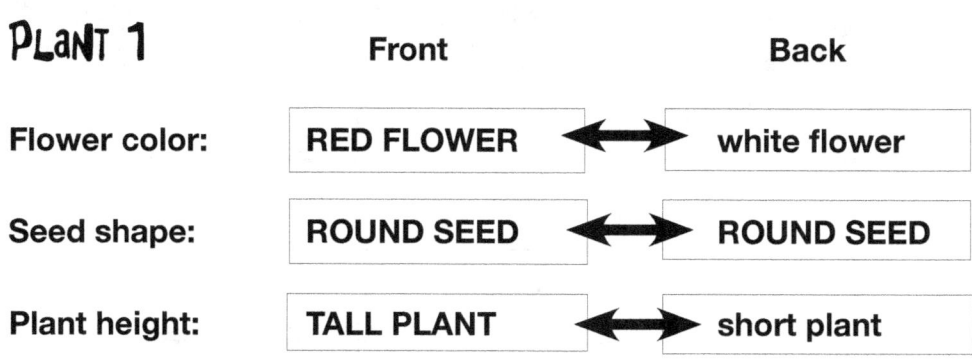

PLANT 2

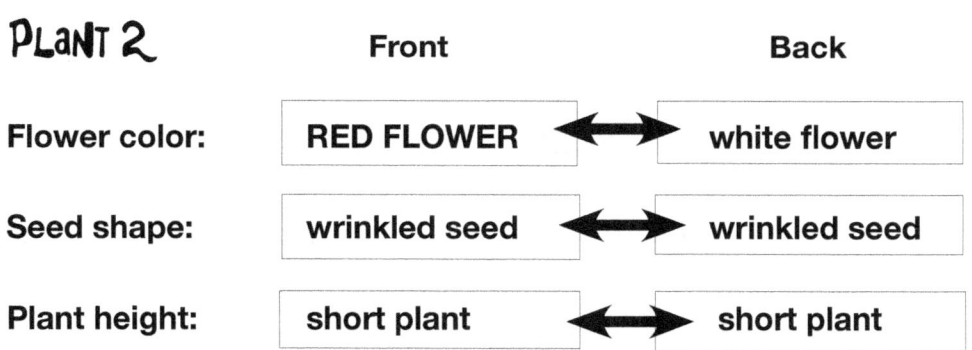

Rules of Heredity:

1. A pea plant receives _____ gene for each characteristic at random from each parent.

2. A pea plant needs _____ copy of a dominant gene (upper case) to show the trait.

3. A pea plant needs _____ copies of a recessive gene (lower case) to show the trait.

PREDICTION OF OFFSPRING FROM PLANT I AND II:

Plant Height	Flower Color	Seed Shape

PLANT BREEDING SIMULATION:

Offspring	Plant Height	Flower Color	Seed Shape
1			
2			
3			
4			
5			
6			
7			
8			
9			
10			

Trait	Number / 10	Percent
RED FLOWER	/ 10	
white flower	/ 10	
ROUND SEED	/ 10	
wrinkled seed	/ 10	
TALL PLANT	/ 10	
short plant	/ 10	

Children's Hospital Oakland Research Institute

Grade: 5
Genetics and Sickle Cell Anemia
Lesson 4: Trait Inheritance

Lesson Time: 1 hour

Reference: Breed-A-Winner Learning Kit from the Imaginarium: www.imaginarium.org

Lesson objectives
- Differentiate between acquired and inherited traits in humans.
- Know that genes are sets of instructions for how your body looks and works and that you get your genes from your parents.
- Know that a person's traits depend on probability and the genes of his or her two parents.
- Hypothesize about possible offspring from parents with various traits.
- Differentiate between recessive and dominant genes in humans.

Overview

The students use Mr. Potato Head toys to reinforce their understanding of dominant and recessive genes. They observe a Mr. Potato Head and decide if an offspring could inherit the traits. Using a coin toss and pictures of mom and dad potato heads, they create an offspring. Then they discover their own dominant and recessive traits. Finally, the class discusses how genetic problems might affect the health of an organism.

Key Term

Genetically inherited traits: Traits that are passed down through DNA from one generation to the next.

Materials

Per student:
- 1 worksheet
- 1 dominant and recessive trait inventory sheet

Per group of 4:
- 2 pennies
- 1 Mr. Potato Head kit

Procedure

> **Question:**
> **How are traits passed down from one generation to the next?**

Activity 1: A Potato Head Family

1. Divide the students into groups of 4. Give a Mr. Potato Head toy with accessories to each group of four students. Ask them to list the acquired and inherited traits. Discuss the answers as a group. Can you genetically inherit a mustache? Can you genetically inherit eyesight? What about a smile?

2. Ask the students to remove all the accessories from their toys to begin the activity. Give each group 2 coins and a worksheet for each student. The worksheet lists dominant and recessive traits. Make sure they understand that these are pretend dominant and recessive traits, not real ones.

3. Tell the students that they are going to make the offspring of a Potato Head mom and a Potato Head dad, each of whom carries one recessive gene and one dominant gene for each trait. Ask them what the Potato Head mom and dad look like (they both show all of the dominant traits.

4. Ask each group to choose a trait from the list on the worksheet. They can choose hair, ears, eyes, nose, mouth, or arms. Ask two people from each group to flip coins at the same time. If two heads appear, or one head and one tail, then the group must place the dominant version of the trait on the offspring. If two tails appear, then the group should choose the recessive version of the trait.

5. Repeat step 4. The group members should take turns flipping the coins.

6. When they have completed all of the "genetic" traits, ask them to choose additional acquired traits including shoes, clothes and hats.

7. Ask each group to show their finished offspring.

Activity 2: Trait Inventory

1. Collect the Mr. Potato Head toys and ask the students to complete the dominant and recessive trait survey.

2. Show examples of the traits in the students.

3. Discuss: What could go wrong with genetic inheritance? Could you inherit a trait that caused a disease?

4. Say that in the next lesson the students will learn about sickle cell anemia, a genetically inherited disease.

Genetics and Sickle Cell Anemia
Lesson 4

Name: _____

Teacher: _____

Date: _____

Genetic Traits for Potato Heads

Trait	Dominant	Recessive
Hair	Bald	Orange
Ears	Round	Flat and invisible
Nose	Red	Orange
Mouth	Big teeth	No teeth, only tongue
Arms	Yellow	White

Coin Toss

1. Decide on one trait. Read the dominant and recessive versions of the trait.
2. Flip two coins.
3. Determine which trait wins:

If you get two heads...

    ...then the dominant trait wins.

If you get two tails...

    ...then the recessive trait wins.

If you get a heads and a tails...

    ...then the dominant trait wins.

4. Place the winning trait on your Potato Head child.
5. Repeat steps 1 to 4 for the remaining traits.

6. What are genes?

_____

7. What are traits?

_____

Draw your Potato Head kid, and draw an arrow to traits inherited through genes.

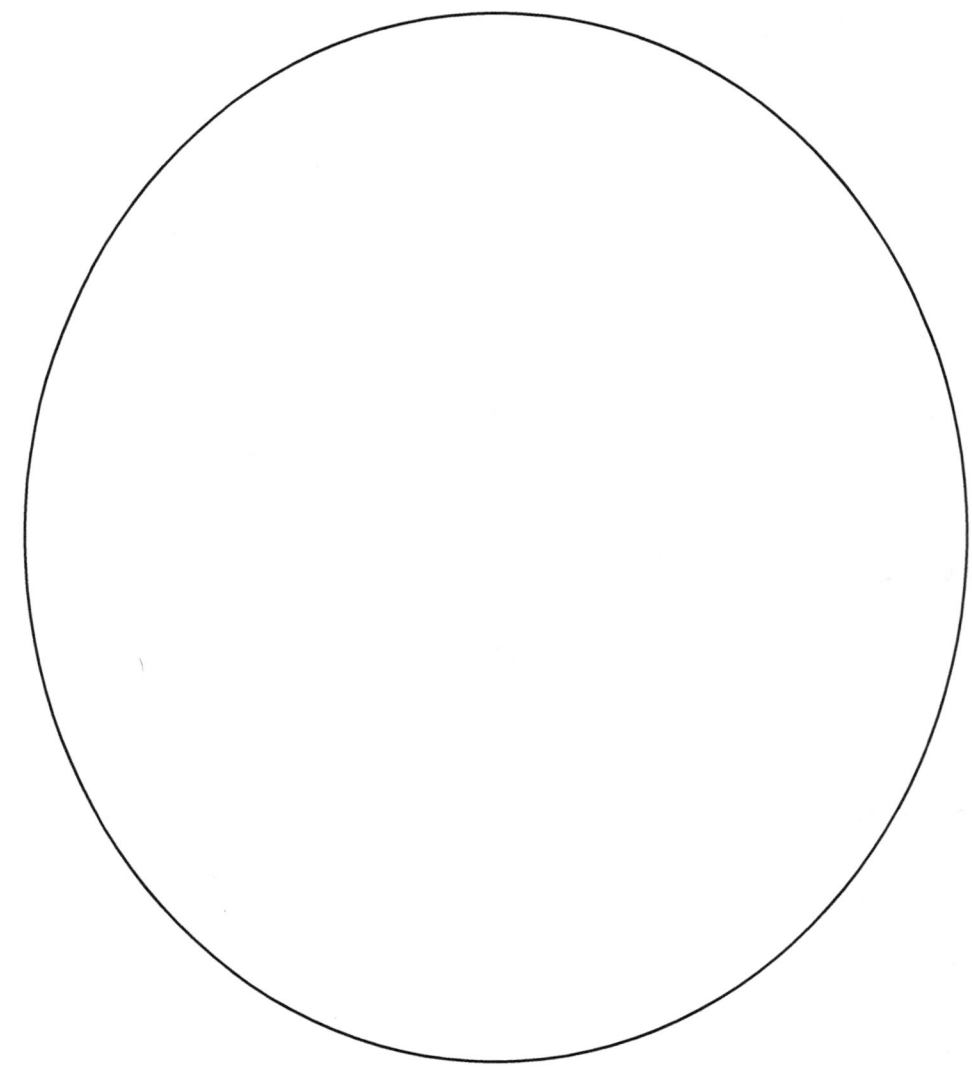

Dominant and Recessive Trait Survey

Trait	Dominant/Recessive	Do you have it?
Freckles	Recessive	
Widow's Peak	Dominant	
Second toe is longer than the first toe	Recessive	
Right-handed	Dominant	
Able to roll your tongue	Dominant	
Cleft chin	Dominant	

Grade: 5
Genetics and Sickle Cell Anemia
Lesson 5: Sickle Cell Anemia

Lesson Time: 1 hour

References: Talking Drums Project, Children's Hospital & Research Center Oakland; Punnett Square Activity from Carolyn Heuer with BodyLink at the Maryland Science Center

Lesson objectives
- That mutations lead to genetic risks and diseases.
- That sickle cell anemia is an example of a genetic disease.
- That sickle cell affects red blood cells.
- How common sickle cell is. One in twelve African Americans is a carrier for the trait.
- That sickle cell is not contagious.
- How they and their families can get tested for the trait if necessary.

Overview

The students assemble and reassemble the DNA models they made in Lesson 2 to better understand how genetic inheritance can go wrong. They meet a patient with sickle cell disease who describes his or her symptoms. Students then draw a family tree and Punnett squares showing how the disease is inherited. A researcher or healthcare practitioner talks to the class about current and future treatments for the disease.

Key Terms

Genotype: The genes carried by an individual, including alleles, or gene forms, that do not show as outward characteristics.

Phenotype: The observable characteristics of an individual.

Genes: The units of heredity in living organisms.

Punnett square: The Punnett square is a genetic diagram that biologists use to determine the probability of an offspring expressing a particular genotype.

Expressed gene: A gene translated into a detectable trait in an organism.

Materials

Per class:
- Large color pictures of regular and sickled red blood cells
- 1 plastic DNA model from Lesson 2 or picture of a DNA model
- 1 map of the world showing areas with a high incidence of malaria, optional

Per student:
- 1 worksheet
- 1 sheet of paper for the family tree
- 1 strand of DNA beads from Lesson 2

Per pair:
- 1 box of colored pencils

Procedure

> **Question:**
> **What can go wrong with DNA?**

Activity 1: The DNA Model Revisited

1. Hand back the strands of beads the students made in Lesson 2. Have one partner switch one bead in the strand. Have partners align their strands of beads together and look at the small change. The students should now make the appropriate change in the second strand to make an A/T or G/C pair. Show the plastic DNA model or photograph to the class and review how the strands of beads relate to the double helix structure.

2. Ask the students what they think can go wrong when just one piece of the DNA sequence is rearranged. Explain how genetic diseases occur when there is a mistake in the genetic code. For example, a gene codes for the shape of red blood cells. When someone has sickle cell disease, one base pair of DNA is switched (like in their DNA bead strands), and as a result, red blood cells are deformed, which causes serious consequences.

Activity 2: Sickle Cell Anemia

1. Introduce the guest speaker, a patient with sickle cell disease. Explain that sickle cell disease is a genetic disease caused by a change or mutation in the genetic code. This change can be passed down from one generation to the next.

2. Ask the guest speaker to talk about the signs and symptoms of sickle cell anemia. Show pictures of normal and sickled red blood cells.

3. Ask the guest speaker to draw his or her family tree on the board to explain how the trait passed from one generation to the next.

4. Pass out paper and colored pencils so that the students can draw their own family trees. Emphasize that many people in the community carry the sickle cell trait and don't know it. One in every 12 African Americans and one in 180 Latinos carry the trait. People who are carriers are at risk for having children with sickle cell disease. It's a good idea to get tested if you don't know if you are a carrier.

5. Ask the guest speaker to talk about the advantage of the sickle cell trait in climates where malaria is common. (Having just one copy of the sickle cell gene provides some resistance to malaria.)

6. Show the malaria map, if available.

Activity 3: Punnett Squares

1. Review that inherited traits come from genes in our DNA that are inherited from our parents.

2. Each of us has two sets of genes – one from our mother and one from our father.

3. Many traits are either dominant or recessive. Explain how capital and lowercase letters can be used to designate dominant and recessive genes. "B" represents the dominant trait, brown hair; and "b" represents the recessive trait, blonde hair. The hair color trait works well because the capital and lowercase letters look different from one another and both traits start with a "B" (it can be difficult to explain that "C" is curly hair and "c" is straight hair).

4. Of the two copies of a gene inherited from the parents, a dominant trait only needs one copy in order to be expressed, or visible. Show how genotypes of BB and Bb will yield offspring with brown hair.

5. A recessive trait needs two copies. The genotype must be bb to yield blonde hair.

6. Now line up the traits with the Punnett square grid. To start, select BB for one parent and bb for the other. Demonstrate how the genes line up in the boxes. Ask the students what the phenotype of the offspring will be (what color hair do the children have?)

	B	B
b		
b		

	B	B
b	Bb	Bb
b	Bb	Bb

7. Repeat this to show that a person with brown hair whose genotype is Bb can mate with another person with blonde hair whose genotype is bb to yield a 50% chance of having offspring with blonde hair. It is also interesting to point out that two people with brown hair and genotype Bb can have offspring with blonde hair. Make sure to use the Punnett square and place the appropriate letters in the grid to make this concept more clear.

	B	b
b	Bb	bb
b	Bb	bb

	B	b
B	BB	Bb
b	Bb	bb

8. The last scenario shows how in the case of dominant traits, a person's appearance does not always reflect their genes.
9. Have the students complete Punnett squares relating to sickle cell anemia.
   SS = A person who has sickle cell disease
   SA = A person who carries the trait
   AA = A person who doesn't have trait

   S stands for sickle cell hemoglobin, and A stands for typical adult hemoglobin.

   If a person with sickle cell disease has a child with a person who doesn't have the trait, what is the chance that the child carries the trait? (100%)

	S	S
A	?	?
A	?	?

	S	S
A	SA	SA
A	SA	SA

If a person who is a carrier of sickle cell disease has a child with a person who doesn't have the trait, what is the chance that the child carries the trait? (50%)

	S	A
A	SA	AA
A	SA	AA

If a person who is a carrier of sickle cell disease has a child with a person who is a carrier of sickle cell disease, what is the chance that the child carries the trait? (50%) What is the chance that the child has sickle cell disease (25%)

	S	A
S	SS	SA
A	SA	AA

10. Emphasize that sickle cell disease is not contagious.

Activity 3: Guest Speaker

Offer information about testing for sickle cell trait. At this point, the second guest speaker, the healthcare worker or researcher, could talk about genetic testing or current and future research on the subject.

Genetics and Sickle Cell Anemia
Lesson 5

Name: _____

Teacher: _____

Date: _____

Hair Color

	B	B
b		
b		

	B	b
b		
b		

	B	b
B		
b		

Sickle Cell Anemia

	A	A
S		
S		

	A	S
S		
S		

	A	S
A		
S		

www.ingramcontent.com/pod-product-compliance
Lightning Source LLC
Chambersburg PA
CBHW081223170426
43198CB00017B/2694